# OUR
# DAY STAR
# RISING

# OUR
# DAY STAR
# RISING

EXPLORING
## THE NEW TESTAMENT
———— WITH ————
## JEFFREY R. HOLLAND

DESERET
BOOK

SALT LAKE CITY, UTAH

Image credits:
Page v: *Shepherd* © Kelsy and Jesse Lightweave; page xiv: Dzmitrock/Shutterstock.com; page 11: Min An/Pexels.com; page 26: ArtMari/Shutterstock.com; page 45: difenbahia/Shutterstock.com; page 60: max shamota/Shutterstock.com; page 67: Patrick Daxenbichler/Shutterstock.com; page 76: vovan/Shutterstock.com; pages 87, 218, 222, 224, 228, 236, 240, 274, 288: John Theodor/Shutterstock.com; page 106: AdamKol/Shutterstock.com; page 116: Protasov AN/Shutterstock.com; page 131: JuliaHermann/Shutterstock.com; page 146: Maxim Khytra/Shutterstock.com; page 160: Subbotina Anna/Shutterstock.com; pages 167, 208: yanikap/Shutterstock.com; page 174: Ooriya Ron/Shutterstock.com; page 179: Romija/Shutterstock.com; page 184: PK Studio/Shutterstock.com; page 191: Jacob_09/Shutterstock.com; page 200: vvvita/Shutterstock.com; pages 204, 244, 266, 278: RnDmS/Shutterstock.com; page 214: Rostislav_Sedlacek/Shutterstock.com; page 230: OW17/Shutterstock.com; page 248: J.F.G.PHOTO/Shutterstock.com; page 252: Kluciar Ivan/Shutterstock.com; page 257: Tanes Ngamsom/Shutterstock.com; page 262: STEKLO/Shutterstock.com; page 270: Dmitry Abezgauz/Shutterstock.com; page 284: Suprun Vitaly/Shutterstock.com; page 292: Felix Mittermeier/Pexels.com.

Visit us at deseretbook.com

Library of Congress Cataloging-in-Publication Data
(CIP on file)
ISBN 978-1-63993-079-1

Printed in the United States of America
1 2 3 4 5 LBC 26 25 24 23 22

TAKE HEED, AS UNTO A LIGHT

THAT SHINETH IN A DARK PLACE,

UNTIL THE DAY DAWN,

AND THE DAY STAR ARISE

IN YOUR HEARTS.

—2 PETER 1:19

# CONTENTS

# PUBLISHER'S PREFACE

In his decades as a teacher and an Apostle of the Lord Jesus Christ, Elder Jeffrey R. Holland has often shared remarkable insights gleaned from his study of the New Testament. A desire to make those teachings more easily accessible in a systematically organized form led to the creation of this unique volume.

Gathered from his talks and writings, these teachings consist basically of two types. Elder Holland teaches *about* the New Testament itself, adding to our understanding of this sacred volume of scripture. He also teaches *from* the New Testament, using its verses to cast new light on various doctrinal themes. Both types of teachings enhance our ability to liken the scriptures unto ourselves and apply their truths in our lives, and both are contained in this book.

The book does not fall in the category of a typical commentary on the scriptures; nor does it include all of Elder Holland's extensive material drawn from the New Testament. Though it runs in the same order as the scripture books themselves, no attempt has been made to standardize the length or number of entries. Some excerpts from his extemporaneous oral sermons lack the polish of Elder Holland's carefully crafted written prose. Some ideas might be presented in a simple paragraph, while others might run several pages. Some chapters of the New Testament will include multiple entries; others will not be represented at all. Some entries quote from multiple chapters of the scriptures. In such cases, we have included the entry under just one chapter, trying to select the chapter quoted most extensively. Minimal editing has been done to standardize style.

The end result is a volume of apostolic teachings organized in such a way as to be especially helpful to readers of the New Testament. We are grateful to Elder Holland for allowing us to present these teachings and to his extraordinarily capable executive assistant, Lisa Atkin, for her help in gathering them.

—Publisher, Deseret Book Company

# AUTHOR'S NOTE

Three years ago, I accepted the invitation President Russell M. Nelson gave to the entire membership of The Church of Jesus Christ of Latter-day Saints to study the various names and titles given to Jesus of Nazareth throughout the scriptures, with most of those names being in the New Testament. That review was so rewarding that it turned into a small book documenting over 430 names for this living Son of God.

Many of the titles struck a deep, spiritual chord in my heart, with a few of them leaving feelings that will be with me for the rest of my life. Two such names that fall into that category are "the Bright and Morning Star" and "Day Star," the latter of which lends itself to the title of this book. It is the promise of Jesus Christ rising as the Day Star—the sun—that "shineth in a dark place until the day dawn . . . in your hearts" (2 Peter 1:19).

When coupled together, they suggest that the light of Christ's being stays with us "24/7," in the vernacular of the day. The "morning star," usually considered to be Venus, is the heavenly body that remains in view latest in the dark morning hours, serving as a harbinger of the day that is coming, eventually intermingling its light with the first rays of the rising sun. It is a precursor of the majestic center of our solar system—the sun—in which we find a new day, a new beginning, a new start, and with it, new hope and new blessings. Through the night (and we might assume through other forms of darkness and sorrow, including through times when we might have temporarily lost our way), one bright star remains in the heavens until morning comes with its greater light and peace, with its safety, strength, and salvation. The night star shines and then "the day star arises in our hearts" (2 Peter 1:19).

These images of light are ultimately all part of the meaning of the Second Coming of the Lord, but they have application in thousands of days—tens of thousands of days—before then. As troublesome as life can sometimes be, with as many painful moments as there are around us, and notwithstanding the promises and prophecies about contentions and wars and people's hearts failing them, nevertheless, Christ (as both the Morning and Day Stars) guides us, leads us, keeps and loves us through the dark of night and into the bright light of day. There never is a place and there never will be a time when we can fall below the redemptive light of the living Son of the living God. His grace and glory are a beacon to us in good times or bad, a lodestar giving reassurance that God is firm and fixed in our life. They also give us the faith that He is always there, that He hears our prayers, and that He keeps His promises.

Some of you have had difficult nights or days—or both—that have gone on for more than one 24-hour period. Some of them go on for weeks and months. Some of them can go on for years—a difficult problem that does not get resolved, a heartache that continues unabated, a conflicted relationship that never seems to heal, the constant presence of poor health or poor finances or poor choices. The list goes on and on. But someday, somewhere, not only when He comes but in anticipation of His coming, we can rest assured that His light will guide us unfailingly through—a star by night and the blazing sun of glory in the day. If we wait for it and watch for it and want it badly enough, our Day Star will most certainly arise in our hearts.

—Jeffrey R. Holland, September 2022

AND JESUS WENT ABOUT . . .

PREACHING THE GOSPEL OF THE KINGDOM,

AND HEALING ALL MANNER OF SICKNESS AND

ALL MANNER OF DISEASE AMONG THE PEOPLE.

—MATTHEW 4:23

# MATTHEW

## MATTHEW 2

*See also Luke 2*

There are so many lessons to be learned from the sacred account of Christ's birth that we hesitate to emphasize one at the expense of all the others. Forgive me while I do just that.

One impression that has persisted with me recently is that—in profound contrast with our own times, generally speaking—this is a story of intense poverty. I wonder if Luke did not have some special meaning when he wrote *not* "there was no room in the inn" but specifically that "there was no room *for them* in the inn" (Luke 2:7; emphasis added). We cannot be certain, but it is my guess that money could talk in those days as well as in our own. I think if Joseph and Mary had been people of influence or means, they would have found lodging even at that busy time of year. I have also wondered if Joseph Smith's translation of the passage is suggesting they did not know the "right people" when it says, "There was none to give room for them in the inns" (JST, Luke 2:7).

We cannot be certain what the New Testament writer intended, but we *do* know this couple was desperately poor. At the purification offering they made after the child's birth, a turtledove was substituted for the required lamb, a substitution the Lord had allowed in the law of Moses to ease the burden of the truly impoverished (see Leviticus 12:8).

The wise men did come later bearing gifts, adding some splendor and wealth to this occasion, but it is important to note that they came from a distance, probably Persia, a trip of several hundred miles at the very least. Unless they started long before the star appeared, it is highly unlikely that they arrived on the night of the babe's birth. Indeed, Matthew records that when they came Jesus was a "young child," and the family was living in a "house" (Matthew 2:11).

Perhaps this provides an important distinction we should remember in our own holiday season. Maybe the purchasing and the making and the wrapping and the decorating—those delightfully generous and important expressions of our love at Christmas—should be separated, if only slightly, from the more quiet, personal moments when we consider the meaning of the Baby (and His birth) who prompts the giving of such gifts.

## MATTHEW 4

Too many lives are buckling when the storms come and the winds blow. In almost every direction, we see those who are dissatisfied with present luxuries because of a gnawing fear that others somewhere have more of them. In a world desperately in need of moral leadership, too often we see what Paul called "spiritual wickedness in high places" (Ephesians 6:12). In an absolutely terrifying way, we see legions who say they are bored with their spouses, their children, and any sense of marital or parental responsibility toward them. Still others, roaring full speed down the dead-end road of hedonism, shout that they will indeed live by bread alone, and the more of it the better. We have it on good word, indeed we have it from the Word Himself, that bread alone—even a lot of it—is not enough (see Matthew 4:4).

"If thou be the Son of God, command that these stones be made bread" (Matthew 4:3).

Whatever else Satan may do, he will certainly appeal to our appetites. Far better to play on natural, acknowledged needs than struggle to plant in us artificial ones. Here Jesus experiences the real and very understandable hunger for food by which He must sustain His mortal life. We would not deny anyone this relief; certainly we would not deny the Son of Man. Israel had its manna in the wilderness. This is Israel's God. He has fasted for forty days and forty nights. Why not eat? He seems ready to break His fast, or surely must soon. Why not simply turn the stones to bread and eat?

The temptation is *not* in the eating. He has eaten before, He will soon eat again, He must eat for the rest of His mortal life. The temptation, at least the part I wish to focus on, is to do it *this way*, to get His bread—His physical satisfaction, relief for His human appetite—the easy way, by abuse of power and without a willingness to wait for the right time and the right way. It is the temptation to be the convenient Messiah. Why do things the hard way? Why walk to the shop or bakery? Why travel all the way home? Why deny yourself satisfaction when with ever such a slight compromise you might enjoy this much-needed nourishment? But Christ will not selfishly ask for unearned bread. He will postpone gratification, indefinitely if necessary, rather than appease appetite—even ravenous appetite—with what is not His.

"Then Jesus was taken up into the holy city, and the Spirit setteth him on the pinnacle of the temple." And Satan came to him there "and said, If thou be the Son of God, cast thyself down" (JST, Matthew 4:5–6).

Satan knows this holy structure is the center of religious life for Israel's people. It is the edifice to which the promised Messiah must come. Many are even now coming and going from their worship, many who through their traditions and disbelief will never accept Jesus as their Redeemer. Why not cast yourself down in a dramatic way and then, when the angels bear you up, as the scriptures say they must, legions will follow you and believe? They need you. You need them—to save their souls. These are covenant people. How better to help them see than to cast yourself off this holy temple unharmed and unafraid? The Messiah has indeed come.

The temptation here is even more subtle than the first. It is a temptation of the spirit, of a private hunger more real than the need for bread. Would God save Him? Would He? Is Jesus to have divine companionship in this awesome ministry He now begins? He knows that among the children of men only suffering, denunciation, betrayal, and rejection lie ahead. But what about heaven? How lonely does a Messiah have to be? Perhaps before venturing forth He ought to get final reassurance. And shouldn't Satan be silenced with his insidious "If," "If," "If"? Why not get spiritual confirmation, a loyal congregation, and answer this Imp who heckles—all at once, all with one stunning appeal to God's power? Right now. The easy way. Off the temple spire.

But Jesus refuses the temptation of the spirit. Denial and restraint there are also part of divine preparation. He will gain followers and He will receive reassurance. But *not this way*. Neither the converts nor the comfort He will so richly deserve has been earned yet. His ministry has hardly begun. The rewards will come by and by. But even the Son of God must wait. The Redeemer who would never bestow cheap grace on others was not likely to ask for any Himself.

And so, I ask you to be patient with things of the spirit. Perhaps your life has been different from mine, but I doubt it. I have had to struggle to know my standing before God. As a teenager I found it hard to pray and harder to fast. My mission was not easy. I struggled as a student only to find that I had to struggle afterwards, too. In my present assignment I have wept and ached for guidance. It seems no worthy accomplishment has ever come easily for me and maybe it won't for you—but I am living long enough to be grateful for that.

It is ordained that we come to know our worth as a child of God *without* something as dramatic as a leap from the pinnacle of the temple. All but a prophetic few must go about God's work in very quiet, very unspectacular ways. And as you labor to know Him, and to know that He knows you; as you invest your time—and inconvenience—in quiet, unassuming service, you will indeed find that His angels have "charge concerning thee: and in their hands they shall bear thee up" (Matthew 4:6). It may not come quickly. It probably *won't* come quickly, but there is purpose in the time it takes. Cherish your spiritual burdens because God will converse with you through them and will use you to do His work if you carry them well.

Now in some frustration Satan moves right to the point. If he cannot tempt physically and cannot tempt spiritually, he will simply make an outright proposition. From a high mountain where they might look over the kingdoms of the world and the glory of them, Satan says, "All these things will I give thee, if thou wilt fall down and worship me" (Matthew 4:9).

Satan makes up for lack of subtlety here with the grandeur of his offer. Never mind that these kingdoms are ultimately not his to give. He simply asks of the great Jehovah, God of heaven and earth, "What is your price? Cheap bread you resist. Tawdry Messianic drama you resist. But no man can resist this world's wealth. *Name your price.*" Satan is proceeding under his first article of faithlessness—the unequivocal belief that you can buy anything in this world for money.

Jesus will one day rule the world. He will govern every principality and power in it. He will be King of kings and Lord of lords. *But not this way.* Indeed, to arrive at the point at all He has to follow a most inconvenient course. Nothing so simple as worshipping Satan or, for that matter, nothing so simple as worshipping God. At least not in the way some of us think worshipping is simple. His arrival at the throne of grace is to lead through travail and sorrow and sacrifice.

Should earning our place in the kingdom of God be so difficult as that? Surely there is an easier way? Can't we buy our way in? Every man or woman does have a price, don't they? Can you not, in fact, buy almost everything in this world for money? Sometimes we wonder.

No, not everyone *does* have a price. Some of the best things *can't* be purchased. Money and fame and earthly glory are not our eternal standard. Indeed these can, if we are not careful, lead to eternal torment.

We are tempted to think there is an easy way, a fast buck, that in the world's goods and the glories of men's kingdoms, we may ride through reaping, as the very convenient Messiah. But why do we think it when it was never so for Him? What do we do with a stable for birthplace and a borrowed tomb at His death? And in His lifetime? Not one single mention of earthly possessions. "The foxes have holes, and the birds . . . have nests; but the Son of man hath not where to lay his head" (Matthew 8:20).

It is not easy to go without—without physical gratifications, or spiritual assurances, or material possessions—but sometimes we must, inasmuch as there is no guarantee of convenience written into our Christian covenant. We must work hard and do right, and sometimes our chance will come. And when we have tried, really tried, and waited for what seemed never to be ours, *then*, as Matthew states in his Gospel account, "angels came and ministered unto him" (Matthew 4:11). For that ministration in your life, I pray.

From the beginning down through the dispensations, God has used angels as His emissaries in conveying love and concern for His children. The scriptures and our own latter-day history are filled with accounts of angels ministering to those on earth. It is rich doctrine and rich history indeed.

Usually such beings are *not* seen. Sometimes they are. But seen or unseen, they are *always* near. Sometimes their assignments are very grand and have significance for the whole world. Sometimes the messages are more private. Occasionally the angelic purpose is to warn. But most often it is to comfort, to provide some form of merciful attention, to give guidance in difficult times.

Our present day is filled with global distress over financial crises, energy problems, terrorist attacks, and natural calamities. These translate into individual and family concerns not only about homes in which to live and food available to eat but also about the ultimate safety and well-being of our children and the latter-day prophecies about our planet. More serious than these—and sometimes related to them—are matters of ethical, moral, and spiritual decay seen in populations large and small, at home and abroad. But I testify that angels are *still* sent to help *us*, even as they were sent to help Adam and Eve, to help the prophets, and indeed to help the Savior of the world Himself. Matthew records in his gospel that after Satan had tempted Christ in the wilderness, "angels came and ministered unto him" (Matthew 4:11). Even the Son of God, a God Himself, had need for heavenly comfort during His sojourn in mortality.

※※※

We quickly and readily think of Christ as a teacher—the greatest teacher who ever lived or ever will live. But even as He taught, He was consciously doing something in addition to that, something that put teaching in perspective.

As His ministry began, Matthew says:

"And Jesus went about all Galilee, *teaching* in their synagogues, and *preaching* the gospel of the kingdom, and *healing* all manner of sickness and all manner of disease among the people" (Matthew 4:23; emphasis added).

Now, the teaching and the preaching we know and would expect. But I remember the first time I realized that from this earliest beginning, *healing* is mentioned as if it were a synonym for *teaching* and *preaching*. In fact, the passage being cited goes on to say more about the healing than the teaching.

"And his fame went throughout all Syria: and they brought unto him all sick people that were taken with divers diseases and torments, and those which were possessed with devils, and those which were lunatic, and those that had the palsy; and he healed them" (Matthew 4:24).

We know that Jesus's life was filled with the performance of many kinds of miracles, but in light of what I have just said it will not be surprising to learn that of all the miracles of Jesus recorded in the New Testament, three-fourths of them are healings of one kind or another. Over and over again His heart was drawn out to those who pled for health and wholeness. He who would become the great example of human suffering sought to ease the pains of others when *they* suffered. In His infinite mercy He regularly healed the blind and the deaf, the lame and the lifeless. We do not give the Savior whimsical names, but He rightfully could be recognized as the Great Physician.

What scenes could be more tender than the pleading leper, a beseeching centurion, or a desperate parent, each in the need of a healing miracle? These and so many more repeatedly turned to Christ acknowledging the wonder of His touch even if they did not always recognize or respond to His divine mission. For many it was as simple as one man said of Jesus: "Whether he be a sinner or no, I know not: one thing I know, that, whereas I was blind, now I see" (John 9:25). When it came to His miracles, Jesus was beyond the reach of Pharisaical haggling. The evidence spoke for itself.

## MATTHEW 5

In the most famous sermon ever given, Jesus began by pronouncing wonderfully gentle blessings that every one of us wants to claim—blessings promised to the poor in spirit, the pure in heart, the peacemakers, and the meek (see Matthew 5:3–12). How edifying those beatitudes are and how soothing they are to the soul. They are true. But in that same sermon the Savior went on, showing how increasingly strait the way of the peacemaker and the pure in heart would need to be. "Ye have heard that it was said by them of old time, Thou shalt not kill," He observed. "But I say unto you, That whosoever is angry with his brother . . . shall be in danger of the judgment" (Matthew 5:21–22).

And likewise, "Ye have heard that it was said by them of old time, Thou shalt not commit adultery: But I say unto you, That whosoever looketh on a woman to lust after her hath committed adultery with her already in his heart" (Matthew 5:27–28).

Obviously as the path of discipleship ascends, that trail gets ever more narrow until we come to that knee-buckling pinnacle: "Be ye therefore perfect, even as your Father which is in heaven is perfect" (Matthew 5:48). What was gentle in the lowlands of initial loyalty becomes deeply strenuous and very demanding at the summit of true discipleship. Clearly anyone who thinks Jesus taught no-fault theology did not read the fine print in the contract! No, in matters of discipleship The Church of Jesus Christ of Latter-day Saints is not a fast-food outlet; we can't always have it "our way." Someday *every* knee shall bow and *every* tongue confess that Jesus is the Christ and that salvation can only come *His* way (see Romans 14:11; Mosiah 27:31).

I ask you to consider for example Christ's teaching in the Sermon on the Mount when He declared, "Ye have heard that it was said by them of old time, Thou shalt not commit adultery: But I say unto you, That whosoever looketh on a woman [or I might readily add, a man] to lust after her [or him] hath committed adultery . . . in his heart" (Matthew 5:27–28).

Surely *no* "commandment," if we may use that language, could more directly address and condemn the sin of pornography than that passage! We can't help but wonder if Christ in the meridian of time might have seen such a latter-day threat, not unlike but well beyond whatever salacious or unseemly looks a man or woman might have given one another in the centuries before photos and films, before the internet and Snapchat. Note also how pornography defiles both the letter and the spirit of that entire legendary Sermon on the Mount. Jesus said as a foundational charge to His disciples there: "Ye are the light of the world. . . . Let your light so shine before men, that they may see your good works, and glorify your Father which is in heaven" (Matthew 5:14, 16). "Light of the world"? The trash that goes on in both the production and the viewing of pornography is almost always in the darkest of hovels, the dingiest of settings, the dirtiest of environments. "Let your light so shine before men"? The one great rule of pornography is that *no* light is to shine on it; it is secretive, hidden, after hours, unsuspecting, unrecognized, as unknown as possible. "Good works"? These are the most destructive and evil works of modern times. "Glorify your Father which is in heaven"? It is the most inglorious, deceitful, and destructive work known on such a wide basis in the society of our day, affecting young and old by the millions on a wholesale basis. There is *no* glory in this business, no glory of God or of the man, woman, or child who produces, performs, purchases, views or perpetuates it. Catholic bishops, Protestant ministers, Jewish rabbis, and Muslim mullahs have spoken out on this sin because God Himself has spoken out on it. Yes, heaven itself abhors this practice.

Sadly enough, it is a characteristic of our age that if people want any gods at all, they want them to be gods who do not demand much, comfortable gods, smooth gods who not only don't rock the boat but don't even row it, gods who pat us on the head, make us giggle, then tell us to run along and pick marigolds. Talk about man creating God in his own image! Sometimes—and this seems the greatest irony of all—these folks invoke the name of Jesus as one who was this kind of "comfortable" God. Really? He who said not only should we not break commandments, but we should not even *think* about breaking them. And if we do think about breaking them, we have already broken them in our heart. Does that sound like "comfortable" doctrine, easy on the ear and popular down at the village love-in?

And what of those who just want to look at sin or touch it from a distance? Jesus said with a flash, if your eye offends you, pluck it out. If your hand offends you, cut it off (see Matthew 5:29–30). "I came not to [bring] peace, but a sword" (Matthew 10:34), He warned those who thought He spoke only soothing platitudes. No wonder that sermon after sermon, the local communities "pray[ed] him to depart out of their coasts" (Mark 5:17). No wonder miracle after miracle, His power was attributed not to God, but to the devil (see Matthew 9:34). It is obvious that the bumper sticker question "What would Jesus do?" will not always bring a popular response.

Jesus said in the culmination of His most remarkable sermon ever, "If ye love them which love you, what reward have ye? do not even the publicans the same?

"And if ye salute your brethren only, what do ye more than others? do not even the publicans so?" (Matthew 5:46–47).

It is with some apostolic sorrow that I acknowledge I have never known what it is like not to have a date when everyone else had one, nor to be painfully shy, nor to be chosen last for basketball, nor to be truly poor, nor to face the memories and emotions of a broken home—nor any one of a hundred other things I know many have had to contend with in the past or are contending with right now. In acknowledging that, I make an appeal for us to reach beyond our own contentment, move out of our own comfort and companion zone, to reach those who may not always be so easy to reach.

If we do less, what distinguishes us from the biblical publican? I might not have been able to heal all the wounds of those I met in my young adult years, but I can't help think if I had tried even harder to be more of a healer, more of a helper, a little less focused on myself, and a little more centered on others, some days in the lives of those God placed in my path would have been much better.

The scriptures were written to bless and encourage us, and surely they do that. We thank heaven for every chapter and verse we have ever been given. But have you noticed that every now and then a passage will appear that reminds us we *are* falling a little short? For example, the Sermon on the Mount begins with soothing, gentle beatitudes, but in the verses that follow, we are told—among other things—not only not to kill but also not even to be angry. We are told not only not to commit adultery but also not even to have impure thoughts. To those who ask for it, we are to give our coat and then give our cloak also. We are to love our enemies, bless those who curse us, and do good to them who hate us (see Matthew 5:1–47).

If that is your morning scripture study, and after reading just that far you are pretty certain you are not going to get good marks on your gospel report card, then the final commandment in the chain is sure to finish the job: "Be ye therefore perfect, even as your Father . . . in heaven is perfect" (Matthew 5:48). With that concluding imperative, we want to go back to bed and pull the covers over our head. Such celestial goals seem beyond our reach. Yet surely the Lord would never give us a commandment He knew we could not keep. Let's see where this quandary takes us.

Around the Church I hear many who struggle with this issue: "I am just not good enough." "I fall so far short." "I will never measure up." I hear this from teenagers. I hear it from missionaries. I hear it from new converts. I hear it from lifelong members.

What I now say in no way denies or diminishes any commandment God has ever given us. I believe in His perfection, and I know we are His spiritual sons and daughters with divine potential to become as He is. I also know that as children of God we should not demean or vilify ourselves, as if beating up on ourselves is somehow going to make us the person God wants us to become. No! With a willingness to repent and a desire for increased righteousness in our hearts, I would hope we could pursue personal improvement in a way that does not include getting ulcers or anorexia, feeling depressed, or demolishing our self-esteem. That is *not* what the Lord wants for Primary children or anyone else who honestly sings, "I'm trying to be like Jesus" (*Children's Songbook*, 78–79).

To put this issue in context, may I remind all of us that we live in a fallen world and for now we are a fallen people. We are in the *telestial* kingdom; that is spelled with a *t*, not a *c*. As President Russell M. Nelson has taught, here in mortality perfection is still "pending" ("Perfection Pending," *Ensign*, November 1995). So I believe that Jesus did not intend His sermon on this subject to be a verbal hammer for battering us about our shortcomings. No, I believe He intended it to be a tribute to who and what God the Eternal Father is and what we can achieve with Him in eternity. In any case, I am grateful to know that in spite of *my* imperfections at least God is perfect—that at least He is, for example, able to love His enemies, because too often, due to the "natural man" (Mosiah 3:19) and woman in us, you and I are sometimes that enemy. How grateful I am that at least God can bless those who despitefully use Him because, without wanting or intending to do so, we *all* despitefully use Him sometimes. I am grateful that God is merciful and a peacemaker because I need mercy and the world needs peace. Of course, all we say of the Father's virtues we also say of His Only Begotten Son, who lived and died unto the same perfection.

I hasten to say that focusing on the Father's and the Son's achievements rather than our failures does not give us one ounce of justification for undisciplined lives or dumbing down our standards. No, from the beginning the gospel has been "for the perfecting of the saints, . . . till we . . . come . . . unto a perfect man, unto the measure of the stature of the fulness of Christ" (Ephesians 4:12–13). I am simply suggesting that at least one purpose of a scripture or a commandment can be to remind us just how magnificent "the measure of the stature of the fulness of Christ" really is, inspiring in us greater love and admiration for Him and a greater desire to be like Him. "Yea, come unto Christ, and be perfected in him," Moroni pleads. "Love God with all your might, mind and strength, then . . . *by his grace ye may be perfect in Christ*" (Moroni 10:32; emphasis added). Our only hope for true perfection is in receiving it as a gift from heaven—we can't "earn" it. Thus, the grace of Christ offers us not only salvation from sorrow and sin and death but also salvation from our own persistent self-criticism.

Brothers and sisters, every one of us aspires to a more Christlike life than we often succeed in living. If we admit that honestly and are trying to improve, we are not hypocrites; we are human. May we refuse to let our own mortal follies, and the inevitable shortcomings of even the best men and women around us, make us cynical about the truths of the gospel, the truthfulness of The Church of Jesus Christ of Latter-day Saints, our hope for our future, or the possibility of godliness. If we persevere, then somewhere in eternity our refinement will be finished and complete—which is the New Testament meaning of perfection.

## MATTHEW 6

We live in troubled times. You read the newspaper. You watch the evening news. You catch something on the Internet. However you get your news or whatever talk you have with each other, you are aware that we have a lot of problems in the world.

Those problems include the reality of war. Places like Afghanistan and Iraq and Iran have come into our everyday conversations. More recently Ukraine and Russia have as well. At one time we hardly even knew where some of these were on the map, and now we think about them every day. Perhaps the problem is the potential for a nuclear holocaust or harm to the environment or some other worldwide catastrophe such as the COVID-19 pandemic.

There is a lot to worry about in life.

But it's always been that way. Don't think you have been singled out for some particular burden at a uniquely troublesome time in the history of the world. It has always been a troubling time in the history of the world. This is a fallen world. It is mortal, and it is filled with thorns and thistles and noxious weeds at local, national, and international levels, at home and abroad, in private and in public.

That is the way it always will be until the Lord comes. We apparently understood that when we agreed to come here. In fact, the scriptures say we shouted for joy at the prospect of coming. Some days we wonder what all the shouting was about. But we saw it better then, and we will see it better later. Right now we grope a little in the second act of a play with a first act we are not allowed to remember except in broad brushstrokes and a third act we have yet to see in any detail.

So join hands and be filled with faith and enjoy life to the fullest. Embrace the promises and possibilities of this stage of life and this moment in history. Don't worry about what lies ahead. Live your life and have faith. Faith begins with faith in the Lord Jesus Christ, and that leads to faith in everything else: faith in the future and faith in our families and faith in our prospects and our promises and our possibilities.

I am convinced that faith was designated as the first principle of the gospel because somehow our Father in Heaven knew that fear would always be with us. We have to start with faith, because fear, if we let it, can be at every turn. Please don't yield to fear. Fear comes of ignoring what we know. When you truly understand why faith is the first principle of the gospel, you will embrace your faith, live your faith, and declare it to those who are faltering, who are giving in to fear.

When bombs were dropping on London in the middle of World War II, students were saying then, as they do today, "Why should I go to school? Why should I get married? Why should we have children? Why should I plan anything? I am going to walk out of here and a bomb will probably drop on me." Well, maybe it will. But it might have happened yesterday, and it could happen tomorrow. Nothing is any different for anyone anytime.

It is just that when bombs are dropping, we tend to think a little more seriously, and that is good. We ought to be a little more serious some of the time, and a bomb tends to get your attention. But don't be a suicide bomber. Don't bring on the very thing you fear. Keep moving, keep believing, keep growing, keep trying. Don't give up, don't give in. Don't worry so much.

Edward Everett Hale reportedly said, "Never bear more than one kind of trouble at a time." I know some people who bear three kinds at once—all they have had, all they now have, and all they expect to have in the future. But life will be better if you discipline yourself to never bear more than one kind of trouble at a time.

In the New Testament, the Savior is recorded as saying, "Take no thought, saying, What shall we eat? or, What shall we drink? or, Wherewithal shall we be clothed?

"(For after all these things do the Gentiles seek:) for your heavenly Father knoweth that ye have need of all these things.

"But seek ye first the kingdom of God, and His righteousness; and all these things shall be added unto you.

"Take therefore no thought for the morrow: for the morrow shall take thought for the things of itself. Sufficient unto the day is the evil thereof" (Matthew 6:31–34).

Now, technically and officially, those words were spoken to the Twelve who followed Jesus, and I suppose they have very special application to my Brethren and me. We really aren't supposed to worry about anything of a personal, temporal nature—not any kind of food or clothing or housing or whatever. We just go wherever we are sent on the Lord's work, and we come back when we are told to come back. But the principle of that divine counsel still applies to you.

Yes, you have to do some planning. You have to be realistic about making some progress, about preparing for the future. But you worry too much. We take too much heed about things that need not worry us—what we will eat, what we will drink, how we will be clothed. Take no thought, or at least less thought, for that, as measured against thinking about the kingdom of God and His righteousness.

"All these things shall be added unto you." That is the part of the scripture almost no one remembers. We always quote "Seek first the kingdom of God." We always quote "Take no thought for the morrow." But we frequently forget that the Savior said "All these things shall be added unto you."

God knows what you need. He wants you to pray about what you need, and He wants you to work for it. But mostly He wants you to believe He can and will provide. He knows what you need. Seek the kingdom of God and His righteousness and remember that the troubles of this day are enough. Don't worry about yesterday, and don't worry about tomorrow. Don't be one of those victims who worry about all the troubles they can think of that have ever existed or ever will exist.

## MATTHEW 7

In the call for compassion and loyalty to the commandments there is sometimes a chance for a misunderstanding, especially among young people who may think we are not supposed to judge anything, that we are never to make a value assessment of any kind. We have to help each other with that because the Savior makes it clear that in some situations we *have* to judge, we are under obligation to judge—as when He said, "Give not that which is holy unto the dogs, neither cast ye your pearls before swine" (Matthew 7:6). That sounds like a judgment to me. The alternative is to surrender to the moral relativism of a deconstructionist, postmodern world that, pushed far enough, posits that ultimately *nothing* is eternally true or especially sacred and, therefore, no one position on any given issue matters more than any other. And that simply is not true.

In this process of evaluation, we are not called on to *condemn* others, but we are called upon to make decisions every day that reflect judgment—we hope good judgment. President Dallin H. Oaks once referred to these kinds of decisions as "intermediate judgments," which we often have to make for our own safety or for the safety of others, as opposed to what he called "final judgments," which can only be made by God, who knows all the facts (see "'Judge Not' and Judging," *Ensign,* August 1999).

For example, parents have to exercise good judgment regarding the safety and welfare of their children every day. No one would fault a parent who says children must eat their vegetables or who restricts a child from running into a street roaring with traffic. So why should a parent be faulted who cares, at a little later age, what time those children come home at night, or what the moral and behavioral standards of their friends are, or at what age they date, or whether or not they experiment with drugs or pornography or engage in sexual transgression? No, we are making decisions and taking stands and reaffirming our values—in short, making "intermediate judgments"—all the time, or at least we should be.

When we face such situations in complex social issues in a democratic society, it can be very challenging and, to some, confusing. Young people may ask about this position taken or that policy made by the Church, saying: "Well, we don't believe we should live or behave in such and such a way, but why do we have to make other people do the same? Don't they have their free agency? Aren't we being self-righteous and judgmental, forcing our beliefs on others, demanding that *they* act in a certain way?" In those situations, you are going to have to explain sensitively why *some* principles are defended and *some* sins opposed *wherever they are found* because the issues and the laws involved are *not* just social or political but eternal in their consequence. And while not wishing to offend those who believe differently from us, we are even more anxious not to offend God.

But to make the point, let me use the example of a lesser law. It is a little like a teenager saying, "Now that I can drive, I know I am supposed to stop at a red light, but do we really have to be judgmental and try to get everyone else to stop at red lights? Does *everyone* have to do what we do? Don't others have their agency? Must they behave as we do?" You then have to explain why, yes, we do hope *all* will stop at a red light. And you have to do this *without* demeaning those who transgress or who believe differently than we believe because, yes, they *do* have their moral agency.

There is a wide variety of beliefs in this world, and there is moral agency for all, but no one is entitled to act as if God is mute on these subjects or as if commandments only matter if there is public agreement over them. In the twenty-first century we cannot flee any longer. We are going to have to fight for laws and circumstances and environments that allow the free exercise of religion and our franchise in it. That is one way we can tolerate being in Babylon but not of it.

I know of no more important ability and no greater integrity for us to demonstrate in a world from which we cannot flee than to walk that careful path—taking a moral stand according to what God has declared and the laws He has given, but doing it compassionately and with understanding and great charity. Talk about a hard thing to do—to distinguish perfectly between the sin and the sinner. I know of few distinctions that are harder to make, or at least harder to articulate, but we must lovingly try to do exactly that. Believe me, brothers and sisters, in the world into which we are moving, we are going to have a lot of opportunity to develop such strength, display such courage, and demonstrate such compassion—all at the same time.

※※

I am devastated that sometimes Latter-day Saints feel "somehow I have to stand on my head, I have to twist myself into a pretzel, I have to be something I cannot be, I have to do something I cannot do, in order for God to even smile on me."

We have to start with a much more generous, wholesome, and true view of the God who loves us. There is nothing, *nothing* in righteousness I would not do for my children. There is no forest fire I would not enter; there is no violent guerilla warfare in which I wouldn't engage; there is nothing in terms of a drowning child or desperate teenager that I would not do to bless and help and protect my child. There is nowhere I would not go; there is nothing I would not face. If I can say that as a mortal, limited, defective, imperfect person, if I can feel that way about a child, what on earth does it mean about God's love for us?

That is why the Savior said we are not talking about a Father who, if you ask for bread, gives you a stone and chuckles about it (see Matthew 7:8–9). He is not a referee at third base who is anxious to call us out. We really have to change our view. We are fighting a long cultural and theological tradition to make sure that we don't see this hellfire-and-brimstone God that is trying to keep us from His kingdom.

※※

Prepare. Plan. Work. Sacrifice. Rework. Spend cheerfully on matters of worth. Carry the calm, and wear the assurance of having done the best you could with what you had. If you work hard and prepare earnestly, it will be very difficult for you to give in or give up or wear down. If you labor with faith in God and in yourself and in your future, you will have built upon a rock. Then, when the winds blow and the rains come—as surely they will—you shall not fall (see Matthew 7:24–25).

"Therefore whosoever heareth these sayings of mine, *and doeth them*, I will liken him unto a wise man, which built his house upon a rock:

"And the rain descended, and the floods came, and the winds blew, and beat upon that house; and it fell not: for it was founded upon a rock.

"And every one that heareth these sayings of mine, *and doeth them not*, shall be likened unto a foolish man, which built his house upon the sand:

"And the rain descended, and the floods came, and the winds blew, and beat upon that house; and it fell: and great was the fall of it" (Matthew 7:24–27; emphasis added).

Hearing and doing—putting the counsel of the Lord into action—is what strong lives are built upon. Rain descends on every life. Floods can sweep over every family. The winds of economic and social and moral force beat upon every house I know. But strong homes and families and lives will stand if we have *heard* and *acted upon* the words of our prophets, teachers, and leaders. That practice will protect us from the Savior's observation about an apostate world in 1820 that "they draw near to me with their lips, but their hearts are far from me" (Joseph Smith—History 1:19).

The ultimate significance of The Church of Jesus Christ of Latter-day Saints—that which makes it the Church of Jesus Christ, and not just an interesting Christian phenomenon—is found in eternal truth and (does this sound familiar?) its doctrine and its covenants. There is great significance to that title given to the revelations of this last and greatest of all dispensations. The fourth article of faith phrases essentially the same combination as, "principles and ordinances," but you get the point. The gospel consists of things we are supposed to know and things we are supposed to do. Doctrine and covenants. Principles and ordinances.

So, when we speak of doctrine, we are starting exactly where we are supposed to start: learning what we need to know in order to make sure we do what we are to do.

Certainly, that was the issue in 1820 when young Joseph wanted to know something, namely, which church was true—so that he could do something, namely, join that church. In that great epiphany in the Sacred Grove, the Savior of the world Himself told Joseph he couldn't find a true church at that time. Why? What did He say? We don't have a lot of quotes from the Savior of the world from New Testament and Book of Mormon time on. What did He say? He said, "They teach for doctrines the commandments of men, having a form of godliness, but they deny the power thereof" (Joseph Smith—History 1:19). The power of the doctrine.

If Joseph and the entire family of God in these last days were going to find their way back to God, it would have to be on the strength of truth—true doctrine, more powerful than that created by men. It would have to have not only a form of godliness, but actually be godly. It had to be truth from and of our Father in Heaven.

When the Savior completed the Sermon on the Mount, what was it that affected the people? It says it in the New Testament. Was it His gentle manner? Was it His tone of voice? Was it His common touch? Was it His homely application, the daily life? Well, it was probably all of those things. But what the Gospel writers say affected the people was this: "When Jesus had ended these sayings, the people were astonished at his doctrine: for he taught them as one having authority and not as the scribes" (Matthew 7:28–29).

Clearly, an essential element in that setting would have to have been the testifying power of the Spirit, as we try so hard to have our missionaries understand. But remember, the Holy Ghost can't testify in the abstract. It has to testify about something. And that something is always true. Canonized, those truths constitute the doctrine of the truth.

So, no wonder the people in Jesus's day were impressed. Powerful true doctrine was borne to their hearts by the Spirit. That is not what they were getting from the scribes and the Pharisees.

From the divine source on high we all need a fountain of truth, doctrine and principles leading to covenants and ordinances that give us greater power than the minions of Satan who would destroy us and destroy our faith and destroy our people if they could. Knowledge is power, literally.

## MATTHEW 9

As the Savior's ministry in the New Testament began, Matthew records:

"And Jesus went about all Galilee, teaching in their synagogues, and preaching the gospel of the kingdom, and healing all manner of sickness and all manner of disease among the people.

"And his fame went throughout all Syria: and they brought unto him all sick people that were taken with divers diseases and torments, and those which were possessed with devils, and those which were lunatic, and those that had the palsy; and he healed them" (Matthew 4:23–24).

Then following the Sermon on the Mount, in rapid succession, He heals a leper, the servant of a centurion, Peter's mother-in-law, and "many that were possessed with devils . . . and healed all that were sick: That it might be fulfilled which was spoken by Esaias the prophet, saying, Himself took our infirmities, and bare our sicknesses" (Matthew 8:16–17). This is then followed in equally rapid fashion by the casting out of the devils near Gadarene, the healing of a man with palsy, the miracle of the woman diseased twelve years with an issue of blood, the raising of a young woman from the dead, the sight returned to the eyes of two blind men, and speech returned to one who was dumb.

With all of this work lying before Him, Jesus caps off this almost nonstop scriptural sequence with these verses, which every missionary has heard:

"But when he saw the multitudes, he was moved with compassion on them, because they fainted, and were scattered abroad, as sheep having no shepherd.

"Then saith he unto his disciples, The harvest truly is plenteous, but the labourers are few;

"Pray ye therefore the Lord of the harvest, that he will send forth labourers into his harvest" (Matthew 9:36–38).

We all know that wonderful call for more labourers into the work of the harvest refers primarily to teaching and testifying. It is a wonderful missionary scripture. But I wish to suggest today that in context it surely is a call to heal one another as well. Jesus certainly did His missionary work, and He did that first. But as He went about preaching and teaching, He bound up all manner of wounds in the process. The verse summarizing all of this, coming just before the calling of the Twelve Apostles and their charge to do likewise, says: "And Jesus went about all the cities and villages, teaching in their synagogues, and preaching the gospel of the kingdom, and healing every sickness and every disease among the people" (Matthew 9:35).

On the example of the Savior Himself and His call to His Apostles, and with the need for peace and comfort ringing in our ears, I ask you to be a healer, be a helper, be someone who joins in the work of Christ in lifting burdens, in making the load lighter, in making things better. Isn't that the phrase we used to use as children when we had a bump or a bruise? Didn't we say to Mom or Dad, "Make it better"? Well, lots of people on your right hand and on your left are carrying bumps and bruises that they hope will be healed and made whole. Someone within reasonable proximity to you today is carrying a spiritual or physical or emotional burden of some sort or an affliction drawn from life's catalog of a thousand kinds of sorrow. In the spirit of Christ's first invitation to Philip and Andrew and then to Peter and the whole of His Twelve Apostles, jump into this work. Help people. Heal old wounds, and try to make things better. In short, I ask you to "follow Him."

## MATTHEW 11

I speak to those who are facing personal trials and family struggles, those who endure conflicts fought in the lonely foxholes of the heart, those trying to hold back floodwaters of despair that sometimes wash over us like a tsunami of the soul. I wish to speak particularly to you who feel your lives are broken, seemingly beyond repair.

To all such I offer the surest and sweetest remedy that I know. It is found in the clarion call the Savior of the world Himself gave. He said it in the beginning of His ministry, and He said it in the end. He said it to believers, and He said it to those who were not so sure. He said to everyone, whatever their personal problems might be:

"Come unto me, all ye that labour and are heavy laden, and I will give you rest.

"Take my yoke upon you, and learn of me; for I am meek and lowly in heart: and ye shall find rest unto your souls" (Matthew 11:28–29).

In this promise, that introductory phrase, "come unto me," is crucial. It is the key to the peace and rest we seek. He is saying to us, "Trust me, learn of me, do what I do. Then, when you walk where *I* am going," He says, "we can talk about where *you* are going, and the problems you face and the troubles you have. If you will follow me, I will lead you out of darkness," He promises. "I will give you answers to your prayers. I will give you rest to your souls."

My beloved friends, I know of no other way for us to succeed or to be safe amid life's many pitfalls and problems.

I testify that the Atonement of Jesus Christ lifts from us not only the burden of our sins but also the burden of our disappointments and sorrows, our heartaches and our despair. From the beginning, trust in such help was to give us both a reason and a way to improve, an

incentive to lay down our burdens and take up our salvation. There can and will be plenty of difficulties in life. Nevertheless, souls who come unto Christ, who know His voice and strive to do as He did, find strength that exceeds their own capacity. The Savior reminds us that He has "graven [us] upon the palms of [His] hands" (1 Nephi 21:16). Considering the incomprehensible cost of the Crucifixion and the Atonement of Jesus Christ, I promise you He is not going to turn His back on us now. When He says to the poor in spirit, "Come unto me," He means He knows the way out and He knows the way up. He knows it because He has walked it. He knows the way because He *is* the way.

Come unto Him and lay down your burden. Let Him lift the load. Let Him give peace to your soul (see Matthew 11:28–29). Nothing in this world is more burdensome than sin. It is the heaviest cross men and women ever bear.

To anyone struggling under the burden of sin, I say again that you can change. You can be helped. You can be made whole— whatever the problem. All He asks is that you *walk away from the darkness and come into the light,* His light, with meekness and lowliness of heart. That is at the heart of the gospel. That is the very center of our message. That is the beauty of redemption. Christ has "borne our griefs, and carried our sorrows," Isaiah declared, "and with his stripes we are healed"—if we want to be (Isaiah 53:4–5).

For anyone out there seeking the courage to repent and change, I remind you that the Church is not a monastery for the isolation of perfect people. It is more like a hospital provided for those who wish to get well. Do whatever you have to do to come into the fold and be blessed. For some of you that is simply to live with greater faith, to believe more. For some of you it does mean to repent: Right here. Right now. For some it means to be baptized and come into the body and fellowship of Christ. For virtually all of us it means to live more by the promptings and promises of the Holy Ghost and to "press forward with a steadfastness in Christ, having a perfect brightness of hope, and a love of God and of all men" (2 Nephi 31:20).

This reliance upon the forgiving, long-suffering, merciful nature of God was taught from before the very foundation of the world. It was always to give us hope and help, a reason to progress and improve, an incentive to lay down our burdens and take up our salvation. May I be bold enough to suggest that it is impossible for anyone who really knows God to doubt His willingness to receive us with open arms in a divine embrace if we will but come unto Him. There certainly can and will be plenty of external difficulties in life. Nevertheless the soul that comes unto Christ dwells within a personal fortress, a veritable palace of perfect peace. "Whoso hearkeneth unto me," Jehovah says, "shall dwell safely, and shall be quiet from fear of evil" (Proverbs 1:33).

## MATTHEW 13

If justice were to take its toll on Jeff Holland right now, he would be in deep trouble. But, fortunately, even though Jeff has passed the beginning of his accountability (at age eight), the Lord might say, "Jeff's accountability is still increasing. He is learning more. He is doing more. Let's withhold judgment and watch him for a while to see if he can merit more blessings." It is like the story of the wheat and tares—don't jump in too soon in judging people, including yourself. That the tares are there is unmistakable and undeniable, but in His love and mercy the Lord is willing to say, "I will not exercise judgment now. Let's wait a little longer" (see Matthew 13:24–30). This principle has been at work in my life personally, and in all of our lives collectively. We are kept, protected, encircled, and loved until we can work out some of the silly, petty weaknesses in our lives.

But work them out we must. This Church cannot survive forever on people who have not decided yet on which team they want to play. We have to have people who will decisively take a stand and be counted in defense of the gospel of Jesus Christ.

We have a tendency to hedge about this a little, but I don't believe the Lord smiles on that, because He kept telling either/or parables. And we say, "Oh, no, 'either/or' is too simplistic. There are too many shades of gray." But He kept telling those decisive stories. Think of them. We just talked about one, the wheat and the tares. He did not say anything about roses or petunias or onions in the middle. He said there is some wheat and there are some tares. How will He judge against that standard? I don't know, but I do know He is going to be the judge, and it will be a righteous judgment. I don't think we will be surprised with those decisions. I know in my own life the fruitful, righteous, constructive part that is wheat, and I know the destructive, dark, less wholesome part that gets qualified as a tare. He knows that I know that already, but He waits a little longer to see if I will repent of the latter in my maturity.

He talked about sheep and goats. Nothing about lions and tigers and leopards and elephants. Then He gathered fish in the gospel net, and there were some good fish and some bad fish, and we say, "What about the mediocre fish?" Nothing there about mediocre fish. Just some good ones and some bad ones. And we say, "How can that be? Everything in my experience says there are more shades of gray than that"—except, deep down in my soul, I really do know the things I should do and the things I should not do. And I cannot think of a circumstance in which I'm really confused about that. I know the kind of courtesy I should show my wife and my children. I know the kind of kindness I should use when driving a car. I know the kind of literature I should read and the gospel study I should be doing. I struggle and strain and want to come up with some shades of grey, but to no avail. It is almost impossible for me to ever say, "Well, Lord, I just really didn't know what I was supposed to do." When it comes to right and wrong, we always know.

God wants us to stand up and be counted. We have to show up at the welfare assignment. We must serve others. We must pray; we must study; we must pay our tithing. These are moral acts of will. They are assertions of ourselves in which we say, "Here am I." We are not lost in some nebulous maze. No, we know clearly what we are to do. Finally, we are to step forward, shoulder our arms, and say, "I believe in the battle, and if anyone is going to fight it, I have to fight it. And if it is not I, who? And if it is not now, when? And if it is not right here, where?"

Someday there will be a harvest. As surely as we are born and as the rivers run to the sea, there will be a moment of truth. The wheat will be separated from the tares, and each will be bound—one taken to the barn, the other burned as stubble (see Matthew 13:30). That time is not yet, but it will be sometime.

I want to share with you a reminder inspired by the short parable told in Matthew 13:45–46 and taught by President Boyd K. Packer. A man plowing his field finds a gem, a pearl—the most beautiful gem he has ever seen in his life. He buys the field, claims the pearl, and is so smitten with it that he wants to put it on display.

He rents an arena at his own expense. And so that this little pearl can be featured appropriately, he has a beautiful box made for it. He imports wood from the Philippines and Africa and the forests of Russia. He imports stunning blue velvet lining from Asia. He commissions handmade gold hinges. Everything has to be perfect to display this pearl.

He places it in the center of the auditorium. He opens the doors and brings fathers, mothers, and children from everywhere to see this beautiful, priceless gem. Then he sits watching the crowd after day one, after day two, and after day three. Then he closes the exhibit. The people are devastated because there are still lines and lines of them coming from everywhere to see this display.

Why does he close the exhibit? Because everyone coming out of the exhibit was saying the same thing: "What a beautiful box. I wonder where he got that wood. And did you notice that blue velvet lining? That was something. And those little, tiny hinges. Can you imagine anyone hand-making those little, tiny hinges—and out of gold, no less?" But not a single person commented on the pearl.

Now, that is a little of what we do in The Church of Jesus Christ of Latter-day Saints, and we have to guard against it. We need boxes for the pearl of the gospel. We are grateful for them. The temple is technically a box. A stunningly beautiful and sacred box, but a box nevertheless. Other box-like props are budgets and agendas and reports and the ward roller-skating party. They are all important, but if those things do not do something to build faith in the Lord Jesus Christ—the true pearl of the gospel—then we may need to ask exactly what purpose they serve. They have their own merit, but they should all, in their own way, build faith in Christ as well.

Obviously, some activities and meetings lend themselves to a spiritual experience more than others. But they all ought to be gospel oriented, or we had better ask ourselves: Should we be doing this? Do we need to do it? We have only so much time, we have only so many resources, we can ask only so much of the people. Let's ask and do and provide and pursue that which builds faith in the Lord Jesus Christ. That is our highest priority. That is the pearl in the box. And by this formula we can have as many boxes as we need. We will always do the necessary, supportive, ancillary thing, but in the end, those activities and programs need to give people a spiritual experience and assist in saving their souls.

## MATTHEW 14

After Jesus had performed the miracle of feeding the five thousand from five loaves of bread and two fishes, He sent them all away and put His disciples into a fishing boat to cross over to the other side of the Sea of Galilee. He then "went up into a mountain apart to pray" (Matthew 14:23).

We are not told all of the circumstances of the disciples as they set out in their boat, but it was toward evening, and certainly it was a night of storm. The winds must have been ferocious from the start. Because of that, these men probably never even raised the sails but labored only with the oars—and labor it would have been. We know this because by the time of "the fourth watch of the night" (Matthew 14:25)—that is somewhere between three and six in the morning—they had gone only a few miles.

Now the ship was caught up in a truly violent storm, like those that can still sweep down on the Sea of Galilee to this day. But as always, Christ was watching over them. He *always* does, remember? Seeing their difficulty, the Savior simply took the most direct approach to their boat, striding out across the waves to help them, walking on the water as surely as He had walked upon the land. In their moment of great extremity, the disciples looked and saw in the darkness this wonder in a fluttering robe, coming toward them on the ridges of the sea. They cried out in terror at the sight, thinking that it was a phantom upon the waves. Then through the storm and darkness—when the ocean seems so great and little boats seem so small—there came the ultimate and reassuring voice of peace from their Master. "It is I," He said, "be not afraid" (Matthew 14:27).

Finally recognizing the Master that night, Peter exclaimed, "Lord, if it be thou, bid me come unto thee on the water." And Christ's answer to him was as it *always* is—to all of us—"Come," He said. Instantly, as was his nature, Peter sprang over the vessel's side and into the troubled waves. While his eyes were fixed upon the Lord, the wind could toss his hair and the spray could drench his robes, but all was well—he was coming to Christ. Only when his faith and his focus wavered, only when he removed his glance from the Master to see the furious waves and the black gulf beneath him, only then did he begin to sink. In fear he cried out, "Lord, save me" (Matthew 14:28–30). In some disappointment, "the master of ocean and earth and skies" (see "Master, the Tempest Is Raging," *Hymns*, no. 105) stretched out His hand and grasped the drowning disciple with the gentle rebuke, "O thou of little faith, wherefore didst thou doubt?" (Matthew 14:31).

This scriptural account reminds us that the first step in coming to Christ—or His coming to us—may fill us with something very much like sheer terror. It shouldn't, but it sometimes does. One of the grand ironies of the gospel is that the very source of help and safety being offered us is the thing from which we may, in our mortal short-sightedness, flee. For whatever the reason, I have seen investigators run from baptism, I have seen elders run from a mission call, I have seen sweethearts run from marriage, and young couples run from the fear of families and the future. Too often too many of us run from the very things that will bless us and save us and soothe us. Too often we see gospel commitments and commandments as something to be feared and forsaken. Quoting the marvelous James E. Talmage on this matter, "Into every adult human life come experiences like unto the battling of the storm-tossed voyagers with contrary winds and threatening seas; ofttimes the night of struggle and danger is far advanced before succor appears; and then, too frequently the saving aid is mistaken for a greater terror. [But] as came unto [these disciples] in the midst of the turbulent waters, so comes to all who toil in faith, the voice of the Deliverer—'It is I; be not afraid'" (*Jesus the Christ*, 3rd ed. [1916], 337).

I can envision the Savior coming to Peter, walking on the water, offering encouragement and reassurance even as Peter overcomes his fear, exerts his faith, and takes a few steps on the water himself. I regret that we seem quick to criticize Peter for that fear, for losing his faith, and for faltering in this remarkable moment. It seems to me we owe Peter our greatest admiration and commendation for (a) wanting to, for daring to do as his master did, to walk on the water, and (b) actually succeeding in doing so. Granted, he took only a few steps successfully, but he did it. I don't know about you, but I know of no other person in history, besides the Savior, who actually performed such a miraculous feat.

I say this because we need to celebrate faith and encourage faith wherever and whenever we find it, even if it is partial, piecemeal, and inadequate. None of us has the complete, grand faith we ought to have, but we can cherish the faith we do have and commend that which we see in others, commendation that will do more than anything else to encourage even greater accomplishment, encourage the next steps we need to take. Great faith comes from small beginnings. Great mustard trees grow out of tiny mustard seeds, and the great faith of a mature Peter comes from the halting faith of a new and fearful disciple. If we have practiced our faith, believed in God's help, limited our fears, and desired to step where the Master strides, when the moment comes, I believe we too will be able to walk upon the watery concourses of life.

Just a word about fear. First of all, it is ironic that Peter feared the appearance of the safest and most reassuring figure in human history, but sometimes the very best of circumstances can startle us. "What is this?" we say. "Can this possibly be true?" we ask. The fact is, wondrous events can come upon us so unexpectedly that we initially fear them. When such moments come, we need to take a deep breath, maybe pinch ourselves once or twice, wait for things to settle into our minds and onto our hearts, and then rejoice at our good fortune. In the gospel of Jesus Christ, we need to be strong, to believe good things are in store, to persevere until shadows flee and the goodness of God is evident in our lives.

## MATTHEW 16

I wish to share my testimony of—and express my eternal gratitude for—the restoration of the holy priesthood, this hallowed prerogative, this sovereign gift, and the role it plays in our lives on both sides of the veil.

The essential function of the priesthood in linking time and eternity was made explicit by the Savior when He formed His Church during His mortal ministry. To His senior Apostle Peter He said, "I will give unto thee the keys of the kingdom of heaven: and whatsoever thou shalt bind on earth shall be bound in heaven: and whatsoever thou shalt loose on earth shall be loosed in heaven" (Matthew 16:19). Six days later He took Peter, James, and John to a mountaintop where He was transfigured in glory before them. Then prophets from earlier dispensations, including at least Moses and Elijah, appeared in glory also and conferred the various keys and powers that each held.

Unfortunately, those Apostles were soon killed or otherwise taken from the earth, and their priesthood keys were taken with them, resulting in more than 1,400 years of priesthood privation and absence of divine authority among the children of men. But part of the modern miracle and marvelous history we celebrate is the *return* of those same earlier heavenly messengers in *our* day and the restoration of those same powers they held for the blessing of all mankind.

Clearly, acting with divine authority requires more than mere social contract. It cannot be generated by theological training or a commission from the congregation. No, in the authorized work of God there has to be power greater than that already possessed by the people in the pews or in the streets or in the seminaries—a fact that many honest religious seekers had known and openly acknowledged for generations leading up to the Restoration.

It is true that some few in that day did not want their ministers to claim special sacramental authority, but most people longed for priesthood sanctioned by God and were frustrated as to where they might go to find such. We in The Church of Jesus Christ of Latter-day Saints can trace the priesthood line of authority exercised by the newest deacon in the ward, the bishop who presides over him, and the prophet who presides over all of us. That line goes back in an unbroken chain to angelic ministers who came from the Son of God Himself, bearing this incomparable gift from heaven.

### MATTHEW 17

With Jesus leading the way, Peter, James, and John ascended "an high mountain apart" (Matthew 17:1) and there witnessed the transfiguration of the Son of God. His face shone as brightly as the sun at noonday and His raiment was as radiant as light itself. Then heavenly messengers appeared, bestowing upon this "First Presidency" every needful key for their ministry. In benediction to the event, a bright cloud overshadowed them and they heard the voice of Deity declare, "This is my beloved Son, in whom I am well pleased; hear ye him" (Matthew 17:5).

The moment passed. The vision ceased. Peter still had many lessons to learn in the days ahead—of political loyalty and personal forgiveness, of material sacrifice and fruitful service. With his brethren he was yet to receive the sacrament of the Lord's supper, to hear Jesus pray for their unity, and to discover which of their number was "a devil" (John 6:70). But whatever lay before him, the transfer of authority was now complete. Endowed with power from on high and armed with the certainty of his conviction, he descended with Jesus into the valley of the shadow of death.

## MATTHEW 18

A servant was in debt to his king for the amount of 10,000 talents. Hearing the servant's plea for patience and mercy, "the lord of that servant was moved with compassion, and . . . forgave . . . the debt." But then that same servant would not forgive a fellow servant who owed him 100 pence. On hearing this, the king lamented to the one he had forgiven, "Shouldest not thou also have had compassion on thy fellow servant, even as I had pity on thee?" (see Matthew 18:24–33).

There is some difference of opinion among scholars regarding the monetary values mentioned here—and forgive the U.S. monetary reference—but to make the math easy, if the smaller, unforgiven 100-pence debt were, say, $100 in current times, then the 10,000-talent debt so freely forgiven would have approached $1 billion—or more!

As a personal debt, that is an astronomical number—totally beyond our comprehension. No one can spend that much! Well, for the purposes of this parable, it is *supposed* to be incomprehensible; it is *supposed* to be beyond our ability to grasp, to say nothing of beyond our ability to repay. That is because this isn't a story about two servants arguing in the New Testament. It is a story about us, the fallen human family—mortal debtors, transgressors, and prisoners all. Every one of us is a debtor and the verdict was imprisonment for every one of us. And there we would all have remained were it not for the grace of a King who sets us free because He loves us and is "moved with compassion toward us" (D&C 121:4).

Jesus uses an unfathomable measurement here because His Atonement is an unfathomable gift given at an incomprehensible cost. That, it seems to me, is at least part of the meaning behind Jesus's charge to be perfect. We may not be able to demonstrate yet the 10,000-talent perfection the Father and the Son have achieved, but it is *not* too much for Them to ask us to be a little more God-like in little things, that we speak and act, love and forgive, repent and improve at least at the 100-pence level of perfection, which it is clearly within our ability to do.

## MATTHEW 20

I wish to speak of the Savior's parable in which a householder "went out early in the morning to hire labourers." After employing the first group at 6:00 in the morning, he returned at 9:00 a.m., at 12:00 noon, and at 3:00 in the afternoon, hiring more workers as the urgency of the harvest increased. The scripture says he came back a final time, "about the eleventh hour" (approximately 5:00 p.m.), and hired a concluding number. Then just an hour later, all the workers gathered to receive their day's wage. Surprisingly, all received the same wage in spite of the different hours of labor. Immediately, those hired first were angry, saying, "These last have wrought but one hour, and thou hast made them equal unto us, which have borne the burden and heat of the day" (see Matthew 20:1–15). When reading this parable, perhaps you, as well as those workers, have felt there was an injustice being done here. Let me speak briefly to that concern.

First of all, it is important to note that no one has been treated unfairly here. The first workers agreed to the full wage of the day, and they received it. Furthermore, they were, I can only imagine, very grateful to get the work. In the time of the Savior, an average man and his family could not do much more than live on what they made that day. If you didn't work or farm or fish or sell, you likely didn't eat. With more prospective workers than jobs, these first men chosen were the most fortunate in the entire labor pool that morning.

Indeed, if there is any sympathy to be generated, it should at least initially be for the men not chosen who also had mouths to feed and backs to clothe. Luck never seemed to be with some of them. With each visit of the steward throughout the day, they always saw someone else chosen.

But just at day's close, the householder returns a surprising fifth time with a remarkable eleventh-hour offer! These last and most discouraged of laborers, hearing only that they will be treated fairly, accept work without even knowing the wage, knowing that anything will be better than nothing, which is what they have had so far. Then as they gather for their payment, they are stunned to receive the same as all the others! How awestruck they must have been and how very, very grateful! Surely never had such compassion been seen in all their working days.

It is with that reading of the story that I feel the grumbling of the first laborers must be seen. As the householder in the parable tells them (and I paraphrase only slightly): "My friends, I am not being unfair to you. You agreed on the wage for the day, a good wage. You were very happy to get the work, and I am very happy with the way you served. You are paid in full. Take your pay and enjoy the blessing. As for the others, surely I am free to do what I like with my own money." Then this piercing question to anyone then or now who needs to hear it: "Why should you be jealous because I choose to be kind?"

Brothers and sisters, there are going to be times in our lives when someone else gets an unexpected blessing or receives some special recognition. May I plead with us not to be hurt—and certainly not to feel envious—when good fortune comes to another person? We are not diminished when someone else is added upon. We are not in a race against each other to see who is the wealthiest or the most talented or the most beautiful or even the most blessed. The race we are really in is the race against sin, and surely envy is one of the most universal of those.

Furthermore, envy is a mistake that just keeps on giving. Obviously, we suffer a little when some misfortune befalls us, but envy requires us to suffer all good fortune that befalls everyone we know! What a bright prospect that is—downing another quart of pickle juice every time anyone around you has a happy moment! To say nothing of the chagrin in the end, when we find that God really is both just and merciful, giving to all who stand with Him "all that he hath" (Luke 12:44), as the scripture says. So, lesson number one from the Lord's vineyard: coveting, pouting, or tearing others down does not elevate your standing, nor does demeaning someone else improve your self-image. So be kind, and be grateful that God is kind. It is a happy way to live.

A second point I wish to take from this parable is the sorrowful mistake some could make if they were to forgo the receipt of their wages at the end of the day because they were preoccupied with perceived problems earlier in the day. It doesn't say here that anyone threw his coin in the householder's face and stormed off penniless, but I suppose one might have.

My beloved brothers and sisters, what happened in this story at 9:00 or noon or 3:00 is swept up in the grandeur of the universally generous payment at the end of the day. The formula of faith is to hold on, work on, see it through, and let the distress of earlier hours—real or imagined—fall away in the abundance of the final reward. Do not dwell on old issues or grievances—not toward yourself nor your neighbor nor even, I might add, toward this true and living Church. The majesty of your life, of your neighbor's life, and of the gospel of Jesus Christ will be made manifest at the last day, even if such majesty is not always recognized by everyone in the early going. So don't hyperventilate about something that happened at 9:00 in the morning when the grace of God is trying to reward you at 6:00 in the evening—whatever your labor arrangements have been through the day.

We consume such precious emotional and spiritual capital

clinging tenaciously to the memory of a discordant note we struck in a childhood piano recital, or something a spouse said or did twenty years ago that we are determined to hold over his or her head for another twenty, or an incident in Church history that proved no more or less than that mortals will always struggle to measure up to the immortal hopes placed before them. Even if one of those grievances did not originate with you, it can end with you. And what a reward there will be for that contribution when the Lord of the vineyard looks you in the eye and accounts are settled at the end of our earthly day.

Which leads me to my third and last point. This parable—like all parables—is not really about laborers or wages any more than the others are about sheep and goats. This is a story about God's goodness, His patience and forgiveness, and the Atonement of the Lord Jesus Christ. It is a story about generosity and compassion. It is a story about grace. It underscores the thought I heard many years ago that surely the thing God enjoys most about being God is the thrill of being merciful, especially to those who don't expect it and often feel they don't deserve it.

I do not know who may need to hear the message of forgiveness inherent in this parable, but however late you think you are, however many chances you think you have missed, however many mistakes you feel you have made or talents you think you don't have, or however far from home and family and God you feel you have traveled, I testify that you have not traveled beyond the reach of divine love. It is not possible for you to sink lower than the infinite light of the Atonement of Jesus Christ shines.

Whether you are not yet of our faith or were with us once and have not remained, there is nothing in either case that you have done that cannot be undone. There is no problem which you cannot overcome. There is no dream that in the unfolding of time and eternity cannot yet be realized. Even if you feel you are the lost and last laborer of the eleventh hour, the Lord of the vineyard still stands beckoning. "Come boldly [to] the throne of grace" (Hebrews 4:16) and fall at the feet of the Holy One of Israel. Come and feast "without money and without price" (Isaiah 55:1) at the table of the Lord.

To those of you who have been blessed by the gospel for many years because you were fortunate enough to find it early, to those of you who have come to the gospel by stages and phases later, and to those of you who may still be hanging back, to each of you, one and all, I testify of the renewing power of God's love and the miracle of His grace. His concern is for the faith at which you finally arrive, not the hour of the day in which you got there.

In the light of Jesus's discourses on the coming of the Son of Man, undoubtedly all the disciples were looking forward to their thrones, but James and John were for a moment seeking the most distinguished ones. Their mother, kneeling before the Savior, said urgently, "Grant that these my two sons may sit, the one on thy right hand, and the other on the left, in thy kingdom" (Matthew 20:21). We cannot fault this mother in wishing such a noble station for her sons, except that she is asking the Lord Himself to aid in matters of ambition and vanity, however worthy. What was asked could not be granted without Jesus being untrue to His own character and His habitual teachings on selfishness and humility.

Furthermore, hers seems to be a narrow view of the kingdom of God. It is a particularly unwholesome court, even in a secular world, where places of highest distinction can be obtained by solicitation and favor rather than by invitation and merit.

This request apparently caused some bitterness, for it is recorded that "when the ten heard it, they were moved with indignation against the two brethren" (Matthew 20:24). We are, at first, a bit mystified by this scene. If James and John innocently thought that such a request would cause difficulty, they seem to be less wise than we might have assumed. If, on the other hand, they made the request without caring for the disaffection that might ensue, they would appear to be selfish as well as vain.

In fact, they were neither. The gentleness of Jesus's reply suggests that these faithful disciples were not calculating or cruel. They were, along with the other ten, simply children in terms of gospel growth and education. Christ uttered not a word of direct rebuke, but dealt with them as a father might deal with a child who had made a request without thinking of the consequences. He implies no malice—only ignorance.

"Ye know not," He said to them quietly, "what ye ask. Are ye able to drink of the cup that I [am about to drink] . . .?" (Matthew 20:22–23)."

There is more than compassion or correction in this question: there is instruction, concerning the true way of progress in the kingdom of God. Jesus taught His disciples that advancement in His kingdom went not by favor or political solicitation, but rather *via dolorosa*, by the way of the cross. The palm-bearers in the celestial realms of glory will be they who have passed through tribulation, and the princes of the kingdom will be those who have drunk most deeply of His cup of service and sacrifice. For those who refused to drink thereof—the selfish, the self-indulgent, the purely ambitious or vain—there will be lesser places in the kingdom, places without honor on His right hand or His left.

The startling question put to those two Apostles by Jesus did not take them by surprise. Promptly and firmly they replied, "We are able."

His response then: "Ye shall drink indeed of my cup, and be baptized with the baptism that I am baptized with" (Matthew 20:20–24).

This was a strange favor, it seems to me, for the Lord to grant. He was not mockingly offering them the cup of His suffering rather than a throne in His kingdom, but He was obviously very serious. However, perhaps even then James and John knew that the cup and the throne were inextricably linked and could not be given separately.

The single greatest feature in the lesson that Jesus gave His disciples here is the contrast between His kingdom and the other kingdoms of this earth. Both the way of acquiring position and the means of exerting authority were dramatically different. His message to them was that earthly kingdoms were then being ruled by a class of people who possessed hereditary rank, or by those who sought favors from them. The governing class were those whose birthright was to rule, and whose boast it was never to have been in a servile position. In His kingdom, on the other hand, people could only become great—rulers, if you will—by first being servants to those over whom they were to bear rule. In the divine commonwealth, only they rule who account it a privilege to serve.

Having explained by contrast the great principles of the spiritual kingdom over those of mortal men, Jesus next enforced the doctrine by a reference to His one example. "Whosoever will be chief among you," He said to the Twelve, "let him be your servant," and then He added: "Even as the Son of man came not to be ministered unto, but to minister, and to give his life a ransom for many" (Matthew 20:27–28).

These words were spoken by Jesus as one who claimed to be a king, and who was indeed ordained in the very councils of heaven to be the first in a great and mighty kingdom. So the Lord is setting himself forth here not merely as an example of humility, but as one who must illustrate for us all that the way to power in the spiritual world is through service, not intimidation; it is loss of self, not obsession with self, that brings those otherwise mystical icons—meaning and fulfillment and happiness. The truth of the matter is that He would one day be ministered to by legions—yes, worlds—of willing, devoted people, acknowledging Him as their Lord and King. Every knee would someday bow and every tongue confess. The point on which He wishes to fix the attention of His disciples here, however, is the peculiar way in which He must work to obtain that crown. In effect, He says:

"I am a King, and I expect one day to claim my kingdom; James and John are not mistaken in that respect. But I will obtain my kingdom differently from the way secular princes get theirs. They get their thrones by succession or intimidation or selfishness; I will get mine by personal merit alone. They secure their kingdom by right of birth or bombast; I hope to secure mine by the right of service. They inherit their subjects, but I will need to buy mine, with the payment of my body and my blood."

I am sure that you and I, being not only less worthy than Christ but also less worthy than Apostles like James and John, would leave such troublesome issues alone if they would only leave us alone. As a rule, we usually do not seek the bitter cup and the bloody baptism, but sometimes they seek us. The fact of the matter is God *does* draft men and women into the spiritual warfare of this world, and if any of us come to genuine religious faith and conviction as a result of that—as many a drafted soldier has done—it will nevertheless be a faith and a conviction that in the first flames of the battle we did not enjoy and certainly did not expect.

I am asking that we put ourselves in the place of James and John, put ourselves in the place of seemingly committed, believing, faithful Latter-day Saints, and ask ourselves, "If we are Christ's and He is ours, are we willing to stand firm forever? Are we in The Church of Jesus Christ of Latter-day Saints for keeps, for the duration, until it's over? Are we in it through the bitter cup, the bloody baptism, and all?"

## MATTHEW 21

All of the tension, the constant movement between revelation and rejection, between prophets and apostasy, was captured in a parable by Jesus, the very Son of God Himself. Near the end of His mortal ministry, He said by way of both history and prophecy:

"Hear another parable: There was a certain householder, which planted a vineyard, and hedged it round about, and digged a winepress in it, and built a tower, and let it out to husbandmen, and went into a far country:

"And when the time of the fruit drew near, he sent his servants to the husbandmen, that they might receive the fruits of it.

"And the husbandmen took his servants, and beat one, and killed another, and stoned another.

"Again, he sent other servants more than the first: and they did unto them likewise.

"But last of all he sent unto them his son, saying, They will reverence my son.

"But when the husbandmen saw the son, they said among themselves, This is the heir; come, let us kill him, and let us seize on his inheritance.

"And they caught him, and cast him out of the vineyard, and slew him.

"When the lord therefore of the vineyard cometh, what will he do unto those husbandmen?

"They say unto him, He will miserably destroy those wicked men, and will let out his vineyard unto other husbandmen, which shall render him the fruits in their seasons" (Matthew 21:33–41).

That brief parable summarizes the experience of revelation and apostasy as it has been repeated prophet after prophet and dispensation after dispensation. Of course, Jesus gave that parable knowing the cycle would continue, even to the point that His life would be taken and another long night of apostasy would follow.

For those first decades following Jesus's death, the Apostles were able to keep the doctrine pure, but as they died or were killed without passing on their ordinations and without the revelation they had received, truly the vineyard of the Lord was plundered. Eventually priesthood keys and presiding priesthood authority were taken from the earth. Doctrine was corrupted and unauthorized changes were made in Church ordinances and Church organization. Scholasticism replaced inspiration, philosophy obscured what had been simple truths, and false ideas crept in everywhere. Much of the knowledge of the true character and nature of God the Father, His Son Jesus Christ, and the Holy Ghost was lost. The doctrines of faith, repentance, baptism, and the gift of the Holy Ghost became distorted or abused or forgotten. The principle of revelation was denied, and the canon of scripture was declared to be closed. The role of prophets and apostles as had been known in those earlier dispensations ceased. No such men were found upon the earth.

## MATTHEW 23

"O Jerusalem, Jerusalem," Jesus cried, "thou that killest the prophets, and stonest them which are sent unto thee, how often would I have gathered thy children together, even as a hen gathereth her chickens under her wings, and ye would not!

"Behold, your house is left unto you desolate" (Matthew 23:37–38).

And therein lies a message for every young man and young woman in The Church of Jesus Christ of Latter-day Saints. You may wonder if it is worth it to take a courageous moral stand in high school, or to go on a mission only to have your most cherished beliefs reviled, or to strive against much in society that sometimes ridicules a life of religious devotion. Yes, it is worth it, because the alternative is to have our "houses" left unto us "desolate"—desolate individuals, desolate families, desolate neighborhoods, and desolate nations.

So here we have the burden of those called to bear the messianic message. In addition to teaching, encouraging, and cheering people on (that is the pleasant part of discipleship), from time to time these same messengers are called upon to worry, to warn, and sometimes just to weep (that is the painful part). They know full well that the road leading to the promised land "flowing with milk and honey" (Exodus 3:8) of necessity runs by way of Mount Sinai flowing with "thou shalts" and "thou shalt nots" (see Exodus 20:3–17).

## MATTHEW 24

As we follow the prophets, we will become more and more of the people that God expects us to be in preparation for the coming of His Son. I do not know when the Second Coming is, but I know that it is one day closer today than it was yesterday, and it will be one day closer tomorrow than it is today, and it is going to happen sometime.

In fact, the beginnings of the Second Coming started around 200 years ago in a grove of trees outside Palmyra, New York, with the great First Vision of the Father and the Son. And so it has been underway for a long time, and if anyone asks you, as they sometimes ask me, "When is the Second Coming?" you can honestly say, "The initial elements of it are already underway, nearly 200 years' worth." When the grand moment of His ultimate appearance will come, we don't know. We leave that entirely in the hands of the Lord, and He says in the scriptures that even the angels of heaven know not of that final arrival (see Matthew 24:36).

But when that final arrival comes, we need to look like His Church. When He comes, we need to look and act and be like His people. That is a responsibility that has never been required in the history of this dispensation or of any dispensation. No one has ever had to receive the Savior and present to Him His Church. That is our dispensation only.

We are the people. I don't know how we are fortunate enough to do that. I don't know why we were the ones selected in the great councils of heaven before the world was to be that, but we somehow got the privilege to come in the last dispensation, the greatest dispensation of time, to prepare for the return of the living Son of the living God and to present to Him His Church. We are going to give the Church of the Lamb to the Lamb, and no one has ever had to do that before, ever.

And everything that you are seeing—more active priesthood, more engaged Relief Society, more attention to the youth, more temples that are being built, more creations of units, more home-centered experience—as all of that unfolds, every bit of that is an attempt to make us true, living disciples of Christ, 24 hours a day, 7 days a week, 365 days a year, at all times and in all things and in all places that we may be in.

That is what is happening in this Church, and we have been preparing for it for a long time. All the years that I have been a General Authority, we have talked about these things. The timing is such that they are coming to pass now. I don't know what that means. I don't think it means that the Second Coming is tomorrow. I don't think it is the day after tomorrow, but it could be, and it is going to be some to-morrow. It is going to happen someday. And we will be better prepared for it as we follow the living prophets, as we respond to the timing of the Lord and understand bit by bit and step by step and day by day how these improvements, how these adjustments are incorporated into the kingdom of God on earth.

Prophecies regarding the last days often refer to large-scale calamities such as earthquakes or famines or floods. These in turn may be linked to widespread economic or political upheavals of one kind or another.

But there is one kind of latter-day destruction that has always sounded to me more personal than public, more individual than collective, a warning, perhaps more applicable inside The Church of Jesus Christ of Latter-day Saints than outside it. The Savior warned that in the last days even those of the covenant, the very elect, could be deceived by the enemy of truth (see Matthew 24:24). If we think of this as a form of spiritual destruction, it may cast light on another latter-day prophecy. Think of the heart as the figurative center of our faith, the poetic location of our loyalties and our values; then consider Jesus's declaration that in the last days "men's hearts [shall fail] them" (Luke 21:26).

The encouraging thing, of course, is that our Father in Heaven knows all of these latter-day dangers, these troubles of the heart and soul, and has given counsel and protections regarding them.

## MATTHEW 25

We are, we always feel, at very best, one-talent people. And that is probably precisely the reason the Lord directed His parable of the talents to the one-talent servant. You will recall that one servant had five talents and received five more. Another had two talents and received two more. But then came all the rest of us—one-talent servants, in trouble as always, running the risk of losing that little bit that we have.

That parable is a painful one, and we tend to sympathize very readily with the one-talent servant who says, "Lord, I knew thee that thou art a hard man . . . and I was afraid, and went and hid thy talent in the earth" (Matthew 25:24–25). It almost seems unfair to think of the one-talent man losing all that he has. Why not take one talent away from the five-talent servant, and he would still have four? The story reads the way it does because none of us would sympathize with the five-talent servant. We wouldn't even identify with the two-talent one. If the Lord wants to get through to us, He will have to address us the way we see ourselves, even if it is not the way He sees us—poor one-talent people, surrounded by five-talent people, fearing that the Lord is a hard man, being afraid, hiding our talents in the earth.

But the real message of that parable is to go to work—to invest ourselves in our cause and to find a return on that investment.

"And so he that had received five talents came and brought other five talents, saying, Lord, thou deliveredst unto me five talents: behold, I have gained beside them five talents more.

"His lord said unto him, Well done, thou good and faithful servant. . . .

"He also that had received two talents came and said, Lord, thou deliveredst unto me two talents: behold, I have gained two other talents beside them.

"His lord said unto him, Well done, good and faithful servant; thou hast been faithful over a few things, I will make thee ruler over many things" (Matthew 25:20–23).

The same promise could have been given to the man of one talent. I am morally certain that if he had brought kind of a return with any kind of use of the one talent that he had, the Lord would have said to him *exactly* as He said to the five-talent man and the two-talent man, "Well done, thou good and faithful servant, thou hast been faithful over a few things, I will make thee ruler over many things: enter thou into the joy of thy lord."

We need to build. We need to grow. We need to increase.

## MATTHEW 26

I wish to direct my next words in a special way to those who are alone or feel alone or, worse yet, feel abandoned. These might include those longing to be married, those who have lost a spouse, and those who have lost—or have never been blessed with—children. My empathy embraces wives forsaken by their husbands, husbands whose wives have walked away, and children bereft of one or the other of their parents—or both. This group can find within its broad circumference a soldier far from home, a missionary in those first weeks of homesickness, or a father out of work, afraid the fear in his eyes will be visible to his family. In short, it can include all of us at various times in our lives.

To all such I speak of the loneliest journey ever made and the unending blessings it brought to all in the human family. I speak of the Savior's solitary task of shouldering alone the burden of our salvation. Rightly He would say, "I have trodden the winepress alone; and of the people there was none with me. . . . I looked, and there was none to help; and I wondered that there was none to uphold [me]" (Isaiah 63:3, 5).

We know from scripture that Jesus's messianic arrival in Jerusalem on the Sunday preceding Passover was a great public moment. But eagerness to continue walking with Him would quickly begin to wane.

Soon enough He was arraigned before the Israelite leaders of the day—first Annas, the former high priest, then Caiaphas, the current high priest. In their rush to judgment, these men and their councils declared their verdict quickly and angrily. "What further need have we of witnesses?" they cried. "He is [worthy] of death" (Matthew 26:65–66).

With that He was brought before the gentile rulers in the land. Herod Antipas, the tetrarch of Galilee, interrogated Him once, and Pontius Pilate, the Roman governor in Judea, did so twice, the second time declaring to the crowd, "I, having examined him before you, have found no fault in this man" (Luke 23:14). Then, in an act as unconscionable as it was illogical, Pilate "scourged Jesus, [and] delivered him to be crucified" (Matthew 27:26). Pilate's freshly washed hands could not have been more stained or more unclean.

This was also a telling time among those who knew Jesus more personally. The most difficult to understand in this group is Judas Iscariot. We know the divine plan required Jesus to be crucified, but it is wrenching to think that one of His special witnesses who sat at His feet, heard Him pray, watched Him heal, and felt His touch could betray Him and all that He was for thirty pieces of silver. Never in the history of this world has so little money purchased so much infamy. We are not the ones to judge Judas's fate, but Jesus said of His betrayer, "Good [were it] for that man if he had not been born" (Matthew 26:24).

Of course, others among the believers had their difficult moments as well. Following the Last Supper, Jesus left Peter, James, and John to wait while He ventured into the Garden of Gethsemane alone. Falling on His face in prayer, "sorrowful . . . unto death" (Matthew 26:38), the record says, His sweat came as great drops of blood as He pled with the Father to let this crushing, brutal cup pass from Him. But, of course, it could not pass. Returning from such anguished prayer, He found His three chief disciples asleep, prompting Him to ask, "Could ye not watch with me one hour?" (Matthew 26:40). So it happens two more times until on His third return He says compassionately, "Sleep on now, and take your rest" (Matthew 26:45), though there would be no rest for Him.

Later, after Jesus's arrest and appearance at trial, Peter, accused of knowing Jesus and being one of His confidants, denies that accusation not once but three times. We don't know all that was going on here, nor do we know of protective counsel which the Savior may have given to His Apostles privately, but we do know Jesus was aware that even these precious ones would not stand with Him in the end, and He had warned Peter accordingly (see Mark 14:27–31). Then, with the crowing of the cock, "the Lord turned, and looked upon Peter. And Peter remembered the word of the Lord. . . . And [he] went out, and wept bitterly" (Luke 22:61–62).

Thus, of divine necessity, the supporting circle around Jesus gets smaller and smaller and smaller, giving significance to Matthew's words: "All the disciples forsook him, and fled" (Matthew 26:56). Peter stayed near enough to be recognized and confronted. John stood at the foot of the cross with Jesus's mother. Especially and always the blessed women in the Savior's life stayed as close to Him as they could. But essentially His lonely journey back to His Father continued without comfort or companionship.

One of the great consolations of the gospel is that because Jesus walked such a long, lonely path utterly alone, *we* do not have to do so. His solitary journey brought great company for our little version of that path—the merciful care of our Father in Heaven, the unfailing companionship of His Beloved Son, the consummate gift of the Holy Ghost, angels in heaven, family members on both sides of the veil, prophets and apostles, teachers, leaders, friends. All of these and more have been given as companions for our mortal journey because of the Atonement of Jesus Christ and the Restoration of His gospel. Trumpeted from the summit of Calvary is the truth that we will never be left alone nor unaided, even if sometimes we may feel that we are.

## MATTHEW 27

Jesus should have had some protection from the government. But how much help does Herod provide? He doesn't want to do anything that will offend Rome. He is ensconced in a castle with wine, women, and song, taking off the head of John the Baptist for the Baptist's indictment of his lifestyle. He is not going to be sympathetic to Jesus. He does not want any more trouble than he has already got.

And Pilate? This is one of the great ironies of scripture: "I find no fault" in this man, he said of Jesus (John 19:4). You remember that Pilate washed his hands of the whole matter, literally and figuratively, and then demanded that Jesus be lashed, that He be excoriated with a whip that had small pieces of steel and glass embedded in the tips (see Matthew 27:22–26).

So He is not getting any help in the political community. He certainly is not going to get any help in the religious community. But perhaps the populace, the people in the street will come to His aid. One might think that at least they would be behind Him. When He entered the city a week earlier, riding on a colt, a little donkey, all prescribed and prophesied, the scripture says of His reception, "a very great multitude" thronged to meet Him, "saying, Hosanna to the Son of David: Blessed is he that cometh in the name of the Lord" (Matthew 21:8–9). Where were all those people now? Can one lose that many friends in seven days?

To these people in the street, Pilate makes an offer. He says in effect, "I feel a little guilty about how we are treating this innocent man. Furthermore, my wife has had a dream about his innocence and that makes me really nervous. I can give you this man. I am entitled to release Him. By Roman authority and the Jewish tradition, I can spare Him on this Passover week. Do you want Jesus? Or do you want a *real* criminal, Barabbas?"

And the people say (forgive my derisive interpretation), "Oh, no, we don't want Him. We would not want anyone who heals and blesses and prays and gives sight to the blind and hearing to the deaf and lets the lame walk and raises people from the dead. We certainly wouldn't want anyone like that loose in our city. Give us a blood-thirsty heathen. Give us Barabbas" (see Matthew 27:13–31).

I don't know whether you know that *Barabbas* was a title more than it was a man. He was a man, but it is a title. In Aramaic, it literally meant "son of the father." How ironic! It was a mafia-like term—a secret combination, undercover, underworld title.

So this choice comes down to the people. Caiaphas and Annas don't help. Pilate and Herod don't help. But we had hopes in the people. They have seen Him. They have felt His presence, and they have seen His miracles. Yet they say, "No, no. Don't give us the Son of the Father. Give us the son of the father." It is one of the most discouraging moments in all of scripture for me personally—that decency and kindness, humility and love could matter so little to so many. Of no great credit to the people, Christ moved on toward Calvary.

"Eli, Eli, lama sabachthani? My God, my God, why hast thou forsaken me?" (Matthew 27:46).

What father or mother could stand by and listen to the cry of their children in distress and not render aid and assistance? I have heard of mothers throwing themselves into raging streams when they could not swim a stroke. I have heard of fathers rushing into burning buildings at the expense of their own lives. All this to rescue those whom they love.

We cannot stand by and listen to crying without it touching our hearts. God the Father had the power to save, and He loved His Son. He could have saved Him. He might have rescued Him from the crowds, or when the crown of thorns was placed on His head. He saw the Son condemned, faint under the load. He saw Him dragged through the streets. He saw His body stretched out, cruel nails driven through His hands and feet, blows that broke the skin, and tore the flesh, and let out life's blood of His beloved Son.

He could have rescued Him when they mocked, "Save thyself. If thou be the Son of God, come down from the cross" (Matthew 27:40).

He looked upon this with great grief and agony over His Only Begotten Son. He heard what must have been the most unbearable words ever uttered, "My God, my God, why hast thou forsaken me?" (Matthew 27:46).

I am willing to testify that God was never, ever closer to the Savior of the world than He was at that moment. But He—even the Father—had to step back a quarter of an inch. He had to step back half a step because it was destiny that the Atonement of Jesus Christ had to be carried out absolutely alone by a mortal man, half-mortal, who could pay the price for mortal sins. It would not work if divinity inserted itself. The payment could not be complete if somehow angels rushed to attend or God the very Father lifted the load. Christ had to do this alone.

In that moment, when the Father might have saved His Son, I thank Him and praise Him that He did not fail us. For He had not only the love for that Son in mind, but He also had the love for all His children.

I rejoice that He did not interfere, that His love for us made it possible for Him to endure, to look upon the sufferings of His Son and to give Him finally to us, our Savior and our Redeemer.

I know now why God is a jealous God. I believe God is jealous, lest we should ever ignore or slight or forget this, His greatest of all gifts to us. Remember, remember.

When the veil was rent and the boulders were thrown and the earth trembled, God in His heaven seemed to be saying, "You cannot do this to my Son with impunity. I am charitable and merciful. I will not exact the uttermost farthing, but I will tell you just for a moment or two how I feel about this cruelty." Thus, the old legalistic remnant of Judaism was rent, the veil of the temple from top to bottom.

God also rent the very earth, a message to the Roman Empire about how impressed He was with material things—political power, geographical dominion, or anything else that the hand of man might conceive. All of that was figuratively and literally shaken.

In the middle of all that, with skies having been darkened, rocks rent, and a temple nearly destroyed, a non-believing Roman centurion looked up and said for all of us, for time and for all eternity, "Truly this was the Son of God" (Matthew 27:54).

I testify to you that He is the Son of God. I can't talk about it without being emotional. In my mind's eye I stand with that centurion, testifying with him that this was the Son of God, the Redeemer of the world, the Savior of all humankind. This pagan soldier is evidence that someday *every* knee shall bow and every tongue confess that this is the truth.

## MATTHEW 28

When Nicodemus came to Jesus early in the Savior's ministry, he spoke for all of us when he said, "Rabbi, we know that thou art a teacher come from God" (John 3:2). Christ was, of course, much more than a teacher. By the time He had successfully fulfilled His earthly mission He was the Savior and Redeemer of the world. But while He moved toward His Atonement, Resurrection, and all that would return Him to the right hand of the Father, He taught—even at age twelve. He was always teaching.

That is what characterized His mortal ministry and that is the charge He left with us as His disciples. In His final earthly admonition to the Apostles He said, "Go ye therefore, and *teach* all nations. . . . *Teaching* them to observe all things whatsoever I have commanded you" (Matthew 28:19–20; emphasis added).

Whether it be from our parents or full-time missionaries or fellow members in the classrooms of The Church of Jesus Christ of Latter-day Saints, our testimonies begin and grow at the hands of inspiring teachers. Perhaps that is why Paul said that God placed in the Church "first apostles, secondarily prophets, thirdly teachers" (1 Corinthians 12:28). Linking teachers with the presiding officers of the Church suggests how important teachers are in the eyes of our Father in Heaven.

This is the missionary's purpose as the Savior phrased it two centuries ago:

"Go ye therefore, and teach all nations, baptizing them in the name of the Father, and of the Son, and of the Holy Ghost:

"Teaching them to observe all things whatsoever I have commanded you: and, lo, I am with you alway, even unto the end of the world. Amen" (Matthew 28:19–20).

That is the charge Christ gave to the original Twelve Apostles, who were, of course, the first missionaries. Now, here is our twenty-first-century expression of that purpose given to missionaries, as recorded in the first paragraph of the first page of *Preach My Gospel*:

"Invite others to come unto Christ by helping them receive the restored gospel through faith in Jesus Christ and His Atonement, repentance, baptism, receiving the gift of the Holy Ghost, and enduring to the end" (*Preach My Gospel* [2018], 1).

Whether using ancient or modern text, this will always be the essence of our gospel responsibility and the commission we as missionaries have. We are to teach the first principles and ordinances of the gospel, all of which draw their meaning and efficacy from the Atonement of Jesus Christ. It is no coincidence that the word *Atonement* sits glaringly right in the middle of your missionary purpose for a reason.

Every truth that a missionary teaches—whether that be faith, repentance, baptism, or any other element of the gospel message— is only an appendage to the central message of all time: that Jesus is the Christ, the Only Begotten Son of God, the Holy Messiah, the Promised One, the Savior and Redeemer of the World, that He alone burst the bands of death and triumphed over the captivity of hell, that not one of us could ever have those blessings without His merciful, grace-filled intervention in our behalf, and that there never shall be any "other name given nor any other way nor means whereby salvation can come unto the children of men, only in and through the name of Christ, the Lord Omnipotent" (Mosiah 3:17).

Your missionary message is that with a complete offering of His body, His blood, and the anguish of His spirit, Christ atoned for the initial transgression of Adam and Eve in the Garden of Eden, and also paid the personal price for the accumulated sins of everyone else who would ever live in this world from Adam to the end of time.

WHAT MANNER OF MAN IS THIS,

THAT EVEN THE WIND AND THE SEA OBEY HIM?

—MARK 4:41

# MARK

The Savior, beleaguered and tired—I don't know if you ever think of the Savior being tired—weary from crowds that surround Him and the blessings that He has given, the love that He feels and the strength that is drained from Him, says, "Let us cross over the lake."

"The same day," after he'd been speaking to the people, "when [evening] was come, he saith unto them, Let us pass over unto the other side. And when they had sent away the multitude, they took him even as he was in the ship. And there were also with him other little ships" (Mark 4:35–36).

If I said only that much and you were a student of the New Testament, you would know what Gospel I am quoting. I am quoting Mark. Mark is like a journalist. Mark is like the Eyewitness News at 6:00 p.m. Mark tells you precise details. He is the only writer that would have said there were other little ships with Him.

"And there arose a great storm of wind, and the waves beat into the ship, so that it was now full. And he was in the hinder part of the ship, asleep on a pillow" (Mark 4:37–38). Another small but exquisite point, someone—almost certainly a woman—was kind enough to have provided Him with a pillow. He is tired, really tired, because one has to be exhausted to sleep through a storm in which the boat is taking water. Furthermore, these were experienced men on board with Him—eleven of the original Twelve were Galileans (only Judas Iscariot was a Judean). And six of those eleven were fishermen. They had lived on this lake. They had made their living by fishing on it.

They had been there since they were children. Their fathers had them mending nets and making repairs on the boat when they were very young. They know this sea; they know the winds and the waves. They are experienced men—but they are terrified. And if *they* are afraid, this is a legitimate storm.

"He was in the hinder part of the ship, asleep on a pillow: and they awake him, and say unto him, Master, carest thou not that we perish?" (Mark 4:38).

I am sure they thought about their situation. I am sure they wondered, *Should we wake Him? He is absolutely exhausted. He has to be, to be sleeping through this.* But they are legitimately afraid and fear the boat is going down. So with some trepidation, I am certain, they shake Him a little, and then have to shake Him a lot, saying, "Master, carest thou not that we perish?" He arose—I have often wondered how He looked at them; I will leave that to you—"He arose and rebuked the wind, and said unto the sea, Peace, be still. And the wind ceased, and there was a great calm."

But He is not through rebuking. He has rebuked the elements, but now there is a gentle rebuke for these His brethren. "And [then] he said unto them, Why are ye so fearful? how is it that ye have no faith?" (Mark 4:39–40).

Is that fair? Wouldn't you be afraid? I would be afraid. I do not like water sports. I swim, I water-ski, I have fun in the water, but I am very respectful of it. I am mindful of the power of water, and I have seen its force in nature. I can honestly say when my children go on a boating excursion of any kind, I am always uneasy until they are home and we can count all the noses. I am sure I would have been afraid at least for the others if I had been on that boat and that storm had come. I am sure I would have thought the boat was going down. Would He have said to me, "Why are you so afraid? How is it that you have no faith?"

Surely it is not that they don't have *any* faith. This is early in their ministry. It is only the fourth chapter of Mark. But Jesus has them on an accelerated schedule. He has to create a Quorum of the Twelve Apostles, in thirty-six months, made up of brand-new converts—no small task indeed. Here, in the middle of a storm, the Savior is trying to teach them, and it is a hard lesson indeed. They cannot afford to be afraid, particularly in light of what lies ahead of them.

Fortunately, the next line relieves the tension a little, at least for the reader—the scriptures can make you smile—"And they feared exceedingly." So much for a lesson about being fearful. Except now it is a different fear. Now it is not about the storm; it is about Him. "They feared exceedingly and said one to another, What manner of man is this, that even the wind and the sea obey him?" (Mark 4:41).

They are not quite sure what they have signed on for here. We can be sure they are going to see much more that will make them stand in greater awe.

Why does Jesus push these twelve men as much as He does, with the line, "Why do you have no faith?" The answer to that is embedded in the first line of this story. Did you miss it? I passed over it quickly in hopes you would. The first line of the story is, "That same day, when even was come, he saith unto them, Let us pass over unto the other side." If the living Son of the living God says, "Let us pass over to the other side," we can be absolutely certain they are going to "pass over to the other side." However much the wind blows, however much the rain pelts, however much stress the boat experiences, and however fearful it all may be, it is going to be all right. Peter, James, John, Andrew, Bartholomew, Philip, and the rest—be calm. Ride out the storm. You are going to go to the other side because He said you would.

Do you think for one moment that God in His heaven would let that boat go down with the living Son of the living God and Redeemer of the world on it? With all He was and all He had left to do? They are "going to the other side."

That is why the Savior can say, "You are too fearful. You have too little faith." He needs them to know who He is and what their new obligations are going to be. He needs them to believe.

I invite us all to realize in the depths of our soul that whatever the storm, whatever the disruption, whatever the travail, whatever the pain, whatever the challenge, externally or internally, we have reason to rejoice and celebrate, assured that we will be triumphant. We have reason *not* to fear. And we have every reason to have faith, because Jesus is the Christ.

I testify that our ship is not going to go down in the sea of eternity. We are not going to lose in our quest for eternal life. We are sailing with the Master of ocean and sky. We are sailing with the Master of heaven and earth. We are sailing with the Master who created the sea and causes the wind to blow. We are in the safest hands available in all of time and eternity. Be peaceful. Be reassured. Be happy. And be strong.

## MARK 5

I wish to celebrate the otherwise unknown woman who strained to touch even the hem of Jesus's robe in an effort to heal the issue of blood that had plagued her for more than a decade.

This woman is a true heroine to me. She is nameless and faceless and anonymous in the story, but we love her dearly for her faith. Perhaps only if we lived in her day would we understand her desperation. She has had this affliction for twelve years and, depending on the exact nature of the malady, has probably been considered "unclean" by her leaders, banned from any temple experience, and ostracized in society generally. We are told that she "had spent all that she had" seeking a cure from physicians (Mark 5:26). To say she is desperate would be a gross understatement.

What were her feelings that day? What had she heard of Jesus and His miracles? How reluctant and shy may she have been? How large was the crowd? What were the chances, realistically speaking, that she could get a blessing from Him amidst all this throng and clamor? Even if she could somehow actually get His attention, surely she would not be able to speak with Him, would have no way or time to tell her story, even to describe her ailment. Her situation was hopeless. Or was it? Can we keep hoping when all else, including twelve years of disappointment, tell us it is fruitless to do so? Something in her—call it hope or faith or determination or all of these—said to her: "Perhaps I can fight through the crowd with enough faith to at least touch the fabric that touches Him. Perhaps if I can just feel the hem of His garment, then perhaps He can feel my need. Perhaps just a touch will be enough." And the rest is history. She had, perhaps unknowingly, obeyed the most basic commandment Jesus ever uttered. "Come unto me," He said repeatedly, and she had come. The rest of that crowd had come to observe or cheer or jeer or just have a great day in the street. But this woman came with single-minded purpose; she came to make true contact, spiritual and physical contact, with the Savior. She came, as the scriptures say, "with real intent" (Moroni 10:4).

No wonder Jesus recognized the touch, even amidst all the jostling and shoving and tugging and pulling. Hers wasn't that kind of bumping, boisterous touch. It was the reach of faith, the grasp of hope. Those contacts are always recognized by the Savior, and, in due time, they are always rewarded. Some blessings come immediately, some come later, some may not come until heaven—but they come to those who come to Him. Always. I love this woman and the faith she represents.

## MARK 9

On one occasion Jesus came upon a group arguing vehemently with His disciples. When the Savior inquired as to the cause of this contention, the father of an afflicted child stepped forward saying he had approached Jesus's disciples for a blessing for his son, but they were not able to provide it. With the boy still gnashing his teeth, foaming from the mouth, and thrashing on the ground in front of them, the father appealed to Jesus with what must have been last-resort desperation in his voice:

"If thou canst do any thing," he said, "have compassion on us, and help us.

"Jesus said unto him, If thou canst believe, all things are possible to him that believeth.

"And straightway the father of the child cried out, and said with tears, Lord, I believe; help thou mine unbelief" (Mark 9:22–24).

This man's initial conviction, by his own admission, is limited. But he has an urgent, emphatic desire in behalf of his only child. We are told that is good enough for a beginning. "Even if you can no more than *desire to believe*," Alma declares, "let this desire work in you, even until ye believe" (Alma 32:27; emphasis added). With no other hope remaining, this father asserts what faith he has and pleads with the Savior of the world, "If *thou* canst do *any thing*, have compassion on *us,* and help *us*" (Mark 9:22; emphasis added). I can hardly read those words without weeping. The plural pronoun *us* is obviously used intentionally. This man is saying, in effect: "Our whole family is pleading. Our struggle never ceases. We are exhausted. Our son falls into the water. He falls into the fire. He is continually in danger, and we are continually afraid. We don't know where else to turn. Can *you* help us? We will be grateful for *anything*—a partial blessing, a glimmer of hope, some small lifting of the burden carried by this boy's mother every day of her life."

"If *thou* canst do *any thing,*" spoken by the father, comes back to him "If *thou* canst *believe,*" spoken by the Master (Mark 9:22–23; emphasis added).

"Straightway" the scripture says—not slowly nor skeptically nor cynically, but "straightway"—the father cries out in his unvarnished parental pain: "Lord, I believe; help thou mine unbelief." In response to new and still partial faith, Jesus heals the boy, almost literally raising him from the dead, as Mark describes the incident (see Mark 9:23–27).

With this tender scriptural record as a backdrop, I wish to speak directly to the young people of The Church of Jesus Christ of Latter-day Saints—young in years of age or young in years of membership or young in years of faith. One way or another that should include just about all of us.

Observation number one regarding this account is that when facing the challenge of faith, the father asserts his strength first, and only then acknowledges his limitation. His initial declaration is affirmative and without hesitation: "Lord, I believe." I would say to all who wish for more faith, remember this man! In moments of fear or doubt or troubling times, hold the ground you have already won, even if that ground is limited. In the growth we all have to experience in mortality, the spiritual equivalent of this boy's affliction or this parent's desperation is going to come to all of us. When those moments come and issues surface the resolution of which is not immediately forthcoming, *hold fast to what you already know and stand strong until additional knowledge comes.* It was of this very incident, this specific miracle, that Jesus said, "If ye have faith as a grain of mustard seed, ye shall say unto this mountain, Remove hence to yonder place; and it shall remove; and nothing shall be impossible unto you" (Matthew 17:20). The size of your faith or the degree of your knowledge is not the issue—it is the integrity you demonstrate toward the faith you do have and the truth you already know.

The second observation is a variation of the first. When problems come and questions arise, do not start your quest for faith by saying how much you do *not* have, leading as it were with your "unbelief." That is like trying to stuff a turkey through the beak! Let me be clear on this point: I am not asking you to pretend to faith you do not have. I *am* asking you to be true to the faith you *do* have. Sometimes we act as if an honest declaration of doubt is a higher manifestation of moral courage than is an honest declaration of faith. It is not! So let us all remember the clear message of this scriptural account: Be as candid about your questions as you need to be; life is full of them on one subject or another. But if you and your family want to be healed, don't let those questions stand in the way of faith working its miracle.

Furthermore, you have more faith than you think you do because of what the Book of Mormon calls "the greatness of the evidences" (Helaman 5:50). "Ye shall know them by their fruits," Jesus said

(Matthew 7:16), and the fruit of living the gospel is evident in the lives of Latter-day Saints everywhere. As Peter and John said once to an ancient audience, I say today, "We cannot but speak the things which we have seen and heard," and what we have seen and heard is that "a notable miracle hath been done" in the lives of millions of members of this The Church of Jesus Christ of Latter-day Saints. That cannot be denied (see Acts 4:20, 16).

This is a divine work in process with the manifestations and blessings of it abounding in every direction, so please don't hyperventilate if from time to time issues arise that need to be examined, understood, and resolved. They do and they will. *In this Church, what we know will always trump what we do not know. And remember, in this world everyone is to walk by faith.*

So be kind regarding human frailty—your own as well as that of those who serve with you in a Church led by volunteer mortal men and women. Except in the case of His only perfect Begotten Son, imperfect people are all God has ever had to work with. That must be terribly frustrating to Him, but He deals with it. So should we. And when you see imperfection, remember that the limitation is *not* in the divinity of the work. As one gifted writer has suggested: When the infinite fullness is poured forth, it is not the oil's fault if there is some loss because finite vessels can't quite contain it all (adapted from Alfred Edersheim, *The Life and Times of Jesus the Messiah,* 2 vols. [1883], 2:108).

Those finite vessels include you and me, so be patient and kind and forgiving.

Last observation. When doubt or difficulty come, do not be afraid to ask for help. If we want it as humbly and honestly as this father did, we can get it. The scriptures phrase such earnest desire as being pursued "with full purpose of heart, acting no hypocrisy and no deception before God" (2 Nephi 31:13). In response to *that* kind of importuning, I testify God will send help from both sides of the veil to strengthen our belief.

One of the principles that we use in the gospel for drawing close to God is fasting. We know there is great power in fasting based, if for no other reason, on a powerful story in the New Testament, where a man approached the Savior for a blessing for his son (see Mark 9:17–29). His son had seizures, and the father said he was uncontrollable. The boy would throw himself into water. He would throw himself into the fire. He was uncontrollable in great measure. The parents were exhausted and in great fear. They first went to the disciples, to the Apostles who were following Jesus, and sought a blessing at their hands. But it was not entirely successful—apparently partly successful, but not entirely so.

So the man went further, so to speak. He went to the Savior Himself and asked for a blessing for this boy. Christ gave him the blessing and the boy was healed. He became gentle and subdued, perfectly calm and free from his seizures.

The only people more stunned than the father and mother, who were so grateful, were the Apostles. They asked the Master, "What happened? Why couldn't we do that? The father asked us first, we did our best, gave the best blessing we could. Why didn't it work for us?"

Now, you have to remember that the Apostles are very, very young at this time in the Church. By the time that story comes along, the Apostles have only been following Him for six or eight months. So they were still learning and maturing in their own faith. But Christ was also willing to help them mature and help them learn. He taught them, saying simply about this incident, pointing to the boy, "This kind"—and I don't know how many kinds there are, but it would be the serious kind—"this kind can come forth by nothing, but by prayer and fasting" (Mark 9:29).

I really believe that part of the reason the Apostles didn't see success entirely with their blessing is that God wanted to teach them a lesson they would not have learned otherwise—namely, that on occasion fasting adds additional power no matter how efficacious a given blessing might be.

One of the reasons we fast, even if we don't need a miracle, even if we don't need to heal someone, even if we don't need a great, grand answer to prayer, is to remember that were it not for the goodness of God, we would starve to death and we would die of thirst. A fast is a mini famine. It is a self-imposed famine of only twenty-four hours. But it is a reminder that we know—and say to God—that every blessing we have comes at His hand. Many of us have access to more food than we will ever use. And we probably waste water even where it is scarce.

Yet, there are many who do not have enough to eat or drink. They don't have enough to stay healthy or nutritionally sound. When we fast, especially when we contribute a fast offering, we are saying voluntarily to God, "I know that could happen to me, and I am grateful, Father in Heaven, for food to eat and water to drink and health to keep going."

## MARK 10

Christ always gave credit to His Father for everything. Indeed, for me, one of the sweetest things in all of the scriptures is His love for His Father. He repeatedly said, "I have come to say only what I heard my Father say. I have come to do only what I have seen my Father do." The Gospels are replete with marvelous, repeated references and examples of Christ paying tribute to His Father, saying in effect, "I am a loyal son. I am doing what I was sent to do by my Father," and that His Father is the greater of the two.

When someone came to Jesus and asked, "Good Master, what shall I do that I may inherit eternal life?" His immediate response was, "Why callest thou me good?" I certainly would have done so. I can't blame this young man for so saying. But Christ says, "Why callest thou me good? there is none good but one, that is, God [the Father]" (Mark 10:17–18).

A little later in the New Testament we read, "Ye have heard how

I said unto you, I go away, and [then] come again unto you. If ye loved
me, ye would rejoice, because I said, I go unto the Father: for my Father
is greater than I" (John 14:28). From start to finish, for all the grandeur of His life, for all the magnificence of His perfect leadership, He
would deflect that credit and, in His humility, offer the compliment to
His Father in Heaven.

## MARK 12

Of the many magnificent purposes served in the life and ministry
of the Lord Jesus Christ, one great aspect of that mission often goes
uncelebrated. His followers did not fully understand it at the time,
and many in modern Christianity do not grasp it now, but the Savior
Himself spoke of it repeatedly and emphatically. It is the grand truth
that in all that Jesus came to say and do, including and especially in
His atoning suffering and sacrifice, He was showing us who and what
God our Eternal Father is like, how completely devoted He is to His
children in every age and nation. In word and in deed Jesus was trying
to reveal and make personal to us the true nature of His Father, our
Father in Heaven.

He did this at least in part because then and now all of us need to
know God more fully in order to love Him more deeply and obey Him
more completely. As both Old and New Testaments declare, "The first
of all the commandments is . . . thou shalt love the Lord thy God with
all thy heart, and with all thy soul, and with all thy mind, and with
all thy strength: this is the first [and great] commandment" (Mark
12:29–30).

After generations of prophets had tried to teach the family of man
the will and the way of the Father, usually with little success, God,
in His ultimate effort to have us know Him, sent to earth His Only
Begotten and perfect Son, created in His very likeness and image, to
live and serve among mortals in the everyday rigors of life.

To come to earth with such a responsibility, to stand in place of
Elohim—speaking as He would speak, judging and serving, loving

and warning, forbearing and forgiving as He would do—this is a duty of such staggering proportions that you and I cannot comprehend such a thing. But in the loyalty and determination that would be characteristic of a divine child, Jesus could comprehend it and He did it.

Jesus did not come to improve God's view of humankind nearly so much as He came to improve mortals' view of God and to plead with them to love their Heavenly Father as He has always and will always love them. The plan of God, the power of God, the holiness of God, yes, even the anger and the judgment of God they had occasion to understand. But the love of God, the profound depth of His devotion to His children, they still did not fully know—until Christ came.

## MARK 14

Given the monumental challenge of addressing inequity in the world, what can one man or woman do? The Master Himself offered an answer. When prior to His betrayal and Crucifixion Mary anointed Jesus's head with an expensive burial ointment, Judas Iscariot protested this extravagance and "murmured against her."

"Jesus said, . . . why trouble ye her? she hath wrought a good work. . . .

"*She hath done what she could*" (Mark 14:5–6, 8; emphasis added).

She hath done what she could! What a succinct formula! A journalist once questioned Mother Teresa of Calcutta about her hopeless task of rescuing the destitute in that city. He said that, statistically speaking, she was accomplishing absolutely nothing. This remarkable little woman shot back that her work was about love, not statistics. Notwithstanding the staggering number *beyond* her reach, she said she could keep the commandment to love God and her neighbor by serving those *within* her reach with whatever resources she had. The journalist reasoned that if there would be more joy in heaven over one sinner who repents than over the ninety and nine who need no repentance, then apparently God is not overly preoccupied with percentages (see Malcolm Muggeridge, *Something Beautiful for God* [1971], 28).

So how might we "do what we can"?

For one thing, we can, as King Benjamin taught, cease withholding our means because we see the poor as having brought their misery upon themselves. Perhaps some *have* created their own difficulties, but don't the rest of us do exactly the same thing? Isn't that why this compassionate ruler asks, "Are we not all beggars?" (Mosiah 4:19). Don't we all cry out for help and hope and answers to prayers? Don't we all beg for forgiveness for mistakes we have made and troubles we have caused? Don't we all implore that grace will compensate for our weaknesses, that mercy will triumph over justice at least in our case? Little wonder then that King Benjamin says we *obtain* a remission of our sins by pleading to God, who compassionately responds, but we *retain* a remission of our sins by compassionately responding to the poor who plead to us (see Mosiah 4:26).

Now, lest I be accused of proposing quixotic, global social programs or of endorsing panhandling as a growth industry, I reassure you that my reverence for principles of industry, thrift, self-reliance, and ambition is as strong as that of any man or woman alive. We are always expected to help ourselves before we seek help from others. Furthermore, I don't know exactly how each of you should fulfill your obligation to those who do not or cannot always help themselves. But I know that God knows, and He will guide you in compassionate acts of discipleship if you are conscientiously wanting and praying and looking for ways to keep a commandment He has given us again and again.

Mark says Jesus fell to His knees and cried, "Abba, Father" (Mark 14:36). *Papa*, we would say, or *Daddy*. This is not abstract theology now. This is a Son pleading with His Dad. "Abba [Daddy, Papa] . . . all things are possible unto thee; take away this cup from me."

Who could resist that? God in His heavens—in His righteousness, for this, His only perfect child—who could resist? "You can do anything. I know you can do anything. Take this cup from me."

That whole prayer, Mark noted, had been to plead that if it were possible, this hour would be stricken from the plan. Christ said, in effect, "If there is another path, I would rather walk it. If there is any other way—*any* other way—I will gladly embrace it." But in the end the cup does not pass.

Then He said and did that which most characterizes His life in time and in eternity, the words and the act that made Jesus the Son of God, according to the great Book of Mormon prophet Abinadi. He said and did what He had to do to become the Son (with a capital S) of God. He yielded to the will of His Father and said, "Not my will, but thine, be done" (Luke 22:42). That is, for all intents and purposes, the last moment in the divine conversation between Father and Son in Jesus's mortal ministry.

From there on the die has been cast. He will see it through no matter what.

Without likening ourselves to Him too much, that symbol of the cup that cannot pass is a cup that comes in our life as well as in His. It is in a much lesser way, to a much lesser degree, but it comes often enough to teach us that we have to yield, we have to obey.

AND SHE BROUGHT FORTH HER FIRST-BORN

SON, AND WRAPPED HIM IN SWADDLING

CLOTHES, AND LAID HIM IN A MANGER; BECAUSE

THERE WAS NO ROOM FOR THEM IN THE INN.

—LUKE 2:7

# LUKE

This is a story before the Nativity account of Joseph and Mary and the baby Jesus. This happened six months before, when an angel appeared to Zacharias and told him they were going to have a baby. Now, he and Elizabeth were old people. And, like Abraham and Sarah, they wondered, "How are we going to have a baby at our age?"

Zacharias was the priest selected to enter the temple that day. His duties were to offer a prayer for all of Israel and light the incense on the altar located in the Holy Place, in front of the curtain that separated him from the Holy of Holies. While he was there, he took righteous advantage of the moment and offered a personal prayer.

You would have done so too, and I would if I were there for that once-in-a-lifetime experience. Even though the scriptures don't spell it out, we know that Zacharias had been making a personal prayer, because the account says:

"There appeared unto him [Zacharias], an angel of the Lord standing on the right side of the altar of incense. And when Zacharias saw him, he was troubled, and fear fell upon him" (Luke 1:11–12).

"But the angel said unto him,"—and here is the reason we know he had been praying—"Fear not, Zacharias, for thy prayer is heard" (Luke 1:13). What prayer? Because of what follows, we can suppose this is a prayer about having a baby, even in their old age. "Fear not, Zacharias, for thy prayer is heard; and thy wife Elisabeth shall bear thee a son, and thou shalt call his name John" (Luke 1:13). They knew all about this prayer in heaven. The answer to it was all arranged. This was going to be the birth of John the Baptist. It was a magnificent moment, promising a precursor to the birth of the Savior.

"And thou shalt have joy and gladness, and many shall rejoice at his birth.

"For he shall be great in the sight of the Lord, and shall drink neither wine nor strong drink; and he shall be filled with the Holy Ghost, even from his mother's womb.

"And many of the children of Israel shall he turn to the Lord their God.

"And he shall go before him in the spirit and power of Elias, to turn the hearts of the fathers to the children, and the disobedient to the wisdom of the just; to make ready a people prepared for the Lord" (Luke 1:14–17).

There is the angel's declaration: a powerful, sweet, sacred, unique moment. And here is the next verse:

"Zacharias said unto the angel, Whereby shall I know this?" Or, how can I know this; is this really true? "For I am an old man, and my wife well stricken in years" (Luke 1:18).

It would seem that this was a serious mistake on Zacharias's part. "The angel answering said unto him, I am Gabriel, that stand in the presence of God; and am sent to speak unto thee, and to shew thee these glad tidings" (Luke 1:19). Now, I don't know how you read that verse, but I have got to think he said that with some passion.

He does not put it in print—these are not the words that he uses—but he could have said, "How dare you question this experience? How dare you ask me if this is true? Do you understand that I am an angel, that I am Gabriel standing before you in the temple? This does not happen to you every day. This does not happen to you every week. This has never happened to you in your entire life, and it is never going to happen again. I am Gabriel, and I stand in the presence of God."

"Behold, thou shalt be dumb, and not able to speak, until the day that these things shall be performed, because thou believest not my words, which shall be fulfilled in their season" (Luke 1:20). Gabriel was saying in a very angelic, sweet way, "Zacharias, you are going to get a chance to be quiet for the next nine months and think about this experience. You won't ever again have to ask if this is true. You are going to be taught what it is like to stand in the presence of an angel, which angel stands in the presence of God."

Why such punishment to an old man? "Because thou believest not my words, all of which shall be fulfilled in their season." Elisabeth *is* going to get pregnant, and she does. That baby *is* going to be born, and he is. And Zacharias *is* going to repent, and he does. But he has nine months during which he does not say a word because he treated lightly the special thing he was given.

When some people say, "How can I believe this story of the Restoration? How can I know this is true?" I feel like Gabriel! "Do you know who we are? Do you know Whose Church this is? Do you know Whose gospel this is? Do you know who Joseph Smith really, truly is? Do you know who Gabriel and Moroni are, really, truly?"

If you don't know these things, I am tempted to ask that you be dumb, not able to speak for eight or nine months, so you can think about this, because it is all true. Every single, solitary word that God has ever declared is going to be fulfilled. Every word! And that was the lesson that Zacharias did not initially understand.

I have thought a lot about Mary, this most favored mortal woman in the history of the world, who as a mere child received an angel who uttered to her those words that would change the course not only of her own life but also that of all human history: "Hail thou virgin who art highly favoured of the Lord. The Lord is with thee; for thou art chosen and blessed among women" (JST, Luke 1:28). The nature of her spirit and the depth of her preparation were revealed in a response that shows both innocence and maturity: "Behold the handmaid of the Lord; be it unto me according to thy word" (Luke 1:38).

It is here I stumble, here that I grasp for the feelings a mother has when she knows she has conceived a living soul, feels life quicken and grow within her womb, and carries a child to delivery. At such times fathers stand aside and watch, but mothers feel and never forget.

## LUKE 2

*See also Matthew 2*

As a father I have recently begun to think more often of Joseph, that strong, silent, almost unknown man who must have been more worthy than any other mortal man to be the guiding foster father of the living Son of God. It was Joseph selected from among all men who would teach Jesus to work. It was Joseph who taught Him the books of the law. It was Joseph who, in the seclusion of the shop, helped Him begin to understand who He was and ultimately what He was to become.

I was a student at Brigham Young University just finishing my first year of graduate work when our first child, a son, was born. We were very poor, though not so poor as Joseph and Mary. My wife and I were both going to school, both holding jobs, and in addition worked as head residents of an off-campus apartment complex to help defray our rent. We drove a little Volkswagen that had a half-dead battery because we could not afford a new one (Volkswagen *or* battery).

Nevertheless, when I realized that our own night of nights was coming, I believe I would have done any honorable thing in this world, and mortgaged any future I had, to make sure my wife had the clean sheets, the sterile utensils, the attentive nurses, and the skilled doctors who brought forth our firstborn son. If she or that child had needed special care at the Mayo Clinic, I believe I would have ransomed my very life to get it.

I compare those feelings (which I have had with each succeeding child) with what Joseph must have felt as he moved through the streets of a city not his own, with not a friend or kinsman in sight, nor anyone willing to extend a helping hand. In these very last and most painful hours of her "confinement," Mary had ridden or walked approximately 100 miles from Nazareth in Galilee to Bethlehem in Judea. Surely Joseph must have wept at her silent courage. Now, alone and unnoticed, they had to descend from human company to a stable, a grotto full of animals, there to bring forth the Son of God.

I wonder what emotions Joseph might have had as he cleared away the dung and debris. I wonder if he felt the sting of tears as he hurriedly tried to find the cleanest straw and hold the animals back. I wonder if he wondered: "Could there be a more unhealthy, a more disease-ridden, a more despicable circumstance in which a child could be born? Is this a place fit for a King? Should the mother of the Son of God be asked to enter the valley of the shadow of death in such a foul and unfamiliar place as this? Is it wrong to wish her some comfort? Is it right He should be born here?"

But I am certain Joseph did not mutter and Mary did not wail. They knew a great deal and did the best they could. Perhaps these parents knew even then that in the beginning of His mortal life, as well as in the end, this baby son born to them would have to descend beneath every human pain and disappointment. He would do so to help those who also felt they had been born without advantage.

Again, I have thought of Luke's careful phrasing about that holy night in Bethlehem:

"The days were accomplished that *she* should be delivered.

"And *she* brought forth *her* firstborn son, and [she] wrapped him in swaddling clothes, and [she] laid him in a manger" (Luke 2:6–7; emphasis added).

Those brief pronouns trumpet in our ears that, second only to the child himself, Mary is the chiefest figure, the regal queen, mother of mothers—holding center stage in this grandest of all dramatic moments. And those same pronouns also trumpet that, save for her beloved husband, she was very much alone.

I have wondered if this young woman, something of a child herself, here bearing her first baby, might have wished her mother, or an aunt, or her sister, or a friend, to be near her through the labor. Surely the birth of such a son as this should command the aid and attention of every midwife in Judea! We all might wish that someone could have held her hand, cooled her brow, and when the ordeal was over, given her rest in crisp, cool linen.

But it was not to be so. With only Joseph's inexperienced assistance, she herself brought forth her firstborn son, wrapped him in the little clothes she had knowingly brought on her journey, and perhaps laid him on a pillow of hay.

Then on both sides of the veil a heavenly host broke into song. "Glory to God in the highest," they sang, "and on earth, peace among men of good will" (Luke 2:14; Phillips Translation). But except for heavenly witnesses, these three were alone: Joseph, Mary, the baby to be named Jesus.

At this focal point of all human history, a point illuminated by a new star in the heavens revealed for just such a purpose, probably no other mortal watched—none but a poor young carpenter, a beautiful virgin mother, and silent stabled animals who had not the power to utter the sacredness they had seen.

The setting was as peaceful as nature could provide. The coming of night in early spring. Skies crystal clear, with stars coming out first by tens, then by hundreds, and finally by thousands. Shepherds in the field finding relief from the glare of day and the fatigue of honest labor. The only unusual—but remarkably beautiful—element in this pastoral scene was in a hillside stable close to the village, in which two human figures huddled over an infant lying in a manger with only a few domestic animals witnessing the wonder they had seen.

These three, who had found no friend or willing host in crowded Bethlehem town, were, first: a beautiful young virgin mother named Mary (probably only in her early or mid-teens if the traditions of the

day were in force), whose courage and conspicuous faith are as striking as anything ever recorded in scripture; second: her husband called
Joseph, older than his young wife but one who by definition must
have been the most worthy man on earth to raise a baby that was not
his physical son but who would, in time, become Joseph's spiritual father; third: last and most beautiful of all, the baby to be named Jesus,
lying in swaddling clothes on the cleanest hay an anxious father could
collect.

One irony this quiet, unpublicized scene belied was the fact
that no baby had ever been born about whom so much was already
known, of whom so much had already been written, and regarding
whom so much was already expected. Indeed, knowledge about who
and what He was started in the realms of heaven before *anyone* had
been born! As Firstborn of the Father in the world of spirits, He was
designated there to be the Savior of the world, foreordained to be the
Lamb "slain from the foundation of the world" (Revelation 13:8).
Later, but still prior to His birth, He would be the grand Jehovah of
the Old Testament, helping Noah save his family in time of flood and
aiding Joseph save his family in time of famine. He was the magiste-
rial Jehovah whose names would include "Wonderful, Counselor, The
Mighty God, The Everlasting Father, The Prince of Peace" (2 Nephi
19:6). He was the Alpha and Omega in the great plan of mercy who
would eventually "preach good tidings unto the meek; . . . bind up the
brokenhearted, . . . proclaim liberty to the captives, and [open] the
prison to them that are bound" (Isaiah 61:1).

To accomplish this, He would tread the winepress of redemption
utterly and entirely alone, with no mortal companion who would aid
Him and no heavenly companion who could. In bearing all the sins
and sorrows of mortality, He would bring the incomprehensible gift
of salvation to the entire human family from Adam to the end of the
world. In the full course of His journey, He would be the Shepherd
and Bishop of our Souls, the Great High Priest of our Profession, the
free-flowing Fountain of all Righteousness (see 1 Peter 2:25; Hebrews

3:1; Ether 8:26). All of these mortal duties and demands had yet to be met. But not tonight. Not this night. Here He was just a baby in the arms of a mother who adored Him, watched over by a father who was gentle and strong.

⁓❦⁓

I have had an interesting thought about Christmas. It is not unique; I am sure other people have thought it better and sooner. But it has come to my mind that the Lord so often deals with pairs of things. I don't think it is a coincidence that our missionaries go out two by two. There is something in the nature of a second witness, there is something in the nature of the two-part experience that we have in life.

I think in the great creative process, in the heart of every family, the future of eternity is basically built around a man and a woman. We have those pairs, as it were, to take us through eternity. In the scriptures, when the Lord wants to declare some things, He will occasionally emphasize it by using the same phrase over, like "the law shall go forth of Zion, and the word of the Lord from Jerusalem" (Micah 4:2). Well, that really means the same thing, but He says it twice, in pairs. Those are similar, those are parallel.

And then He does it with opposites. Wheat and tares and sheep and goats, and we get great parables and twosomes. There, in those particular cases, they happen to be contrary.

But the thought I have had at Christmas is that part of the heart of the plan of salvation and of Christ's message to us is built around birth and death and that they are essentially inseparable. The surest thing we have in life, once we are born, is that we are going to die, and, of course, there is no one who has ever died who has not already been born. You know, it seems kind of silly to say that, but those two are linked, I think, in an important way.

President Gordon B. Hinckley once talked about Christmas in the context of Easter. He said that the minute we celebrate Christmas we ought to, in some sense, almost in the same breath, be celebrating Easter. You get that idea of the unity of Christ's birth and Christ's death as a two-part experience, an A and B experience, this shared, paired commonality that we are talking about.

At a Christmas Eve family home evening once, my son-in-law led the discussion and gave a little Christmas message based on a phrase from the hymn "Silent Night." The phrase was from the third verse, one that we don't know as well and don't sing as often as we sing the first verse. In that hymn, it speaks of Christmas as being "the dawn of redeeming grace." That really struck me: that the redeeming grace really, technically would not come until the Atonement of Jesus Christ. The redeeming grace that we sing about in "Silent Night" would not be in effect, the real mission would not be accomplished, the success of the plan of salvation would not be complete until that death and Resurrection, until the Atonement of Jesus Christ was complete.

But the birth, the Bethlehem birth, was the dawn of it. It was the beginning, the sun rising, if you will, on the idea of redemption and grace. It would take the Savior's lifetime—thirty-three years, more or less—for that baby to mature and to finally go to Gethsemane and to the Garden Tomb and the Resurrection. But that little manger scene was the dawn of that and inseparable from it. You would not have the one without the other.

So surely that is why those shepherds were so adoring, and that is why those wise men came. There is another duality: the two extremes in the culture. The shepherds were workmen, the lowest on the social scale, not very well received or respected in the downtown community. That is who the shepherds represent on one end.

Then these kings came, these wise men representing the highest, most sophisticated, wealthiest people in society, bringing gold and frankincense and myrrh. There again is a kind of pairing: the poorest with the most well-off, the least educated with the most educated. That little twosome comes together in the manger scene as well.

Also, a part of that Christmas scene were the angels who came and sang hosannas—legions of angels; the whole heaven was filled with angels. And obviously, they were not just celebrating the birth. The reason they were so excited is that it meant the beginning of the Atonement of Jesus Christ. It meant the beginning of the Resurrection and of eternal life. That was the exciting thing.

Without that, this would have been just another baby. Mary and Joseph would have been just another poor couple who did not have enough money to get a hotel room and so ended up in a stable, in a cave in the side of the hill. That night would have been lost in history and would have meant nothing had this baby not been the baby that it was. And the baby that it was, was the baby that was going on to be crucified for our sins and our sorrows and to be resurrected for eternal life, that every single, solitary one of us would be able to enjoy. Every human being who had ever lived or would yet live would be resurrected because of Christ.

And so, when the angels were singing or the shepherds were adoring or the wise men were coming, whether they knew it or not, they were celebrating both of those events. They were celebrating the birth because of the life that would be lived and the triumph that would come to the end of it.

⁂

Approximately forty days after Mary's delivery of her child, she and Joseph took the baby named Jesus to the temple, where the infant was to be formally presented unto the Lord.

As they made their way toward the temple, the Holy Spirit was resting upon a beloved elderly man named Simeon. It was revealed to this gentle and venerable man that he would not die before seeing the Messiah—"the Lord's Christ," as Luke phrases it (Luke 2:26). The Spirit then led him to the temple, where he saw a young carpenter and his wife enter the sanctuary with a newborn babe cradled in his mother's arms.

Simeon, who had waited all his life for "the consolation of Israel," took that consolation in his arms, praised God, and said, "Lord, now lettest thou thy servant depart in peace . . . for mine eyes have seen thy salvation, . . . a light to lighten the Gentiles, and the glory of thy people Israel" (Luke 2:25, 29–30, 32).

Luke goes on to say: "And Joseph and his mother marveled at those things which were spoken of him. And Simeon blessed them, and said unto Mary His mother, Behold, this child is set for the fall and rising again of many in Israel; and for a sign which shall be spoken against; (yea, a sword shall pierce through thy own soul also) that the thoughts of many hearts may be revealed" (Luke 2:33–35).

There is a profound Christmas message in the one this dear old man gave to beloved Mary in that first Christmas season. He was joyously happy. But his joy was not of the superficial kind. It was not without its testing and trying, the warning that this child's life—or at least His death—would be like a sword piercing through His beloved mother's soul. We might well ask, "Was such an ominous warning, such a fateful prophecy, appropriate in this season of joy? Surely such was untimely, even unseemly, at that moment—when the Son of God was so young and tender and safe, and His mother so thrilled with His birth and His beauty?"

Our answer is, it *was* appropriate *and* important. I submit that unless we see all the meaning and joy of Christmas the way old Simeon saw it all (and in a sense forced Joseph and Mary to see it)—the whole of Christ's life, the profound mission, the end as well as the beginning—then Christmas will be just another day off work, with food and fun and football for many and a measure of personal loneliness and family sorrow for others. The true meaning, the unique, joyous meaning of the birth of this baby, was not confined to those first hours in Bethlehem but would be realized in the life He would lead and in His death, in His triumphant atoning sacrifice (remember why Joseph and Mary were in the temple), and in His prison-bursting Resurrection. These are the realities that make Christmas joyful.

⁂

I believe it is most significant and very instructive that the first recorded words attributed to the Son of God in His mortality are, "Wist ye not that I must be about my Father's business?" (Luke 2:49). That question surely must speak volumes about who He is, what lies ahead of Him, and the ultimate measurement of His mission. And it just as surely must speak something of us, who have been invited to be about the same business.

## LUKE 4

As I understand it, the purpose of the Savior's ministry, the highest and holiest consummating central fact of the plan of salvation, the plan of happiness, the plan of mercy (pick your favorite scriptural phrase), it all focuses on the Atonement of the Lord Jesus Christ—the reason for which there was a plan, the reason for which there was a Creation, certainly the reason for which there was a Fall, and certainly the reason for which there was redemption thereafter.

"The Spirit of the Lord is upon me, because he hath anointed me to preach the gospel to the poor; he hath sent me to heal the brokenhearted, to preach deliverance to the captives, and recovering of sight to the blind, to set at liberty them that are bruised, to preach the acceptable year of the Lord" (Luke 4:18–19).

That was the first official declaration that Christ made to His home synagogue in Nazareth, and for that they took Him to the brow of a hill and attempted to throw Him over to His death. He majestically and miraculously and, with powers that are not filled in in the text, walked through them and past them and never went back to Nazareth (see Luke 4:28–30).

That is often how a declaration about the Atonement of Jesus Christ has been received, or a declaration about the gospel, or sometimes the declarations and truths and our feelings about the temple. There are some who don't feel as keen and warm about it as we do. But it is central to our worship, and it is the crystalizing, crowning, consummate event in the plan of salvation.

Everywhere He went, the forces of evil went before Him, and they knew Him from the beginning, even if mortals did not. In the same day that some were saying, "Is not this Joseph's son?" (Luke 4:22), the devils were calling out, "Let us alone; what have we to do with thee, thou Jesus of Nazareth? art thou come to destroy us? [We] know thee who thou art: the Holy One of God" (Luke 4:34).

## LUKE 5

Time was short. Much had to be done in a matter of months. Jesus prepared Peter as quickly as possible for the call that was to come.

"Launch out into the deep," He counseled this fisherman one morning in Galilee, "and let down your nets for a draught" (Luke 5:4). After an unsuccessful night of effort, Peter's expert judgment told him a final effort was useless. But this was a man of genuinely childlike faith, and he lowered the net. The number of fish taken in that single attempt strained the strings until they began to break and filled two boats until they began to sink. In that small ship Peter kneeled, stunned, at the feet of the Master. Jesus said lovingly, "Henceforth thou shalt catch men" (Luke 5:10).

*Launch out into the deep!* Peter could not have known the everwidening circles that single command would make in the stream of his plain and simple life. He was launching out into the expanse of godliness, into the eternal possibilities of redeemed and celestial life. He would be learning the mysteries of the kingdom. He would be hearing unspeakable things. To launch out into that limitless sea of the gospel of Jesus Christ, Peter brought his craft to shore, turned his back on the most spectacular single catch ever taken from Galilee, "forsook all, and followed him" (Luke 5:11).

## LUKE 6

I wish to discuss the apostleship and the importance of its perpetuation in the true Church of Jesus Christ. In so doing I speak not of the men who hold that office but rather of the office itself, a calling in the holy Melchizedek Priesthood that the Savior Himself has designated for the watch care of His people and the witnessing of His name.

In order to establish a church that would continue under His direction even after He was taken from the earth, Jesus "went . . . into a mountain to pray, and continued all night in prayer to God. And when it was day, he called unto him his disciples: and of them he chose twelve, whom also he named apostles" (Luke 6:12–13).

Later on, Paul would teach that the Savior, knowing the inevitability of His death, had done this to give the Church a "foundation of . . . apostles and prophets" (Ephesians 2:19–20). These brethren and the other officers of the Church would serve under the direction of the resurrected Christ.

Why? Among other reasons, so "that we henceforth be no more children, tossed to and fro, and carried about with every wind of doctrine, by the sleight of men, and cunning craftiness, whereby they lie in wait to deceive" (Ephesians 4:14).

Thus, the apostolic and prophetic foundation of the Church was to bless in all times, but *especially* in times of adversity or danger, times when we might feel like children, confused or disoriented, perhaps a little fearful, times in which the devious hand of men or the maliciousness of the devil would attempt to unsettle or mislead. Against such times as come in our modern day, the First Presidency and Quorum of the Twelve are commissioned by God and sustained by you as "prophets, seers, and revelators," with the President of The Church of Jesus Christ of Latter-day Saints sustained as *the* prophet, seer, and revelator, the *senior* Apostle, and as such the only man authorized to exercise all of the revelatory and administrative keys for the Church. In New Testament times, in Book of Mormon times, and in modern times these officers form the foundation stones of the true

Church, positioned around and gaining their strength from the chief cornerstone, "the rock of our Redeemer, who is [Jesus] Christ, the Son of God" (Helaman 5:12), the great "Apostle and High Priest of our profession," to use Paul's phrase (Hebrews 3:1). Such a foundation in Christ was and is always to be a protection in days "when the devil shall send forth his mighty winds, yea, his shafts in the whirlwind, yea, when all his hail and his mighty storm shall beat upon you." In such days as we are now in—and will more or less always be in—the storms of life "shall have no power over you . . . because of the rock upon which ye are built, which is a sure foundation, a foundation whereon if men build they cannot fall" (Helaman 5:12).

To those who may feel they have somehow forfeited their place at the table of the Lord, we say again with the Prophet Joseph Smith and his brethren that God has "a forgiving disposition," that Christ is "merciful and gracious, slow to anger, [is] long-suffering and full of goodness" (*Lectures on Faith* [1985], 42). I have always loved that when Matthew records Jesus's great injunction, "Be ye therefore perfect, even as your Father which is in heaven is perfect" (Matthew 5:48), Luke adds the Savior's additional commentary: "Be ye therefore merciful, as your Father also is merciful" (Luke 6:36)—as if to suggest that mercy is at least a beginning synonym for the perfection God has and for which all of us must strive. Mercy, with its sister virtue forgiveness, is at the very heart of the Atonement of Jesus Christ and the eternal plan of salvation. Everything in the gospel teaches us that we can change if we need to, that we can be helped if we truly want it, that we can be made whole, whatever the problems of the past.

"Forgive, and ye shall be forgiven" (Luke 6:37), Christ taught in New Testament times. And in our day, "I, the Lord, will forgive whom I will forgive, but of you it is required to forgive all men" (D&C

64:10). It is, however, important for some of you living in real anguish to note what He did *not* say. He did *not* say, "You are not allowed to feel true pain or real sorrow from the shattering experiences you have had at the hand of another." *Nor* did He say, "In order to forgive fully you have to reenter a toxic relationship or return to an abusive, destructive circumstance." But notwithstanding even the most terrible offenses that might come to us, we can rise above our pain only when we put our feet onto the path of true healing. That path is the forgiving one walked by Jesus of Nazareth, who calls out to each of us, "Come, follow me" (Luke 18:22).

## LUKE 11

I find it interesting that the first thing light reveals when a candle is lighted is the hand holding it. The Lord made this fascinating observation about personal light.

"The light of the body is the eye: therefore when thine eye is single, thy whole body also is full of light; but when thine eye is evil, thy body also is full of darkness.

"Take heed therefore that the light which is in thee be not darkness.

"If thy whole body therefore be full of light, having no part dark, the whole shall be full of light, as when the bright shining of a candle doth give thee light" (Luke 11:33–36).

The candles we hold up for others to see ought to be extensions of the light within ourselves. What we are shines more brightly than anything we say or do. If we are to fill the world with light, we must first face any tattered remnant of darkness that remains in our own souls. I invite you to join me in regularly turning inward to confront there *anything* we wouldn't want others to see—arrogance or unkindness, impatience or vanity, or any number of other flaws we need to remedy. Whatever it is, let us trim our lamps, add oil, and make those changes necessary that allow us to hold up a brighter candle, a purer light. Christ focused some of His most pointed opprobrium for the hypocrite. We must never be guilty of that in this battle. We must be the best person we can be in every way we can.

Light is not the absence of darkness; rather, darkness is the absence of light. Light and truth exist independently. This being the case, the more light we have, the more independent we are—the freer we are to choose. With truth lighting the way, we are able to see and make choices we otherwise could not make.

Since we are agents with the ability to choose, the responsibility for our education rests first with us. Others may help—teachers, parents, leaders, friends, even those who are not friends but whose negative examples and misguided perspectives serve to instruct what not to do or what not to believe. Ultimately, however, the responsibility for getting the facts straight is ours. The work is ours. The choices are ours.

Keep in mind that any knowledge we gather can be both negative and positive. Yes, we will gather statistics and horror stories about the impact of the darkness on our society. But more important, we must also fill our hearts and minds with truth and light, with love and the Spirit of God. Too often we allow ourselves to be forced into a defensive, remedial position when we could be more effective by taking positive, constructive action. And nothing is more constructive than a good, powerful, pure personal life.

As we educate ourselves, we need to educate others. The promoters of darkness often seem to have direct access to the media microphone. We may not be able to take that away from them, but we can at least raise our own voices. We can teach correct principles often and in as many ways as possible.

Since darkness is the absence of light, surely the most powerful way to counter darkness is to fill the world with light. Is it not part of our work as sons and daughters of God to encourage creative efforts that dispel darkness and replace it with light? How powerful a force for good would be a renaissance in literature, art, technology, and science that adds light rather than takes it away! Such a renaissance is possible. There are among us artists and artisans who need only to receive a little more support and encouragement from men and women of conscience to produce works that could rival those that half a millennium ago marked the end of Europe's Dark Age and the rise of a wonderful new cultural and spiritual Renaissance.

As we fill the earth with art (and media) that is good and uplifting—as we fill the earth with light and knowledge—our children will see the darkness for what it is. They will see that it is counterfeit, that it brings only sorrow, pain, and emptiness. They will come to prefer light and be attracted to that which is good and true.

## LUKE 14

We read in the fourteenth chapter of Luke:

"Then said he unto him, A certain man made a great supper, and bade many:

"And sent his servant at supper time to say to them that were bidden, Come; for all things are now ready."

These people were not being invited for the first time. They knew about it. They just hadn't been aware of the time and the place.

"And they all with one consent began to make excuse. The first said unto him, I have bought a piece of ground, and I must needs go and see it: I pray thee have me excused.

"And another said, I have bought five yoke of oxen, and I go to prove them: I pray thee have me excused.

"And another said, I have married a wife, and therefore I cannot come.

"So the servant came, and shewed his lord these things. Then the master of the house being angry said to his servant, Go out quickly into the streets and lanes of the city, and bring in hither the poor, and the maimed, and the halt, and the blind."

These people had *not* been invited before. They did not know about the meal or the time and the place. But they were now being invited.

"And the servant said, Lord, it is done as thou hast commanded, and yet there is room.

"And the lord said unto the servant, Go out into the highways and hedges, and compel them to come in, that my house may be filled."

Now we are declining on the social scale as we move from the poor, and the halt, and the maimed to the highwaymen and those who are working in dark places.

"Compel them to come in, that my house may be filled.

"For I say unto you, That none of those men which were bidden shall taste of my supper.

"And there went great multitudes with him: and he turned, and said unto them,

"If any man come to me, and hate not his father, and mother, and wife, and children, and brethren, and sisters, yea, and his own life also, he cannot be my disciple.

"And whosoever doth not bear his cross, and come after me, cannot be my disciple. . . .

"Salt is good: but if the salt have lost his savour, wherewith shall it be seasoned?" (Luke 14:16–27, 34).

I have scribbled in the margin of my scriptures, "f" and "t." I have done that now and again in the other verses as well. Those are my "fear and trembling" scriptures. Those are verses that really scare me. This is a simple story about being bidden to the feast, and we hear a lot of excuses as to why people can't make it—because they just got married, or just bought a new piece of ground, or simply have more important things to do. Then the Son of God, who teaches more about love and family, and fathers and mothers, and brothers and sisters than anyone who has ever walked the face of the earth, wheels and says: "If any man come to me, and hate not his father, and mother, and wife, and children, and brethren, and sisters, yea, and his own life also, he cannot be my disciple" (Luke 14:26).

Now, I don't think He is telling us to hate our parents, or our brothers or sisters, or our wives or our children. But He is saying something about taking up a cross and following Him, and what that may entail for a disciple of Jesus Christ.

You have had some choices to make, and you will have choices for the rest of your life. If there is anything that we understand, it is that that freedom will continue, that you have possibilities, you have options. And I am trying to suggest that there is one major decision that can color and, in fact, help make most of the other decisions, and that is, "What will I do with Jesus?" We have to decide if He was what He said He was, the Son of God, the Redeemer of this world, and that He died for our sins.

With all my heart I know in a way I have never known before that this is the Church and kingdom of God. I have wondered how it must feel for someone who does not know, or has not heard, or perhaps does not even have any inclination—how it must feel to them to have someone say, "We know that God lives because He has appeared. We know that Jesus is the Christ and also lives because He appeared also. We have prophets who speak with heavenly beings. It is the same as when Moses, and Elijah, and Jeremiah, and Isaiah were here. The true Church is on the earth, and there really is such a thing as a true Church. It really does matter what you do, and there really are ultimate issues in life." Those of us who have been raised in the shadows of the everlasting hills sometimes are not sure we understand what that kind of declaration may mean to someone not of our faith. I am not sure we fully appreciate the kind of challenge that might be for them.

You see, we are talking about absolutes, in a world that is really quite taken with relativism. I am wondering if perhaps there is someone, any one of you, who does not know, who is not sure, who is "halting between two opinions." And I am afraid too many of us are.

Where is the blood of the Lamb in our lives right now? Where is the power of testimony that casts out that enemy of all good things? That persecution is going on in some of your lives right now. I *know* that it is because it goes on in mine from time to time. I also know that you and I will stand accountable before God, a loving Father who cares dearly and eternally and deeply about us.

I know with all my heart that this is the Church and kingdom of God, that Jesus lives and reigns, and whether the world understands or not, that He *is* King of kings and Lord of lords. I know we will meet Him, and we will be accountable for keeping His name sacred and His image pure, for we have so covenanted to do.

## LUKE 15

We believe in vicarious work in The Church of Jesus Christ of Latter-day Saints. We believe that the righteous action, participation, and loyalty of one person can materially aid in the salvation of another. That principle is at the heart of work for the dead in our temples.

The greatest example of a vicarious blessing is the Atonement of Jesus Christ. It is the greatest evidence that the righteousness of one can influence the salvation of another. That gift is for all of us. We all claim its power.

That same principle is in force in your lives. In your own way you can vicariously bless your children and your children's children, and your children's children's children. We have promises regarding our posterity, promises made in response to faithfulness and loyalty. If you keep your covenants, your children will be fortified and blessed in their effort to keep theirs. In short, the best thing you can do for your children is to stay faithful, to keep believing, to keep loving, to keep trying to stay faithful yourself. And like the prodigal son or the prodigal daughter, one day they will come to themselves. I love that line from the parable of the prodigal son: "He came to himself." He said, "I have got to go home. I have got to get back to my roots. To be a servant in my father's house would be better than this life among swine."

And there is his father, perhaps out on the porch rocking, a quilt put over his legs in case the evening chill would affect this aging man. He waits and rocks and rocks and waits.

And then one day way, way down the lane he sees his boy coming home. He runs, even as an older man he runs, falls on the boy's neck, and kisses him. Through his tears he says, "We have a robe and a ring and a fatted calf waiting. Our family is back together" (see Luke 15:11–24).

Believe. Trust. Have faith. Do all you can to save your children and trust that God can make up the rest.

Satan is certainly not subtle in his teachings; why should we be? Let us never make our faith difficult to detect. Live the gospel as conspicuously as you can. Keep the covenants your children know you have made. Give priesthood blessings. And bear your testimony! Don't just assume your children will somehow get the drift of your beliefs on their own.

Even then we know that some children will make decisions that break their parents' hearts. Moms and dads can do everything right and yet have children who stray. Moral agency still prevails. But even in such painful hours it will be comforting to us to know that our children know of our abiding faith in Christ, in His true Church, in the keys of the priesthood and in those who hold them. It will be comforting then to us to know that if our children choose to leave the strait and narrow way, they leave it very conscious that their parents were firmly in it. Furthermore, they will be much more likely to return to that path when they come to themselves (see Luke 15:17) and recall the loving example and gentle teachings we offered them.

Among the most memorable parables the Savior ever told is the story of a foolish younger brother who went to his father, asked for his portion of the estate, and left home to squander his inheritance, the scripture says, in "riotous living" (Luke 15:13). His money and his friends disappeared sooner than he thought possible—they always do—and a day of terrible reckoning came thereafter—it always does.

In the downward course of all this he became a keeper of pigs, one so hungry, so stripped of sustenance and dignity that he "would fain have filled his belly with the husks that the swine did eat" (Luke 15:16). But even that consolation was not available to him.

Then the scripture says encouragingly, "He came to himself" (Luke 15:17). He determined to find his way home, hoping to be accepted at least as a servant in his father's household. The tender image of this boy's anxious, faithful father running to meet him and showering him with kisses is one of the most moving and compassionate scenes in all of holy writ. It tells every child of God, wayward or otherwise, how much God wants us back in the protection of His arms.

But being caught up in this younger son's story, we can miss, if we are not careful, the account of an elder son, for the opening line of the Savior's account reads, "A certain man had *two* sons"—and He might have added, "both of whom were lost and both of whom needed to come home."

The younger son has returned, a robe has been placed on his shoulders and a ring on his finger, when the older son comes on the scene. He has been dutifully, loyally working in the field, and now he is returning. The language of parallel journeys home, though from very different locations, is central to this story.

As he approaches the house, he hears the sounds of music and laughter.

"And he called one of the servants [note that he has servants], and asked what these things meant.

"And [the servant] said unto him, Thy brother is come; and thy father hath killed the fatted calf, because he hath received him safe and sound.

"And [the older brother] was angry, and would not go in: therefore came his father out, and entreated him" (Luke 15:26–28).

You know the conversation they then had. Surely, for this father, the pain over a wayward child who had run from home and wallowed with swine is now compounded with the realization that this older, wiser brother, the younger boy's childhood hero, as older brothers always are, is angry that his brother has come home.

No, I correct myself. This son is not so much angry that the other has come home as he is angry that his parents are so happy about it. Feeling unappreciated and perhaps more than a little self-pity, this dutiful son—and he is *wonderfully* dutiful—forgets for a moment that he has never had to know filth or despair, fear or self-loathing. He forgets for a moment that every calf on the ranch is already his and so are all the robes in the closet and every ring in the drawer. He forgets for a moment that his faithfulness has been and always will be rewarded.

No, he who has virtually everything, and who has in his hardworking, wonderful way earned it, lacks the one thing that might make him the complete man of the Lord he nearly is. He has yet to come to the compassion and mercy, the charitable breadth of vision to see that *this is not a rival returning.* It is his brother. As his father pled with him to see, it is one who was dead and now is alive. It is one who was lost and now is found.

Certainly, this younger brother had been a prisoner—a prisoner of sin, stupidity, and a pigsty. But the older brother lives in some confinement too. He has, as yet, been unable to break out of the prison of himself. He is haunted by the green-eyed monster of jealousy. He feels taken for granted by his father and disenfranchised by his brother, when neither is the case. He has fallen victim to a fictional affront. As such he is like Tantalus of Greek mythology—he is up to his chin in water, but he remains thirsty nevertheless. One who has heretofore presumably been very happy with his life and content with his good fortune suddenly feels very unhappy simply because another has had some good fortune as well.

Who is it that whispers so subtly in our ear that a gift given to another somehow diminishes the blessings we have received? Who makes us feel that if God is smiling on another, then He surely must somehow be frowning on us? You and I both know who does this—it is the father of all lies. It is Lucifer, our common enemy, whose cry down through the corridors of time is always and to everyone, "Give me thine honor."

It has been said that envy is the one sin to which no one readily confesses, but just how widespread that tendency can be is suggested in the old Danish proverb, "If envy were a fever, all the world would be ill." The parson in Chaucer's *Canterbury Tales* laments it because it is so far-reaching—it can resent anything, including any virtue and talent, and it can be offended by everything, including every goodness and joy. As others seem to grow larger in our sight, we think we must therefore be smaller. So, unfortunately, we occasionally act that way.

How does this happen, especially when we wish so much that it would not? I think one of the reasons is that every day we see allurements of one kind or another that tell us what we have is not enough. Someone or something is forever telling us we need to be more handsome or more wealthy, more applauded or more admired than we see ourselves as being. We are told we have not collected enough possessions or gone to enough fun places. We are bombarded with the message that on the *world's* scale of things we have been weighed in the balance and found wanting. Some days it is as if we have been locked in a cubicle of a great and spacious building where the only thing on the TV is a never-ending soap opera entitled *Vain Imaginations* (see 1 Nephi 12:18).

But God does not work this way. The father in this story does not tantalize his children. He does not mercilessly measure them against their neighbors. He doesn't even compare them with each other. His gestures of compassion toward one do not require a withdrawal or denial of love for the other. He is divinely generous to both of these sons. Toward both of his children he extends charity.

One observer has written: "In a world that constantly compares people, ranking them as more or less intelligent, more or less attractive, more or less successful, it is not easy to really believe in a [divine] love that does not do the same. When I hear someone praised," he says, "it is hard not to think of myself as less praiseworthy; when I read about the goodness and kindness of other people, it is hard not to wonder whether I myself am as good and kind as they; and when I see trophies, rewards, and prizes being handed out to special people, I cannot avoid asking myself why that didn't happen to me" (Henri J. M. Nouwen, *The Return of the Prodigal Son* [1992], 103). If left unresisted, we can see how this inclination so embellished by the world will ultimately bring a resentful, demeaning view of God and a terribly destructive view of ourselves. Most "thou shalt not" commandments are meant to keep us from hurting others, but I am convinced the commandment not to covet is meant to keep us from hurting ourselves.

How can we overcome such a tendency so common in almost everyone? For one thing, we can do as these two sons did and start making our way back to the Father. We should do so with as much haste and humility as we can summon. Along the way we can count our many blessings and we can applaud the accomplishments of others. Best of all, we can serve others, the finest exercise for the heart ever prescribed. But finally these will not be enough. When we are lost, we can "come to ourselves," but we may not always be able to "find ourselves," and, worlds without end, we cannot "save ourselves." Only the Father and His Only Begotten Son can do that. Salvation is in Them only. So we pray that They will help us, that They will "come out" to meet and embrace us and bring us into the feast They have prepared.

## LUKE 18

I invoke this scene from Luke's New Testament account:

"It came to pass, that as [Jesus] was come nigh unto Jericho, a certain blind man sat by the way side begging:

"... *Hearing [a] multitude pass by, he asked what it meant.*

"... They told him, that Jesus of Nazareth passeth by.

"And he cried, saying, Jesus, thou Son of David, have mercy on me."

Startled at his boldness, the crowd tried to silence the man, but "he cried so much the more," it says. As a result of his persistence, he was brought to Jesus, who heard his faith-filled plea for the restoration of his sight and healed him (Luke 18:35–43; emphasis added).

I am moved by this vivid little vignette every time I read it. We can sense the man's distress. We can almost hear him shouting for the Savior's attention. We smile at his refusal to be silenced—indeed, his determination to turn the volume *up* when everyone else was telling him to turn it *down*. It is, in and of itself, a sweet story of very determined faith. But as with all scripture, the more we read it, the more we find in it.

One thought that struck me only recently is the good sense this man had in having spiritually sensitive people around him. The entire significance of this story hinges on a handful of anonymous women and men who, when asked by their colleague, "What does this commotion mean?" had the vision, if you will, to identify Christ as the reason for the clamor; He was "Meaning Personified." There is a lesson in this little exchange for all of us. In matters of faith and conviction, it helps to direct your inquiry toward those who actually have some! "Can the blind lead the blind?" Jesus once asked. "[If so] shall they not both fall into the ditch?" (Luke 6:39).

## LUKE 22

The setting was Jerusalem. The season was that of the Passover, a celebration rich in symbolism for what was about to come. Long ago the troubled and enslaved Israelites had been "passed over," spared, finally made free by the blood of a lamb sprinkled on the lintel and doorposts of their Egyptian homes (see Exodus 12:21–24). That, in turn, had been only a symbolic reiteration of what Adam and all succeeding prophets were taught from the beginning—that the pure and unblemished lambs offered from the firstlings of Israel's flocks were a similitude, a token, a prefiguration of the great and last sacrifice of Christ which was to come (see Moses 5:5–8).

Now, after all those years and all those prophecies and all those symbolic offerings, the type and shadow was to become reality. On this night when Jesus's mortal ministry was concluding, the declaration made by John the Baptist when that ministry had begun now meant more than ever—"Behold the Lamb of God" (John 1:29).

As a final and specially prepared Passover supper was ending, Jesus took bread, blessed and broke it, and gave it to His Apostles, saying, "This is my body which is given for you: this do in remembrance of me" (Luke 22:19). In a similar manner He took the cup of wine, traditionally diluted with water, said a blessing of thanks for it, and passed it to those gathered about Him, saying, "This cup is the new testament in my blood," "which is shed . . . for the remission of sins." "This do in remembrance of me." "For as often as ye eat this bread, and drink this cup, ye do shew the Lord's death till he come" (Luke 22:20; Matthew 26:28; Luke 22:19; 1 Corinthians 11:26).

Since that upper-room experience on the eve of Gethsemane and Golgotha, children of the promise have been under covenant to remember Christ's sacrifice in this newer, higher, more holy and personal way.

With a crust of bread, always broken, blessed, and offered first, we remember His bruised body and broken heart, His physical suffering on the cross where He cried, "I thirst," and finally, "My God, my God, why hast thou forsaken me?" (John 19:28; Matthew 27:46).

The Savior's physical suffering guarantees that through His mercy and grace every member of the human family shall be freed from the bonds of death and be resurrected triumphantly from the grave. Of course, the time of that resurrection and the degree of exaltation it leads to are based upon our faithfulness.

With a small cup of water we remember the shedding of Christ's blood and the depth of His spiritual suffering, anguish which began in the Garden of Gethsemane. There He said, "My soul is exceeding sorrowful, even unto death." He was in agony and "prayed more earnestly: and his sweat was as it were great drops of blood falling down to the ground" (Luke 22:44).

The Savior's spiritual suffering and the shedding of His innocent blood, so lovingly and freely given, paid the debt for what the scriptures call the "original guilt" of Adam's transgression (see Moses 6:54). Furthermore, Christ suffered for the sins and sorrows and pains of all the rest of the human family, providing remission for all of our sins as well, upon conditions of obedience to the principles and ordinances of the gospel He taught (see 2 Nephi 9:21–23). As the Apostle Paul wrote, we were "bought with a price" (1 Corinthians 6:20). What an expensive price and what a merciful purchase!

That is why every ordinance of the gospel focuses in one way or another on the Atonement of the Lord Jesus Christ, and surely that is why this particular ordinance with all its symbolism and imagery comes to us more readily and more repeatedly than any other in our life. It comes in what has been called "the most sacred, the most holy, of all the meetings of the Church" (Joseph Fielding Smith, *Doctrines of Salvation*, 3 vols. [1954–56], 2:340).

Perhaps we do not always attach that kind of meaning to our weekly sacramental service. How "sacred" and how "holy" is it? Do we see it as *our* Passover, remembrance of *our* safety and deliverance and redemption?

With so very much at stake, this ordinance commemorating our escape from the angel of darkness should be taken more seriously than it sometimes is. It should be a powerful, reverent, reflective moment. It should encourage spiritual feelings and impressions. As such it should not be rushed. It is not something to "get over" so that the real purpose of a sacrament meeting can be pursued. This *is* the real purpose of the meeting. And everything that is said or sung or prayed in those services should be consistent with the grandeur of this sacred ordinance.

Everything that He taught was important, but for me, as a personal observation, the greatest declaration of Christ's life of who He was and the quality of His integrity, the quality of His loyalty, His love of His Father in Heaven, as often as that was made manifest in so many different ways—for me, the greatest manifestation was in the suffering of Gethsemane. There He took on the sins and sorrows and heartaches and depression and anxiety and fears and problems of every human being, all of us and everyone who has ever lived. I do not understand His ability to do it, but He did it.

As He suffered that and went into that process from Gethsemane leading to Calvary and the cross and the death that He would suffer and the suffering that would be His death—in all of that, for me, the highest moment is when He asked, "Is there any other way? Is there any other cup? Is there any other path? Do I have any options?" And the answer was no. He is not the only one who has asked, "Is there no other way?"

Because there is no other way, with bowed head and humble heart, He says, "Father, . . . not my will, but thine, be done" (Luke 22:42). That is the most majestic moment in the life of the Son of God in all that I know about Him in holy writ—to do what you have to do, whether you want to do it or not. And I say that is the most majestic because in doing that, He saved my life. He gave me my chance, and He gave you yours. And He gave it even to those who don't care and who vilify Him and curse and misuse His name and defame Him. He did it for them, too. He did it for the ones who surrounded the cross and taunted Him and said, "Oh, oh, if you are the Son of God, well, why don't you come down now? Why don't you come down from that cross and be the King of kings? Be the king you say you were."

He endured that kind of taunting, that spitting and hissing and vilification. He did it for them. He did it for you. He did it for our living prophet. He did it for Joseph Smith. He did it for Adam and Eve, and He certainly did not do it with delightful anticipation of what it was going to be like to bleed from every pore and to suffer the sorrow and depression that has been spoken of here tens of millions of times over. I don't know how that happens, but He did it. It cost Him His life, but that was the arrangement. That was the promise. And for me, He waves the most majestic banner that anyone could wave when He says, "Not my will, but thine, be done" (Luke 22:42).

Peter could not descend completely with Christ; no one could. Furthermore, he was restrained by Jesus Himself when he physically assaulted those who had come to seize the Lord. Peter could not go with Him, but neither could he in his most confused and frightened moment flee from Him. Denying that he knew Him, Peter stood in the courtyard of the accusers and saw the indignities his Lord and Savior suffered. Then he did what all repentant men have cause to do. Silently and alone, he "went out, and wept bitterly" (Luke 22:62). Peter had been so certain that his strength was sufficient for such times—that, if necessary, he would withstand evil alone. Reassuringly he had said to Jesus, "Though all men shall be offended because of thee, yet will I never be offended" (Matthew 26:33). But in the kingdom of God no man's strength is sufficient. This sobering, sorrowing realization—that he was not, of himself, capable of what God requires—was perhaps the final ingredient in Peter's short months of personal preparation. In the years ahead he would preside over the Church of Jesus Christ with dignity and great power, not in spite of his need for divine assistance, but clearly and admittedly because of it. Heavenly guidance and spiritual manifestation would be the marks of his administration.

And for Peter, there would never again be a denial of Jesus.

## LUKE 23

For me there is no greater amazement and no more difficult personal challenge than when, after the anguish in Gethsemane, after the charade before Annas and Caiaphas and the Jewish court, and after Pilate's cowardice, Jesus staggers under His load to the crest of Calvary and says, "Father, forgive them; for they know not what they do" (Luke 23:34).

If ever there is a moment where I indeed stand all amazed, it is here, for this is an amazement of a different kind. So much of the mystery of His power and ministry tear at my *mind*. The circumstances of His birth, the breadth and variety of His ministry and miracles, the self-summoned power of the Resurrection—before all of these I stand all amazed and say, "How did He do it?" But here with disciples who slept through His hour of greatest need and abandoned Him before the cock could crow three times, here fainting under the weight of His cross and the sins of all mankind that were attached to it, here rent with brutal blows on the piercing spikes in His palms and in His wrists and in His feet—here now the amazement tears not at my *mind* but at my *heart*, and I ask not "*How* did He do it?" but "*Why* did He do it?" It is here that I examine my life, not against the miraculousness of His but against the mercifulness of it, and it is here I find how truly short I fall in emulation of the Master.

I cannot speak for you, but for me this is a higher order of amazement and a greater order of magnitude. I am startled enough by His ability to heal the sick and raise the dead, but I have had something of that experience in a limited way, as virtually all of you have as well. We are lesser vessels and undoubtedly unworthy of the privilege, but we have seen the miracles of the Lord repeated in our own lives and in our own homes and with our own portion of the priesthood. But mercy? Forgiveness? Atonement? Reconciliation? Too often that is a different matter.

How could He say this at that moment? With all that pain, with blood from every pore, with a plea that this most bitter of all cups might pass, surely He does not need to be thinking of others *now*, does He? Not every minute all the time, and especially not with this pack of jackals who are laughing and spitting, stripping Him of His clothing and His rights and His dignity? Or is this yet one more staggering evidence—amazing evidence yet again—that He really was perfect and intends us to be also? Is it only coincidental—or absolutely intentional—that as something of a last requirement before stating that goal in the Sermon on the Mount, He reminds us that you must "love your enemies, bless them that curse you, do good to them that hate you, and pray for them which despitefully use you, and persecute you" (Matthew 5:44–48)?

I would rather raise the dead! I would rather restore sight and steady a palsied hand. I would rather do anything than to love my enemies and forgive those who hurt me or my children or my children's children, and especially those who laugh and delight in the brutality of it.

Is there no justice? Shouldn't He cry out, "Be gone with you!" as He did to those other devils? Shouldn't He condemn them all and call down the legions of angels that were always waiting at His very command?

Don't they know that He is doing this for them, and if they are not interested or appreciative or grateful, then what reason on earth is there to do it? Every generation in every dispensation of the world has had its own multitudes crowding around that cross laughing and jeering, breaking commandments and abusing covenants. It is not just a relative handful in the meridian of time who are guilty here. It is most of the people, most of the places, most of the time, including all of us who should have known better.

It has always been a wonderful testimony to me of the greatness of all of our prophets, including and especially the Savior of the world in His magnificence, that in the midst of distress and difficulty they could remain calm and patient, charitable and forgiving—that they could even talk that way, let alone live that way. But they could, and they did. They remembered their covenants, they disciplined themselves, and they knew that we must live the gospel at all times, not just when it is convenient and not just when things are going well. Indeed, they knew that the real test of our faith and our Christian discipleship is when things are *not* going smoothly. That is when we get to see what we are made of and how strong our commitment to the gospel really is.

Surely the classic example of this is that in the most painful hours of the Crucifixion the Savior could say, "Father, forgive them; for they know not what they do" (Luke 23:34). That is a hard thing to ask when we are hurting. That is a hard thing to do when we have been offended or are tired or stressed out or suffering innocently. But that is when Christian behavior may matter the most. Remember, "the powers of heaven cannot be controlled nor handled [except] upon the principles of righteousness" (D&C 121:36). And do we need the powers of heaven with us at such times!

Remaining true to our Christian principles is the only way divine influence can help us. The Spirit has a near-impossible task to get through to a heart that is filled with hate or anger or vengeance or self-pity. Those are all antithetical to the Spirit of the Lord. On the other hand, the Spirit finds instant access to a heart striving to be charitable and forgiving, long-suffering and kind—principles of true discipleship. What a testimony that gospel principles are to apply at all times and in all situations and that if we strive to remain faithful, the triumph of a Christian life can never be vanquished, no matter how grim the circumstance might be.

## LUKE 24

When Christ bids us to yield, to submit, to obey the Father, He knows how to help us do that. He has walked that way, asking us to do what He has done. He has made it safer. He has made it very much easier for our travel. He knows where the sharp stones and the stumbling blocks lie and where the thorns and the thistles are the most severe. He knows where the path is perilous, and He knows which way to go when the road forks and nightfall comes. He knows this because He has suffered "pains and afflictions and temptations of every kind . . .

that he may know . . . how to succor his people according to their infirmities" (Alma 7:11–12).

To those who stagger or stumble, He is there to steady and strengthen us. In the end He is there to save us, and for all this He gave His life. However dim our days may seem, they have been a lot darker for the Savior of the world. As a reminder of those days, Jesus has chosen, even in a resurrected, otherwise perfected body, to retain for the benefit of His disciples the wounds in His hands and in His feet and in His side—signs, if you will, that painful things happen even to the pure and the perfect; signs, if you will, that pain in this world is not evidence that God does not love you; signs, if you will, that problems pass and happiness can be ours. It is the wounded Christ who is the Captain of our souls, He who yet bears the scars of our forgiveness, the lesions of His love and humility, the torn flesh of obedience and sacrifice.

These wounds are the principal way we are to recognize Him when He comes. He may invite us forward, as He has invited others, to see and to feel those marks (see Luke 24:39–40). If not before, then surely at that time, we will remember with Isaiah that it was for us that a God was "despised and rejected . . . ; a man of sorrows, and acquainted with grief," that "he was wounded for our transgressions, he was bruised for our iniquities: the chastisement of our peace was upon him; and with his stripes we are healed" (Isaiah 53:3, 5).

The physical Resurrection of Jesus Christ, representing as it does the meaning of His life, His death, His Atonement, and all that He accomplished in His earthly mission, is the great centerpiece, the culminating triumph, the majestic victory over death and hell that sets Christianity apart from all other religions. Other faiths have holy men. Other faiths have miracles and visions and spiritual manifestations. Other faiths have devout believers who give their lives in defense of their religious convictions. But no other religion and no other individual ever in history speaks of one who voluntarily laid down his own life and three days later took it back up again, never to experience death again. The Resurrection is the great triumphant symbol of Christianity, the symbol of Christian distinctiveness. It is Christ's singular message to the world. "As in Adam all die, even so in Christ shall all be made alive" (1 Corinthians 15:22).

Christ's most intimate associates, the men and women who beheld Him, really knew: their eyes beheld, their ears heard, their hands felt the presence of the risen Lord.

The deep meaning and peace this experience brought can still be vivid to us 2,000 years later, particularly if we remember how devastated and despairing these disciples and followers were at the time. For most of them, if not all, their hopes and dreams had died when the Savior died. Notwithstanding His efforts to tell them He would rise again, even His chief Apostles seemed not to have accepted or at least did not understand that statement as something to be realized literally. Of course, how could they, inasmuch as no such thing had ever happened in the history of the world. For three years they had followed Him, learned from Him, depended on Him, looked to Him to mark the way. Now He was gone and they were bereft of all hope—alone, confused, helpless, and afraid.

Then first to Mary Magdalene, followed by those on the road to Emmaus and a larger group of disciples gathered in Jerusalem, Jesus appeared—resurrected, victorious, body and spirit united never to be separated again (see Luke 24:1–48). His promises had been kept; His Messianic mission had been fulfilled. The final and absolute seal of genuine majesty and Godhood had been put on all that He had said and all that He had done.

This was the message that His believers would take to the world and that would change the world. This was the reality that turned fishermen into Apostles and tent makers into missionaries. This was the reality for which these Apostles would also die, calm in the assurance that they too, as a gift from their beloved Master, would be resurrected at some future day. And from those humble beginnings in which He sat with them to eat honeycomb and fish has come the movement of Christianity across the world, a force that will continue to be victorious and that will see Christ come again as King of kings and Lord of lords.

PEACE I LEAVE WITH YOU,

MY PEACE I GIVE UNTO YOU:

NOT AS THE WORLD GIVETH, GIVE I UNTO YOU.

LET NOT YOUR HEART BE TROUBLED,

NEITHER LET IT BE AFRAID.

—JOHN 14:27

# JOHN

## JOHN 1

Looking up from the water's edge, past the eager crowds seeking baptism at his hand, John, called the Baptist, saw in the distance his cousin, Jesus of Nazareth, striding resolutely toward him to make a request for that same ordinance. Reverently, but audibly enough for those nearby to hear, John uttered the admiration that still moves us two millennia later: "Behold the Lamb of God" (John 1:29).

It is instructive that this long-prophesied forerunner to Jesus did not call Him "Jehovah" or "Savior" or "Redeemer" or even "the Son of God"—all of which were applicable titles. No, John chose the earliest and perhaps most commonly recognized image in the religious tradition of his people. He used the figure of a sacrificial lamb offered in atonement for the sins and sorrows of a fallen world and all the fallen people in it.

I read a biblical scholar once who took poor Andrew to task. He said Andrew had no business being listed with apostolic companions where he was not invited. Those of you who have studied the New Testament will remember that the original Twelve are always listed in three groups of four, and while there is some variation in the second two groups, there is never any variation in the first group of four: it is always Peter, James, John, and Andrew (see, for example, Matthew 10; Mark 13; Luke 6). Peter, James, and John are understandable. That has a little meter to it; it rather trips off the tongue. But Peter, James, John, and *Andrew*? That bothered this scholar. Furthermore, I admit I said to myself, "I think I agree. I don't know much about Andrew; but he doesn't seem to measure up to the other three." Until one day I read this:

"The next day after [Jesus's baptism] John stood, and two of his disciples;

"And looking upon Jesus as he walked, he saith, Behold the Lamb of God!

"And the two disciples heard him speak, and they followed Jesus. . . .

"And one of the two which heard John speak, and followed him, was Andrew, Simon Peter's brother.

"He first findeth his own brother Simon, and saith unto him, We have found the Messias, which is, being interpreted, the Christ.

"And he brought him to Jesus" (John 1:35–37, 40–42).

We know a great deal about Peter. We don't know much about Andrew. But the interesting question is, would there have been a Peter if there had not been an Andrew?

You will recall that when Andrew and another disciple, probably John, first heard Christ speak, they were so moved and attracted to Jesus that they followed Him as He left the crowd. Sensing that He was being pursued, Christ turned and asked the two men, "What seek ye?" Other translations render that simply "What do you want?" They answered, "Where dwellest thou?" or "Where do you live?" Christ said simply, "Come and see" (John 1:38–39). Just a short time later He formally called Peter and other new Apostles with the same spirit of invitation. To them He said, "Follow me" (John 1:43).

It seems that the essence of our mortal journey and the answers to the most significant questions in life are distilled down to these two very brief elements in the opening scenes of the Savior's earthly ministry. One element is the question put to every one of us on this earth: "What seek ye? What do you want?" The second is His response to our answer, *whatever that answer is*. Whoever we are and whatever we reply, His response is *always* the same: "Come," He says lovingly. "Come, follow me." Wherever you are going, first come and see what I do, see where and how I spend my time. Learn of me, walk with me, talk with me, believe. Listen to me pray. In turn you will find answers to your own prayers. God will bring rest to your souls. Come, follow me.

When Jesus walked out of the wilderness after forty days and nights of preparation, His eye fell upon a man who made his living sailing on a turbulent sea. With powers of discernment not of this world, He declared in that first encounter, "Thou art Simon, the son of Jona: thou shalt be called Cephas," or literally "a stone" (John 1:42). Here was a principal building block for the priestly foundation to be laid. Jesus Himself would be the chief cornerstone, but at His side would be apostles and prophets full of courage and strength and integrity. In those earliest hours of His ministry, Jesus had found the man prepared from before the foundation of the world to become His chief Apostle and special witness in the dispensation of the meridian of time.

## JOHN 3

Nicodemus would not have been considered "common" in the Judaic society of his day. But he, like everyone else, was one who nevertheless needed his vision enlarged and his life lifted. His need for the Master's touch revealed how universal that need was. In the sight of God, all needed the "new testament" written in their hearts regardless of social standing or ecclesiastical significance (see Jeremiah 31:33).

John describes Nicodemus as "a man of the Pharisees, . . . a ruler of the Jews" (John 3:1), a member of the powerful Jewish Sanhedrin. But in his groping toward the light he was, in a sense, as plain as all others darkened by apostasy and damaged by life lived without revelation.

Nicodemus was obviously haunted by what he heard and saw and felt coming from Jesus. On the other hand, he was not quite confident enough to come by day, publicly, and acknowledge Jesus's Messiahship. His first remark seems tentative, almost exploratory. "We know that thou art a teacher come from God," he says (John 3:2), but in the record we have, he stops short of admitting the Savior's Messiahship and shies away from asking what he must do to be saved.

Fortunately—as with others coming with other kinds of limitations—Jesus reached out to him, inviting Nicodemus to reach up: "Verily, verily, I say unto thee, Except a man be born again [or "from above"], he cannot see the kingdom of God."

Nicodemus's response is confused. Conditioned by his Pharisaic literalism, he was either unwilling or unable to grasp the Savior's meaning and chose to give the reference to "birth" its most immediate meaning.

"How can a man be born when he is old? can he enter the second time into his mother's womb, and be born?" he asked.

Jesus patiently clarified: "Verily, verily, I say unto thee, Except a man be born of water and of the Spirit, he cannot enter into the kingdom of God."

Nicodemus must have looked either bewildered or incredulous because Jesus continued, bringing down to the rabbi's level a teaching that apparently was too lofty for him to grasp otherwise. Master Teacher that He was, Jesus seized on a double meaning of a Hebrew word and used it to lead Nicodemus from the temporal to the spiritual. In Hebrew the word *spirit* was rendered *ruah*, which also meant "puff" or "gust," as a gust of wind. So, striving to teach of the Spirit, Jesus used the very word.

"Marvel not that I said unto thee, Ye must be born again.

"The wind bloweth where it listeth, and thou hearest the sound thereof, but canst not tell whence it cometh, and whither it goeth: so is every one that is born of the Spirit." But Nicodemus seemed more confused than ever. "How can these things be?" he asked. Jesus answered, "Art thou a master of Israel, and knowest not these things? . . . If I have told you earthly things, and ye believe not, how shall ye believe, if I tell you of heavenly things?" (John 3:3–12).

Indeed, how can we understand spiritual, eternal truths if we are muddled about physical, temporal facts? If we do not understand the whispering source of the Spirit, perhaps we will understand the whispering source of the wind as an earthly application of an otherwise heavenly teaching. We must come to understand heavenly things by starting where we are.

## JOHN 4

While traveling through Samaria among people intensely despised by the Jews of that day, Jesus and His disciples passed by the city of Sychar, "near to the parcel of ground that Jacob gave to his son Joseph" (John 4:5). This area, which included within its borders Jacob's well, was uniquely symbolic of the Jewish-Samaritan animosity. Samaritans spoke strongly for their ancestral tie to Jacob—and the Jews denied them that assertion with equal vehemence. Did Jesus choose just such a location to lift the sight of both groups, too long limited by dark traditions?

While His disciples went into the city to buy food (it was the noon hour), Jesus sat on the stone perimeter of the well and watched a Samaritan woman approach with her waterpot in hand. The woman must have been very surprised to hear this Jewish traveler speak to her as she was preparing to lower her waterpot for water. Not only was a man speaking to a woman He did not know, but more strikingly, He was a Jew addressing a Samaritan. Nevertheless, He said to her, "Give me to drink."

She questioned His request, as well she might, and Jesus had exactly the teaching situation He wanted.

"If thou knewest the gift of God," He said, "and who it is that saith to thee, Give me to drink; thou wouldest have asked of him, and he would have given thee living water."

Here the Savior instantly introduced a hint of His true identity, a revelation that could indeed be "living water" to this woman if she could grasp heavenly things. But she showed no such inclination, wondering aloud how this man could possibly give her any water—living or otherwise—when He had nothing to draw with from such a deep well.

Jesus went on. Referring to temporal sustenance, He said, "Whosoever drinketh of this water shall thirst again." Then He said, "But whosoever drinketh of the water that I shall give him shall never thirst; but the water that I shall give him shall be in him a well of water springing up into everlasting life."

This profound declaration so movingly spoken clearly captured the Samaritan woman's attention. But she was still caught up in the common—rather than the uncommon—possibilities. She could not see His higher purpose, but she was certainly interested in a perpetual source of water that would spare her these difficult daily trips to the well! "Sir," she said respectfully, "give me this water, that I thirst not, neither come hither to draw."

Jesus reached out one more time to help her understand. He tried to help by speaking of her most personal earthly things and asked her to call her husband. She replied that she had no husband. Jesus said, in effect, you certainly do not, and I include in that denial not only the man with whom you are now living but perhaps also the five who preceded him. At this stunning revelation the woman cried out, "Sir, I perceive that thou art a prophet."

Surely it is fair to assume that Christ would have preferred to talk to the woman about living water rather than bogus husbands. But He met the student where she was in order to take her where she needed to go. Indeed, He took the most common of women in one of the most common, yet serious, sins, and lifted her to uncommon opportunity. In response to her confession that "I know that Messias cometh, which is called Christ," He replied powerfully and pointedly: "I that speak unto thee am he" (John 4:5–26).

Jesus seized on earthly things the woman could understand in order to lift her toward heavenly things she did not understand.

But what of others closer to Christ and stronger of spirit? We might suppose that an unfaithful woman of Samaria might have considerable difficulty breaking away from the commonplace that held her down. But what of Jesus's disciples? An answer to that question, at least in part, follows immediately in John's narrative.

Just as Jesus was concluding His discussion with the Samaritan woman, His disciples returned from the village with food for a midday meal, "saying, Master, eat.

"But he said unto them, I have meat to eat that ye know not of" (John 4:31–32).

Obviously, Jesus was referring to the "sustenance" of the experience He had just had with the Samaritan woman. He had, in a very few moments, lifted her from probable hostility and spiritual stupor to a state where she at least began to glimpse spiritual matters and heard in a wonderfully rare moment the Son of God declare Himself to be the long-awaited Messiah. This was "meat" to One who fed on things of the Spirit—more so than a common crust of bread or literal cut of lamb so faithfully obtained in town by His brethren.

But very much like the Samaritan woman before them, the disciples had not yet had enough experience to understand.

"Hath any man brought him ought to eat?" they asked in bewilderment. If He has had meat to eat we know not of, who brought it to Him and why did He send us into the city? they wondered. Why would He have us make such an effort and then eat here with another before we returned?

We smile slightly at this moment of confusion because we know what has transpired in their absence. Perhaps if they had known why Jesus was speaking to the woman and what it was He had said, they would have more readily understood His reference to eating meat of quite a different kind. Christ's "meat," like His "living water," would leave one filled for eternity. In His gentle, patient, uncommon way, Christ lifted His beloved followers from the commonplace.

"My meat is to do the will of him that sent me, and to finish his work.

"Say not ye, there are yet four months, and then cometh harvest? Behold, I say unto you, Lift up your eyes, and look on the fields; for they are white already to harvest."

Jesus had seen an opportunity with eternal significance and seized it. For Him, the field was *always* ready to harvest. He saw past the traditions and the wrangling and the pettiness of men. Indeed, He had even seen past the woman's very serious sins. What He saw was a chance to lift a life, to teach a human soul, to edify a child of God and move her toward salvation. That was His "meat" and His "work." Certainly, it was the will of His Father, which He had come to fulfill. Even these disciples who had become so close to the Master had yet to shed fully the scales of traditional darkness from their view. They too needed the uncommon invitation commonly extended to lift up their eyes to higher purposes, loftier meanings, more spiritual sustenance (see John 4:27–35).

After noting a few such incidents, it becomes clear that this same lesson is taught by the Savior again and again. Jesus spoke of *temples* and the people thought He spoke of temples (see John 2:18–21). He spoke of *bread* and the people thought he spoke of bread (see John 6:30–58). And so on. And these were not merely parables in the allegorical sense of multiple applications of a single saying. They were in every case an invitation to "lift up your eyes," to see heavenly things—specifically to see and understand Him. But they are also repeated manifestations of His willingness to meet people on their own terms, however limited that understanding, and there lead them on to higher ground. Ultimately, if they would, it would lead them beyond time and space altogether, into eternity.

## JOHN 5

One marvelous incident of the Savior's healing is recorded in the fifth chapter of John. It occurred at the time of the feast of the Jews, probably the Passover, and Jesus had come up to Jerusalem to celebrate this sacred occasion. It was the Sabbath, and Jesus, probably on His way to the temple, passed by a pool called Bethesda, or literally "the House of Mercy."

Surrounding the pool was a great multitude of the blind, halt, and withered, all waiting for a chance to step into this legendary pool. The tradition of the time was that when the waters of Bethesda were troubled, it was the work of an angel, therefore the first to enter the water following that divine manifestation would be healed. John's account refers to one man, lame for thirty-eight years, who had not the physical strength to match His faith. Day in and day out He came to the pool to be healed, but day in and day out He was not mobile enough to be able to enter the water first. On this day mentioned, Jesus noticed the man and "knew that he had been a long time in that case." Jesus stopped, looked at him, and said, "Wilt thou be made whole?" The lame man, considering the thirty-eight years of his condition, may well have thought that either a naïve or cruel question. But surely the loving look in the eye of the Stranger not only merited his respect but gave him hope. With honesty he kept looking into those eyes and said, "Sir, I have no man . . . to put me in the pool." Said Jesus, "Rise, take up thy bed, and walk." In that instant the lame man was made whole (John 5:1–11).

My friends, that same loving hand reaches out to us. That same compassionate voice assuredly invites us, "Come unto me, all ye that labour and are heavy laden, and I will give you rest. Take my yoke upon you, and learn of me; for I am meek and lowly in heart: and ye shall find rest unto thy souls. For my yoke is easy and my burden is light" (Matthew 11:28–30). Over and over again we read that the Lord's hand is stretched out still (see, for example, Isaiah 5:25; 9:12, 17). "And how merciful is our God unto us, . . . and he stretches forth his hands . . . all the day long" (Jacob 6:4).

## JOHN 6

Members of The Church of Jesus Christ of Latter-day Saints are not considered "Christian" by some because we are not fourth-century

Christians, we are not Nicene Christians, we are not creedal Christians of the brand that arose hundreds of years after Christ. No, when we speak of "restored Christianity," we speak of the Church as it was in its New Testament purity, not as it became when great councils were called to debate and anguish over what it was they really believed. So, if one means Greek-influenced, council-convening, philosophy-flavored Christianity of post-apostolic times, we are *not* that kind of Christian.

Thus, we teach that God the Father and His Son, Jesus Christ, are separate and distinct Beings with glorified bodies of flesh and bone. As such we stand with the historical position that "the formal doctrine of the Trinity as it was defined by the great church councils of the fourth and fifth centuries is *not* to be found in the [New Testament]" (*Harper's Bible Dictionary*, Paul F. Achtemeier, ed. [1985], 1099; emphasis added). We take Christ literally at His word—that He "came down from heaven, not to do [his] own will, but the will of him that sent [him]" (John 6:38). Of His antagonists He said they have "hated both me and my Father" (John 15:24). These, along with scores of other references, including His pleading prayers, make clear Jesus's physical separation from His Father. However, having affirmed the point of Their separate and distinct physical nature, we declare unequivocally that They are indeed "one" in every other conceivable way—in mind and deed, in will and wish and hope, in faith and purpose and intent and love, but They *are* separate and distinct beings as all fathers and sons are. In this matter we differ from traditional creedal Christianity but agree with the New Testament.

During the Savior's Galilean ministry, He chided those who had heard of Him feeding the five thousand with only five barley loaves and two fishes, and now flocked to Him expecting a free lunch. That food, important as it was, was incidental to the real nourishment He was trying to give them.

"Your fathers did eat manna in the wilderness, and are dead," He admonished them. "I am the living bread which came down from heaven: if any man eat of this bread, he shall live for ever."

But this was not the meal they had come for, and the record says, "From that time many of his disciples went back, and walked no more with him" (John 6:26, 49, 51, 66).

In that little story is something of the danger in our day. It is that in our contemporary success and sophistication we too may walk away from the vitally crucial bread of eternal life, we may actually *choose* to be spiritually malnourished, willfully indulging in a kind of spiritual anorexia. Like those childish Galileans of old, we may turn up our noses when divine sustenance is placed before us. Of course, the tragedy then as now is that one day, as the Lord Himself has said, "In an hour when ye think not the summer shall be past, and the harvest ended," we will find our "souls [are] not saved" (D&C 45:2).

I have wondered if someone reading this might feel he or she or those they love are hungering for something more substantial and asking with the otherwise successful young man of the scriptures, "What lack I yet?" (Matthew 19:20). I have wondered if someone might be wandering "from sea to sea," running "to and fro" as the prophet Amos said (Amos 8:12), wearied by the pace of life in the fast lane or in trying to keep up with the Joneses before the Joneses refinance. I have wondered if any are hoping to find the answer to a deeply personal problem or to have some light cast on the most serious questions of their heart. Such problems or questions often deal with our marriages, our families, our friends, our health, our peace—or the conspicuous lack of such cherished possessions.

It is to those who so hunger that I wish to address my thoughts. Wherever you live, and at whatever point in age or experience you find yourself, I declare that God has through His Only Begotten Son lifted the famine of which Amos spoke. I testify that the Lord Jesus Christ is the Bread of Life and a Well of Living Water springing up unto eternal life. I declare to those who are members of The Church of

Jesus Christ of Latter-day Saints, and especially to those who are not, that our Heavenly Father and His Beloved Firstborn Son did appear to the boy prophet Joseph Smith and restored light and life, hope and direction to a wandering world, a world filled with those who wonder, "Where is hope? Where is peace? What path should I follow? Which way should I go?"

Regardless of past paths taken or not taken, I wish to offer you "the way, the truth, . . . the life" (John 14:6). I invite you to join in the adventure of the earliest disciples of Christ who also yearned for the bread of life—those who did *not* go back but who came to Him, stayed with Him, and who recognized that for safety and salvation there was no other to whom they could ever go (see John 6:68).

## JOHN 9

In the ninth chapter of John, the Savior anoints the eyes of "a man which was blind from his birth." He does so with a little spittle and clay and tells him to go wash in the pool of Siloam. He obeys, and the man has vision.

Soon this man becomes the talk of the town. Everyone knew that he had been blind and now he could see. As a result, more and more people are coming to follow Jesus.

This is particularly concerning to the Pharisees, who go to the man's parents and say, in effect, "We have seen this man from Nazareth, and He is supposedly performing miracles. It is causing trouble, and your son is part of the problem. Tell him to be quiet. Tell him to forget about the whole matter." These Pharisees are important people in town, and the parents are very deferential. They reply, "Our son is of age. Ask him about this. Don't talk to us."

So the Jewish leaders say, "Alright. We will." They confront the son, point their finger at him, and say, "No more of this. Don't cause trouble. Don't talk about any miracle." The sweet young man listens to them for a while, but finally he says, "Wait, wait, wait. You have to understand something here. I am not brilliant. I have never read anything. Those scrolls that you read, those scriptures you are quoting, all those things you are telling me here are foreign to me. I don't know much of anything because I have been blind all my life. In fact, I only know one thing: I was blind, and now I can see" (see John 9:1–25).

That declaration is hard to argue with. What can one say in response to that declaration? "Oh, no, you can't really see, can you?" No, that won't work because he *can* see. We do live by faith. We start with faith; we can't ask for the evidence first. Faith *precedes* the miracle. But with that faith, miracles *do* come. They come in your life and my life and everyone's life. We grow and develop, and He speaks to our mind and to our heart.

And we cannot or should not, with any integrity, deny the evidence.

## JOHN 10

We can be certain that everyone, one way or another, will have his or her share of adversity before life is over. In that spirit, I invite us to remember that the most repeated line in all of scripture is "It came to pass." Painful days do pass. It might seem that they won't, but they do. No regret is forever. No disappointment is fatal or final. No mistake is beyond remedy. Bad times pass, especially if friends are willing to help them pass. And when they do pass, we are able to remember there are wonderful days to come with magnificent blessings arriving with them. Life is not over until it is over, and we have more tread left on our tires than we realize. Even as the years go by, we have a generous amount of life still to live in quality if not always in quantity.

Why? Because there is always a need for more of everything that is good and uplifting and worthwhile. Furthermore, we are the ones who can produce those gifts, wrapped with ribbons of encouragement, courtesy, and friendship of all kinds. Believe it or not, there are people who count on us, and we will find our days more rewarding if we believe that there is something significant, even essential, that perhaps only we can do. We could all cite many examples of men and women who have lived fully with a tremendous impact for good on others regardless of their age or the condition of their health and however limited their income and education, talents and opportunities may have appeared to be. Since there are so many of these people, we can only suppose that there could be many more. To get all out of life that we can, we should put everything into it that we can, for as many people as we can, for as long as we can.

If we can embrace life fully, gratefully, we will all understand a little better what Christ meant when He said, "I am come that they might have life, and that they might have it more abundantly" (John 10:10).

If in times of trial we wander, we need someone wise and concerned to give aid. Jesus said He was the Good Shepherd, one who would leave the ninety and nine safely enfolded to rescue the lamb that is lost. And this Shepherd is not a hireling, one who trembles at the sound of a wolf and flees at the sight of thieves. Ownership of the flock makes a great deal of difference, and this watchman will protect at the very cost of His life. "I . . . know my sheep," He promised, ". . . and I lay down my life for the sheep" (John 10:14–15).

Safely returned, we again graze along, not knowing what the loss of our life might have been like. With staff in hand, Christ must often muse lovingly over such youthful artlessness. "Verily, verily, I say unto you, ye are little children, and ye have not as yet understood how great blessings the Father hath in his own hands and prepared for you;

"And ye cannot bear all things now; nevertheless, be of good cheer, for I will lead you along. The kingdom is yours and the blessings thereof are yours, and the riches of eternity are yours" (D&C 78:17–18). *He is the Good Shepherd.*

## JOHN 11

When Lazarus lay ill, Mary and Martha sent for the Savior, and He didn't come; at least He didn't come quickly. He started toward Bethany, but He had things to do along the way, healing other people as He traveled—a Roman centurion's son and others He encountered. He did not seem to feel much urgency, and Lazarus died before He got there.

Mary handled that all right, but Martha needed things to be done when they needed to be done. She rushed out to greet Him, and she said, "If thou hadst been here, my brother [would not have] died." Jesus said, "Thy brother shall rise again." And she said, "I know that he shall rise again in the resurrection at the last day" (John 11:21–24).

She got just that far and the Savior—I am sure lovingly, I am sure patiently, I am sure with all kinds of generosity—stopped her from going any further. He said with conversation-ending power, "I am the resurrection and the life: he that believeth in me, though he were dead, yet shall he live." And then this word—this line—"And whosoever liveth and believeth in me shall never die" (John 11:25–26).

We need a better vocabulary, because our loved ones who pass away are not dead. We have that on the good word of the Savior of the world, the Light and the Life of the world. We use the word because we have to deal with our loss, but they are not dead. "Whosover liveth and believeth in me *shall never die*."

## JOHN 12

I testify to you in my utmost admiration for you that God loves broken things. They are everywhere, in everyone. But that is what we agreed to in mortality. The scriptures say that we shouted for joy at the chance to come here. There are days when we wonder what the shouting was about. Well, we were thrilled, and we will be again. We need to understand that there are cycles in our lives. It takes broken clouds to nourish the earth. It takes broken earth to grow grain. It takes broken grain to make bread. It takes broken bread to nourish us.

These are the cycles of life! This is how it works! After a while, we can understand that. But think of the first time that idea was introduced. You know that little parable where Jesus said, "Except a corn of wheat fall into the ground and die, it abideth alone: but if it die, it bringeth forth much fruit" (John 12:24). In other words, you have to throw it away to get it back. After a lot of agriculture classes and 4-H work, we know that is the way to get a harvest. But the first man who had to do that (probably Adam?), must have said, "What? You want me to throw this seed corn away? I am starving to death, I am down to this little handful, and you want me to throw it in the ground? To give it up?"

And the Lord says, "That is exactly what I want you to do." And we learn that we can plant, nourish, and water, then harvest, getting a return that is tenfold or perhaps a hundredfold more than we gave up. But we have to be patient. We have to trust and live by faith, understanding that He knows how to fix things that are broken. In fact, you could make a good case that the thing God loves most in this world is broken—it is a broken heart and a contrite spirit.

We are all going to get the chance to break our heart and bring our spirit into contrition, thus identifying with the Savior of the world. And if that broken heart is not for your sins and sorrows over your own personal problems, then you get to break your heart for your neighbors' troubles. You get to feel their sadness and their circumstances and to care for their sorrow. If your heart is joyful (thank heavens!), you get to dry the tears of your neighbor. Everyone gets to practice being godly, trusting that One so endowed can mend broken things.

There is a special moment in the New Testament when the Savior is receiving courage from His Father in Heaven. He is searching His soul as Passion Week begins, knowing that the Atonement is coming. He is probably aware that everyone is going to be with Him at the start of the week and no one is going to be with Him by the end of the week. And He undoubtedly knows something of the suffering that awaits Him in Gethsemane and on Calvary.

Here, as Passion Week begins, He says, "Father, save me from this hour." Spare me, take me, remove me from this hour. Then, in the same breath, almost before He finishes His sentence, He says, "But for this cause came I unto this hour" (John 12:27). It almost seems He is arguing with Himself. It feels that He knows He has to do this but is saying, "I don't want to do it." We know that because in the Garden of Gethsemane, He asks His Father, "If there is any other cup, I would rather drink that" (see Luke 22:42). We ought to understand that about the Atonement of Jesus Christ.

Well, there was not any other way. He knows that because He acknowledges "for this [hour] came I into the world" (John 18:37).

And the Father speaks through the veil saying, in effect, "I am going to glorify You. You are going to be glorified in this world and in the next. You are going to succeed" (see John 12:28). Christ reaches up through the veil, asking for courage, and He receives it from the Father. It is a beautiful, beautiful moment.

How did others respond to hearing the voice of God? Well, it was different for different people; it depends on who you are and where you were.

Some people said, "I think I heard thunder. Is there a storm off in the distance? Are clouds rolling in from Galilee?" (see John 12:29). Others, a little more in tune, said, "I think I heard angels nearby. I think sacred beings were near and perhaps speaking" (see John 12:29). The third group, which in this case was limited to the Savior of the world only, knew that God had spoken. God the Eternal Father, the Father of us all, the Creator of the great plan of salvation and the Father of the Son of God who has to carry the burden of that salvation for each of us.

How does that happen? Why didn't everyone hear the same thing? Why didn't everyone know that God had spoken? Some were in tune enough to at least think angels were present, but a large number thought it had only thundered. All they heard was noise.

The challenge is not with the work, not with the plan, not with heaven, not with God; the challenge is with us. When revelation comes, do we hear thunder? Do we think "perhaps there are angels"? Or can we break through our limitations and recognize "God has spoken"?

## JOHN 13

As the Lord and His disciples prepared the sacred supper of the ultimate Passover week, Jesus was under the strain of deep and profound emotion. Only He knew what lay immediately ahead, but perhaps even He did not fully anticipate the depth of pain to which He must go before it could be said, "The Son of Man hath descended below them all" (D&C 122:8).

In the midst of this meal and such thoughts, Christ quietly arose, girded Himself as a slave or servant would, and knelt to wash the Apostles' feet. This small circle of believers in this scarcely founded kingdom was about to pass through their severest trial, so He would set aside His own increasing anguish in order that He might yet once more serve and strengthen them. It does not matter that no one thought to wash His feet. In transcendent humility He would continue to teach and to cleanse them. He would to the final hour—and beyond—be their sustaining servant. As John wrote, who was there and watched the wonder of it all, "Having loved his own which were in the world, he loved them unto the end" (John 13:1).

So it had been, and so it was to be—through the night, and through the pain, and forever. He will always be our strength, and no anguish in His own soul will ever keep Him from that sustaining role.

In the moonlit silence of that Near Eastern night, every acute pain, every heartfelt grief, every crushing wrong and human hurt experienced since time began was to be heaped upon His weary shoulders.

But in such a moment when someone might well have said it to Him, He rather says to them, "Let not your heart be troubled, neither let it be afraid" (John 14:27).

Internally The Church of Jesus Christ of Latter-day Saints has always been built on a concept of unity. It does not just need such a spirit, it demands it.

We have no church without it.

You will recall that in the thirteenth chapter of John we find passages describing the Savior's preparation to leave His disciples. His ultimate preparation was instituting the sacramental covenant honoring His body and His blood. But He did something just before the meal that mystified me for a long time. I did not fully understand it. I had read it; I had been taught it; I knew what the words said—but I knew there was something more.

"Now before the feast of the passover, when Jesus knew that his hour was come . . .

"He riseth from supper, and laid aside his garments; and took a towel, and girded himself.

"After that he poureth water into a basin, and began to wash the disciples' feet, and to wipe them with the towel wherewith he was girded.

"Then cometh he to Simon Peter: and Peter saith unto him, Lord dost thou wash my feet?

"Jesus answered and said unto him, What I do thou knowest not now; but thou shalt know hereafter."

That is one of the lines that haunted me when I first read them years ago. "What I do thou knowest not now, but thou shalt know hereafter." I knew there was meaning there that I was not getting.

"Peter saith unto him, Thou shalt never wash my feet. Jesus answered him, If I wash thee not, thou hast no part with me.

"Simon Peter saith unto him, Lord not my feet only, but also my hands and my head" (John 13:1, 4–9).

And you know the way it finishes.

I prayed about those verses. I read them and reread them. I went on through John to chapters 17 and 18. Then I would come back to chapter 13. I knew that somehow there was more to washing feet than simply a lesson in humility, more than teaching that the servant is not greater than his Lord. I wondered if section 88 of the Doctrine and Covenants would help me, inasmuch as it referred to the washing of feet as it was introduced in the School of the Prophets. I was at home in the middle of the night, and my documentary *History of the Church* was at the office. I knew I could not get at it, but I thought perhaps I had something in my home library that would refer to this ordinance, so I started throwing books around. After a while I found the comment I had remembered from the Prophet Joseph Smith, given in November 1835 as they prepared to institute the washing of feet in the School of the Prophets in Kirtland.

"The item to which I wish the more particularly to call your attention tonight, is the ordinance of washing of feet. . . . We have not desired as much from the hand of the Lord through faith and obedience, as we ought to have done, yet we have enjoyed great blessings, and we are not so sensible of this as we should be. . . . We must have all things prepared, and call our solemn assembly . . . and in it we must attend to the ordinance of washing of feet. It was never intended for any but official members.

"It is calculated to unite our hearts, that we may be one in feeling and sentiment, and that our faith may be strong, so that Satan cannot overthrow us, nor have any power over us here" (*History of the Church* 2:308–9).

When I read those words, bells started to ring, and rockets went into the air, because I felt I knew then what Jesus meant when He said to Peter, "What I do thou knowest not now, but thou shalt know hereafter."

This *is* a great lesson about humility, showing the Master girding His loins and washing the feet of the servants, including the one who would betray Him. But beyond that there was an urgent attempt on His part to shield and protect and bless them in His absence, for Satan would be coming to destroy.

Then everything else that followed came alive for me—the institution of the sacrament, that great, unifying, accessible opportunity we have every Sunday to keep us united in our own souls with each other and with God; the Atonement, the "at-one-ment," which would keep us together and free us from evil; the great high priestly prayer in which Christ prayed that we could be one, even in this world. Of course, the success of these efforts is suggested in the book of Acts, where, for a time in the Church, all things were held in common, and Zion was established, and Satan was able to do no work within that little Church.

All this was part of what Peter needed to hear, I think, because while he would not fail ultimately, he would, just hours from this washing, flee from the courtyard of Caiaphas and weep at the third crowing of the cock. Jesus knew what lay ahead and Peter did not. And Jesus knew a lot that Peter did not know. Jesus knows a lot that we don't know, and it is important to be united lest Satan sift us as chaff and have power over us here. It is important *"to unite our hearts, that we may be one in feeling and sentiment, and that our faith may be strong, so that Satan cannot overthrow us"* (emphasis added).

That is what we have to do for each other—keep love in and Satan out of our shared life with the Savior.

On the eve of His ultimate suffering and Crucifixion, Jesus was gathered with His disciples in an upper room where He introduced to them the ordinance of the sacrament and left His final teachings with them. Worried about them, fearful for what lay ahead of them, He made a final effort to summarize the gospel for them. Perhaps in the spirit of saying, "If you can only remember *one* thing I have taught you, remember this," He said:

"Little children, yet a little while I am with you. Ye shall seek me: [but] whither I go, ye cannot come; so now I say to you,

"A new commandment I give unto you, That ye love one another; as I have loved you, that ye also love one another.

"By this shall all men know that ye are my disciples, if ye have love one to another" (John 13:33–35).

True to that call and following the Savior's pure, loving example, Peter and the others picked up the torch of the gospel which Jesus had left them—and us—to carry, and in His name went out into the world. Peter characterized that task as "preaching peace by Jesus Christ," testifying "How God anointed Jesus of Nazareth with . . . power: *who went about doing good*, and healing all that were oppressed of the devil; for God was with him" (Acts 10:36, 39; emphasis added).

Brothers and sisters, as I represent the First Presidency and Quorum of the Twelve in expressing love *for* you, I also thank you very personally, every one of you, for love *from* you—for every kind thing you have ever done, every encouraging word you have ever said, every instance of forgiveness you have shown, every time you have helped a child, or greeted someone with a smile, or extended the hand of friendship. I thank you for trying to show that we are disciples of Christ in the manner He commanded, the manner "by [which] shall all men know" us—that includes your patience with people and their problems, your acceptance of callings in The Church of Jesus Christ of Latter-day Saints when you were a new member, or maybe a tired old one, or sometimes just plain frightened.

I thank you for suffering in a righteous cause, and there is no greater or more righteous cause than the message, the brotherhood and sisterhood, of the gospel of Jesus Christ. I thank you for every time you have written a note of encouragement to someone, or followed that impression to make a phone call, or for holding your tongue that time when it would have been very easy (and probably justified) to speak sharply. I thank you from the bottom of my heart for every tear you have helped to wipe away, and every smile you have helped to bring back. I thank you for being living evidence in someone's life that even though the night be dark, God will be there, and Jesus will be there, and people like you will be there—with the eternal promise in such hours that the sun truly does rise and shine warmly, lovingly again.

In short, I love you and thank you for "going about doing good," as quiet and nameless as those acts may be. And you will understand in the spirit of these particular remarks that I am not speaking of big service projects or conspicuous leadership in the Church. Thank heaven for all who do the big things. But that is a topic for another day. No, today I am speaking of little things, small things, probably unpremeditated things where you through your actions "preach peace by Jesus Christ."

In this you are, like He is, a teacher of truth, an emissary from God, a healer of troubled hearts. You are a light in a dark place, a protector, a strong defense, a haven in difficult times. And you are, regularly, often, dramatically, the answer to someone's prayer. I cannot pay you a sweeter or more heartfelt compliment.

## JOHN 14

Repentance and faith, service and compassion—now is always the right time for these. The past is to be learned from, not lived in, and the future is to be planned for, not paralyzed by. God has declared Himself in the present tense: *I am the Great I AM.*

Such a journey from beginning through present to end suggests a path, a course of travel, and Jesus said He was "the Way." He did not say He would *show* the way (although He did); He said He *was* the way (see John 14:6). To travel here suggests something more than merely knowing the terrain, watching for pitfalls, and setting out at a brisk pace. It means all of that plus the sobering admission that we will need His merciful assistance for every step of the journey.

This particular way is impassable alone. He waits patiently for us while we rest. He encourages us when we murmur. He calls us back when we stray. Ultimately, He carries us on His shoulders, rejoicing, because we find the heights are too great and the waters too deep (see Luke 15:5). Only strict adherence—adherence in its most literal sense—to the Lord Jesus Christ will see us through, for there is "none other name under heaven given among men, whereby we must be saved" (Acts 4:12).

Using the metaphor of the sheepfold, He told His disciples, "I am the door: by me if any man enter in, he shall be saved" (John 10:9). Thus, the place the way leads to is not only inevitable by, but also in a sense incidental to, the way itself. "No man cometh unto the Father, but by me," Jesus warned (John 14:6).

Whoever you are and wherever you find yourself as you seek your way in life, I promise you that obedience to and love for Jesus Christ and His gospel should be—*must* be—our highest priority. He is "the way, the truth, and the life" (John 14:6). He must be *our* way, *our* truth, and *our* life. So wherever else you want to go in life, I ask you to "come unto Him" as the imperative first step in getting there, in finding happiness, strength, and success in your journey.

I know of no other way for us to succeed or to be happy or to be safe than to keep that relationship with the Savior strong and spiritual. I know of no other way for us to be able to carry our burdens or find what Jacob called "that happiness which is prepared for the saints" (2 Nephi 9:43). That is why we make solemn covenants with Him beginning with our baptism and continuing on the rest of our lives. We take upon us His name. In as many ways as possible, both figuratively and literally, we try to take upon us His identity. We seek out His teachings and retell His miracles. We send latter-day witnesses, including prophets, apostles, and missionaries, around the world to declare His message. We testify that He is the only source of eternal life. We plead for Him to swing open the gates of heaven in our behalf and trust everlastingly that He will, based upon our faithfulness.

My desire for you is that you might have more straightforward experience with the Savior's life and teachings in whatever setting that may be.

Ultimate happiness, true peace, and anything even remotely close to scriptural joy are found first, foremost, and forever in living the gospel of Jesus Christ. Lots of other philosophies and systems of belief have been tried. Indeed, it seems safe to say that virtually *every* other philosophy and system has been tried down through the centuries of history. But when the Apostle Thomas asked the Lord the question young people often ask today, "How can we know the way?" (and often in life that really translates, "How can we know the way to be happy?") Jesus gave the answer that rings from eternity to all eternity, "I am the way, the truth, and the life . . . And whatsoever ye shall ask in my name, that will I do. . . . If ye shall ask any thing in my name, I will do it" (John 14:5–6, 13–14).

What a promise! Live my way, live my truth, live my life—live *in this manner* that I am showing you and teaching you—and whatsoever you ask will be given, whatsoever you seek you will find, including happiness.

Being called to the Twelve carries with it a sobering education. The Brethren don't talk much about those experiences, but everyone seems to have some kind of a refining, humbling experience.

I remember being in the middle of this personal tutorial. I was probably wearing my feelings like a terrible mask on my face. I am sure I looked terrible, because then-Elder James E. Faust came up and threw his arms around me saying, "We know exactly how you feel. And there's nothing that we can do for you." Which wasn't very encouraging. But it was something I was learning about the Savior and who He is.

I read everything I could about the Apostleship. I spent all the time I could—every spare minute—reading about the Apostleship in the New Testament, the Book of Mormon, the Doctrine and Covenants, Church histories, biographies, anywhere there was a serious reference to the Apostleship. I did everything I knew to do to learn about the Apostles.

Everything I read just made the weight heavier. I was not getting any relief until finally, the straw that broke the camel's back, the final blow, came when I was reading in the fourteenth chapter of John in the New Testament, where the Savior said to the Twelve then, "He that believeth on me, the works that I do shall he do also; and *greater works than these shall he do*" (John 14:12; emphasis added). And that was it, that was too much. Greater works than He, the Savior, had done, the Twelve were going to do? Raise people from the dead? Be the Creator of heaven and earth under the Father? Go out and create a solar system? To say nothing of the traditional miracles of causing the lame to walk and the blind to see.

I know now the Lord was doing this for a purpose. He had my attention. I know we are supposed to be humble; I was humble. If we are supposed to be meek and lowly, I was going to be meek and lowly.

While I was in that condition, the Lord could teach me. Remember that when you have a hard day. Remember that when you are being tested. The Lord can teach us especially well when we are needy, when we are driven to our knees.

I was taught something in those first weeks that I still believe, something I have been clinging to regarding that verse I read. I don't think He meant that "you will do greater works than I have done" *vertically*, like creating heaven and earth or being an atoner, or being a God in mortality. He could not have meant that. What I think He meant was we would do some greater works *laterally*. I think He meant that the Twelve, ancient and modern, including me, would be able to go to places and be with people that He did not go to or be with. In that sense, I can understand the "greater works" we would do that He was unable to do.

In His entire mortal ministry, He traveled some ninety-five miles—from Nazareth and Capernaum on the north to Jerusalem on the south. He performed His ministry for three years, more or less. We don't know exactly, but it was roughly thirty-six months. So, ninety to ninety-five miles, thirty to thirty-six months.

Well, I have been in the Quorum of the Twelve for more than twenty-eight years now. My twenty-eight years, compared to His three? My poor math says I have had over nine times the opportunity He had to spread the gospel. His ninety miles? You may remember that a few years ago Sister Holland and I circled the globe with President and Sister Russell M. Nelson. We started flying east and kept going east until we came home flying from the west. We literally circled the globe. It was not the first time we had done that, and probably won't be the last.

So, the very average Jeff Holland gets to go around the earth with the Prophet and President of The Church of Jesus Christ of Latter-day Saints, while the Savior of the World gets to go up and down the Jordan River valley with some ex-fishermen He is trying to mold into Apostles. I have taken consolation in the idea that this was what He meant in the bold scripture. He meant "Jeff, you are going to get to do things I did not get to do. So go in my name, as my Apostle, and do what I would do."

In teaching us to live the first principles of the gospel, beginning always with faith in Him, the Savior has probably spoken enough encouraging words to supply the whole universe, yet we see all around us unhappy Latter-day Saints, worried Latter-day Saints, gloomy Latter-day Saints into whose troubled hearts not one of these innumerable consoling words seems to be allowed to enter.

Yes, life can be challenging. Yes, we have pain and regrets and real problems to work through. Yes, we have disappointments and sorrow, all kinds of highs and lows. But the Lord and the prophets have spoken enough encouraging words about how to face those problems to fill a cosmic journal. The Savior's benediction upon His disciples even as He moved toward the pain and agony of Gethsemane and Calvary is the most famous of these. On that night, the night of the greatest suffering that has ever taken place in the world or that ever will take place, the Savior said, "Peace I leave with you, my peace I give unto you. . . . Let not your heart be troubled, neither let it be afraid" (John 14:27). What a stunning view of life in the most agonizing of hours! How can He possibly say that, facing what He knows He is facing? Because this is the Church of the happy endings! This victory is already won. Yet I see cheerless Latter-day Saints with a crisis of faith here, a skeptical heart there, and more than enough guilt or depression to go around. I think some of us must have that remnant of Puritan heritage still in us that says it is somehow wrong to be comforted or helped, that we are *supposed* to be miserable about something.

"Let not your heart be troubled, neither let it be afraid" (John 14:27).

I submit to you that may be one of the Savior's commandments that is, even in the hearts of otherwise faithful Latter-day Saints, almost universally disobeyed; and yet I wonder whether our resistance to this invitation could be any more grievous to the Lord's merciful heart. I can tell you this as a parent: as concerned as I would be if somewhere in their lives one of my children were seriously troubled or unhappy or disobedient, nevertheless I would be infinitely more devastated if I felt that at such a time that child could not trust me to help, or should feel his or her interest were unimportant to me or unsafe in my care. In that same spirit, I am convinced that none of us can appreciate how deeply it wounds the loving heart of the Savior of the world when He finds that His people do not feel confident in His care or secure in His hands or trustful in His commandments.

Just because God is God, just because Christ is Christ, They will help and bless us if we will only let Them. It is Their nature to do so.

## JOHN 15

Christ said, "I am the true vine, and . . . ye are the branches" (John 15:1, 5). "Abide in me, and I in you. As the branch cannot bear fruit of itself, except it abide in the vine; no more can ye, except ye abide in me" (John 15:4).

"Abide in me" is an understandable and beautiful enough concept in the elegant English of the King James Bible, but *abide* is not a word we use much anymore. So I gained even more appreciation for this admonition from the Lord when I was introduced to the translation of this passage in another language. In Spanish, that familiar phrase is rendered *"permaneced en mi."* Like the English verb *abide*, *permanecer* means "to remain, to stay," but even gringos like me can hear the root cognate there of *permanence*. The sense of this then is "stay," but stay *forever*. That is the call of the gospel message. Come, but come to remain. Come with conviction and endurance. Come permanently, for your sake and the sake of all the generations who must follow you, and we will help each other be strong to the very end.

"He who picks up one end of the stick, picks up the other," my marvelous mission president taught in his very first message to us (Marion D. Hanks quoting Harry Emerson Fosdick, *Living Under Tension* [1941], 111). And that is the way it is supposed to be when we join this, the true and living Church of the true and living God. When we join The Church of Jesus Christ of Latter-day Saints, we board the *Good Ship Zion* and sail with her wherever she goes until she comes into that millennial port. *We stay in the boat*, through squalls and stills, through storms and sunburn, because that is the only way to the promised land. The Church of Jesus Christ of Latter-day Saints is the Lord's vehicle for crucial doctrines, ordinances, covenants, and keys that are essential to exaltation, and one cannot be fully faithful to the gospel of Jesus Christ without striving to be faithful in His Church, which is its earthly institutional manifestation. To new convert and longtime member alike, we declare in the spirit of Nephi's powerful valedictory exhortation: "Ye have entered in by the gate; . . . [but]

now, . . . after ye have gotten into this strait and narrow path, I would ask if all is done? Behold, I say unto you, Nay; . . . press forward with a steadfastness in Christ, . . . and endure to the end, behold, thus . . . ye shall have eternal life" (2 Nephi 31:18–20).

Jesus said, "Without me ye can do nothing" (John 15:5). I testify that is God's truth. Christ is everything to us and we are to *abide* in Him permanently, unyieldingly, steadfastly, forever. For the fruit of the gospel to blossom and bless our lives, we must be firmly attached to Him, the Savior of us all, and to this His Church, which bears His holy name. He is the vine that is our true source of strength and the only source of eternal life. In Him we not only will endure but also will prevail and triumph in this holy cause that will never fail us. May we never fail it nor fail Him.

⁂

At the zenith of His mortal ministry, Jesus said, "love one another, *as I have loved you*" (John 15:12; emphasis added). To make certain they understood exactly what kind of love that was, He said, "If ye love me, keep my commandments" (John 14:15), and "whosoever . . . shall break one of [the] least commandments, *and shall teach men so,* he shall be . . . the least in the kingdom of heaven" (Matthew 5:19; emphasis added). Christlike love is the greatest need we have on this planet in part because righteousness was always supposed to accompany it. So if love is to be our watchword, as it must be, then by the word of Him who is love personified we must forsake transgression and any hint of advocacy for it in others. Jesus clearly understood what many in our modern culture seem to forget: that there is a crucial difference between the commandment to forgive sin (which He had an infinite capacity to do) and the warning against condoning it (which He never ever did even once).

Friends, especially my young friends, take heart. Pure Christlike love flowing from true righteousness can change the world.

## JOHN 17

From our experience on various assignments around the world, we sense that some Latter-day Saints feel distant from God, cut off from a personal feeling for the mission and Atonement of Jesus Christ, and foreign to everyday experiences with the Holy Ghost and its guidance in their lives. This is a concern for all of us because the Savior Himself said in His great prayerful declaration, "This is life eternal, that they might know thee the only true God, and [me,] Jesus Christ, whom thou hast sent" (John 17:3).

Our knowledge of and relationship to the members of the Godhead is at the heart of our quest for eternal life. So one of the destinations to which The Church of Jesus Christ of Latter-day Saints can take you is to the profound, powerful, stunning realization that your happiness, your safety, your peace of mind, and, yes, ultimately your salvation is at the heart of *everything* these Godly beings do. I don't mean just *some* things They do, I mean *everything* They do. *Everything* God, Christ, and the Holy Ghost do, to say nothing of the angels of heaven at their command, has something to do with granting you your hopes and dreams and your eternal life. If something does not contribute to your happiness and progress, They don't do it.

The Savior said, "And this is life eternal, that they [that is, we] might know thee *the only true God*, and Jesus Christ, whom thou hast sent" (John 17:3; emphasis added). I stress that phrase, "*the only true God*."

May I declare that one of the tragedies of our day is that the true God is not known. Tragically, much of contemporary Christianity has inherited the view of a capricious, imperious, and especially angry God whose primary duty is to frighten little children and add suffering to the lives of already staggering adults. May I unequivocally and unilaterally cry out against that sacrilegious and demeaning view of a loving and compassionate Father in Heaven. I wonder if the Savior may not have known, even in His mortal years, that this would happen, thus His plea for the world to know *the True God,* the Fatherly God, the Forgiving and Redeeming and Benevolent God. To bring that understanding was *one* of the reasons Christ came to the earth.

So feeding the hungry, healing the sick, rebuking cruelty, pleading for faith—and hope and charity—this was Christ showing us the way of the Father. In His life and especially in His death, Christ was declaring, "This is *God's* compassion I am showing you, as well as my own." It is the perfect Son's manifestation of the perfect Father's care. In Their mutual suffering and shared sorrow for the sins and heartaches of the rest of us, we see ultimate meaning in the declaration: "For God so loved the world, that he gave his only begotten Son, that whosoever believeth in him should not perish, but have everlasting life. For God sent not his Son into the world to condemn the world; but that the world through him might be saved" (John 3:16–17).

I bear personal witness of a living, loving God, who knows our names, hears and answers prayers, and cherishes us eternally as His children.

I testify that there is no spiteful or malicious motive in Him. I testify that all He does (He who never sleeps nor slumbers) is seek for ways to bless us, to help us, and to save us. I pray that you will believe that and embrace it. I pray that you will strive to see the wonder and majesty of heaven's concern and compassion for us.

I share a few lines from the Savior's prayer for unity. It is interesting that would be the subject on His mind as He was going to His death. Could He count on the Church as a body to cling together? Could He count on the Apostles and the leaders on down? Could He count on people being unified? It is intriguing to me that of all the things He could pray about, that is what He prayed about.

In John 17:8 we read: "I have given unto them the words . . . thou gavest me." For one thing, I think nothing could be more unifying than to teach the gospel, than to declare the truth, than to find the revelations and have revelation and give that to each other. "I have given unto them the words . . . thou gavest me; and they . . . received [those words]."

In verse 14: "I have given them thy word." Notice the implications. Notice what happens: "The world [hateth] them." "I gave them the word and they were not popular, at least for a few minutes, because they are not of the world, as I was not of the world."

And then a line with which I have always been intrigued. I think it is one of the most powerful lines I can imagine, buried right here in the middle of this prayer for His associates:

"For their sakes I sanctify myself, that they also might be sanctified" (John 17:19). I don't know all that that means, but I know what I am supposed to do: if I want others to be close to the Lord, I had better be close to the Lord. If I want people to be sanctified, I had better be sanctified. I sanctify myself that they may be sanctified, or unified, or cleansed, or repentant, or worthy. That starts with the least part of that unity—it starts with us.

## JOHN 19

The children of Israel have always been under covenant to sacrifice. The first commandment given to Adam and Eve after they left the garden was to sacrifice.

"And he gave unto them commandments, that they should worship the Lord their God, and should offer the firstlings of their flocks, for an offering unto the Lord. And Adam was obedient unto the commandments of the Lord.

"And after many days an angel of the Lord appeared unto Adam, saying: Why dost thou offer sacrifices unto the Lord? And Adam said unto him: I know not, save the Lord commanded me.

"And then the angel spake, saying: This thing is a similitude of the sacrifice of the Only Begotten of the Father, which is full of grace and truth" (Moses 5:5–7).

There may have been other commandments given. We don't know them. We just know that to sacrifice is the first one mentioned outside the garden. And so it went for many years, thousands of years. But it never went very well. Not every story in the Old Testament is a majestic declaration of faith, loving kindness, and an understanding of the gospel of Jesus Christ, but they were taught these virtues partly through symbolism. In the above case, it was the symbolism of sacrifice. So when the great Lamb of God does come and fulfills that symbol that had been offered for nearly four thousand years, it concludes a dispensation. Jesus opens a new dispensation by changing the symbolism. It does not change the covenant. It does not change the principle of sacrifice, but it does change the symbol.

Following His great sacrifice, He says: "Ye shall offer for a sacrifice unto me a broken heart and a contrite spirit. And whoso cometh unto me with a broken heart and a contrite spirit, him will I baptize with fire and with the Holy Ghost. . . . Behold, I have come unto the world to bring redemption unto the world, to save the world from sin" (3 Nephi 9:20–21).

It is still the same lesson taught by that sacrificial lamb in the Old Testament. It is still toward the same purpose: redeeming the children of God from sin. But it involves a different offering, a different symbol. It is more personal. It is deeper in the soul. The sacrificial lamb was a little abstract. No one seemed to understand it completely. The blood was hardly dry on the altar when people would forget why they had made that offering—that is, making a covenant to live like the Savior who would come—and they would return to brutality, violence, and sin.

But it is important to remember that the new symbols—a broken heart and a contrite spirit—retain identification with the Savior. Christ died of a broken heart and His soul was filled with contrition for the sins of the world.

Crucifixion was designed to be the most painful, most excruciating form of death that the Romans could employ. They could put people to death with other quicker, more violent means. But they could not put anyone to death with more suffering than crucifixion caused.

Death was ultimately to come by suffocation. There was not supposed to be any obvious damage to the body. No bruises, no lacerations, no organs scarred. One was supposed to hang on the cross and gasp for breath as the weight of the body bore down on the lungs. If some relief was needed, the crucified could try to "stand" on the nail that had been driven through the feet, securing to the upright beam of the cross—that is, the victim could push up on that nail if he could stand the pain.

And what a severe pain that must have been. Take the pressure off by pushing up and lifting the diaphragm a little, getting another breath or two. Or if you can imagine it—I can't—lifting oneself up with open-arm strength, with shoulder strength, trying to take the pressure off the lungs by lifting one's whole body with arms that are nailed into the crossbeam. Death by crucifixion was supposed to take days to accomplish, and it was supposed to be terrible.

But when the Roman soldier comes around to take those three off the cross before the Sabbath begins, He is surprised by one of them. He comes to the two thieves and breaks their leg bones for the shock that will hasten their death. Then he comes to the Savior and thinks, "I believe he is already dead." This gentile would not have been allowed to break the Savior's bone, because this is to be a perfect offering, just as it was to be a perfect Lamb. God and the angels of heaven would have forbidden that Roman soldier from breaking a bone of this perfect offering.

But none of this was necessary. Sensing that Jesus was already dead, he takes out his sword and pierces the Master's side, His abdomen, down under His rib cage. And, lo and behold, blood and water rush out (see John 19:32–34). And we must ask, Where did that come from? He has not been in a car wreck. He has not fallen down a mountainside. No organs of any kind should have been disturbed by crucifixion except the lungs. One was just supposed to suffocate. No blood loss possible.

I don't know the physiology of this. I don't know the biology or the chemistry. But it would appear that blood and water that was now down in the lower abdomen was there because Jesus's heart was broken. Could it have been the amniotic sack around the heart and the blood flowing to and inside the heart that burst and rushed into the vacant space of that abdomen? In any case, blood was waiting there to flow out when the area was pierced with the Roman's sword. (See Edwards, Gabel, and Hosmer, "On the Physical Death of Jesus Christ," *Journal of the American Medical Association*, March 21, 1986, for a discussion of the medical implications of crucifixion.)

I share that much with you regarding the meaning of the Atonement of Jesus Christ with its symbolism of sacrifice. But I share this thought with you also. When you have bad days, when you have hard times, trust in God's ability to give you your heart back and to renew your spirit when one is broken and the other is contrite. We are not going to be asked to go to Gethsemane. We are not going to bleed from every pore. We are certainly not going to be a sacrifice, on a cross, for the sins of the world. But we are going to be allowed to have our heart hurt for the sins of this generation.

We say we are disciples of Christ. And what does that mean? I think it means to walk where He walked and say what He said and do what He did and shed the tears He shed—not to the degree He shed them, but to share to some degree in His suffering.

But symbolically we are going to shed tears. We are going to feel a little pain. We are going to need to console someone the way He consoled. We are invited to make our sacrificial offering. Yes, the children of Israel will always be under a covenant to sacrifice.

So please, be courageous when you have a hard day, when you have a hard week. Maybe your trial will go on for a month or a year or more. Through it all, we are being allowed to identify with Him whom we know to be the Only Begotten Son of God—the only perfect child that was ever on the earth, He who is our Savior and Redeemer. In this symbolism we demonstrate that we are His disciples, that we have agreed to walk where He walked and to feel something of what He felt. And if we don't have any sins to feel pain of our own, over which to feel a broken heart or a contrite spirit, then bless you. That is a wonderful accomplishment but look to your right and look to your left. You will see someone who is not as fortunate. You can shed a few tears for them. There is pain enough to go around. There is sin and sorrow enough to go around. We are being taught from Adam to the end of the world, in each generation, how to care for each other and how to resist sin. The covenant of sacrifice lets us feel remorse for sin until this world is cleansed from all transgression, is glorified, and we receive our celestial promise. All this through the Lamb of God who was sacrificed from the foundation of the world.

## JOHN 20

Beginning in the spiritual anguish of the Garden of Gethsemane, moving to the Crucifixion on a cross at Calvary, and concluding on a beautiful Sunday morning inside a donated tomb, a sinless, pure, and holy man, the very Son of God Himself, did what no other deceased person had ever done nor ever could do. Under His own power He rose from death, never to have His body separated from His spirit again. Of His own volition He shed the burial linen with which He had been bound, carefully putting the burial napkin that had been placed over His face in "a place by itself" (John 20:7), the scripture says.

That first Easter sequence of Atonement and Resurrection constitutes the most consequential moment, the most generous gift, the most excruciating pain, and the most majestic manifestation of pure love ever to be demonstrated in the history of this world. Jesus Christ, the Only Begotten Son of God, suffered, died, and rose from death in order that He could, like lightning in a summer storm, grasp us as we fall, hold us with His might, and through our obedience to His commandments, lift us to eternal life.

Christ's post-Resurrection greeting and message was probably that which He wanted to give originally, during His mortal life, but that people would not accept it.

Upon visiting His Apostles, He said, "Peace be unto you." He repeated Himself three times: "Peace be unto you." He allowed them to see the nail prints in His hands and thrust their hands into His side. He told them, "Peace be unto you: as my Father hath sent me, even so send I you" (John 20:19, 21, 26).

The tragic irony is that peace is the commodity that is so difficult to find.

I think Christ's initial greeting when we see Him will be "Peace be unto you." Let us try to find it now. We may not make much headway politically, but maybe in our chapels, our homes, and as individuals we can find peace.

It will not be easy; it seems difficult when we are surrounded by so much contention. One event from the Bible gives me hope: the people of Enoch. They were a people who lived in the midst of a world that was not at all peaceful; in fact, it was a very wicked world. But the people of Enoch became so righteous that they were raised to heaven.

The Nephites experienced a similar period of time after Jesus Christ visited them. Their conversion was so powerful that peace lasted among them for more than two hundred years. In the words of the prophet Mormon, "there still continued to be peace in the land" (4 Nephi 1:4).

This can happen for us. It will happen for us. And if we can't find peace internationally right now, we will find it at home.

## JOHN 21

Repeatedly Jesus had tried to tell His followers that He was *not* going to remain physically present with them, but they either could not or would not comprehend such a wrenching thought. Mark writes: "He taught his disciples, and said unto them, The Son of man is delivered into the hands of men, and they shall kill him; and after that he is killed, he shall rise the third day. But they understood not that saying, and were afraid to ask him" (Mark 9:31–32).

Then, after such a short time to learn and even less time to prepare, the unthinkable happened, the unbelievable was true. Their Lord and Master, their Counselor and King was crucified. His mortal ministry was over, and the struggling little Church He had established seemed doomed to scorn and destined for extinction. His Apostles did witness Him in His resurrected state, but that only added to their bewilderment. As they surely must have wondered, "What do we do now?" they turned for an answer to Peter, the senior Apostle.

Here I ask your indulgence as I take some nonscriptural liberty in my portrayal of this exchange. In effect, Peter said to his associates, "Brethren, it has been a glorious three years. None of us could have imagined such a few short months ago the miracles we have seen and the divinity we have enjoyed. We have talked with, prayed with, and labored with the very Son of God Himself. We have walked with Him and wept with Him, and on the night of that horrible ending no one wept more bitterly than I. But that is over. He has finished His work and has risen from the tomb. He has worked out His salvation and ours. So you ask, 'What do we do now?' I don't know more to tell you than to return to your former life rejoicing. I intend to 'go a fishing.'" And at least six of the ten other remaining Apostles said in agreement, "We also go with thee." John, who was one of them, writes, "They went forth, and entered into a ship immediately" (John 21:3).

But, alas, the fishing was not very good. Their first night back on the lake they caught nothing, not a single fish. With the first rays of dawn, they disappointedly turned toward the shore, where they saw in the distance a figure who called out to them, "Children, have you caught anything?" Glumly these Apostles-turned-again-fishermen gave the answer no fisherman wants to give, "We have caught nothing," they muttered, and to add insult to injury they were being called "children" (see John 21:5).

"Cast the net on the right side of the ship, and ye shall find," the stranger calls out (John 21:6)—and with those simple words recognition begins to flood over them. Just three years earlier these very men had been fishing in this very sea. On that occasion, too, they had "toiled all the night, and [had] taken nothing," the scripture says. But a fellow Galilean on the shore had called out to them to let down their nets and they drew "a great multitude of fishes," enough that their nets broke, the catch filling two boats so heavily they had begun to sink (Luke 5:5–6).

Now it was happening again. These "children," as they were rightly called, eagerly lowered their net and, "they were not able to draw it for the multitude of fishes." John said the obvious, "It is the Lord." And over the edge of the boat the irrepressible Peter leaped (John 21:6–7).

After a joyful reunion with the resurrected Jesus, Peter had an exchange with the Savior that I consider the crucial turning point of the apostolic ministry generally and certainly for Peter personally, moving this great rock of a man to a majestic life of devoted service and leadership. Looking at their battered boats, their frayed nets, and a stunning pile of 153 fish, Jesus said to His senior Apostle, "Peter, do you love me more than you love all this?" Peter said, "Yea, Lord; thou knowest that I love thee" (see John 21:15).

The Savior responds to that reply, but continues to look into the eyes of His disciple and says again, "Peter, do you love me?" Undoubtedly confused a bit by the repetition of the question, the great fisherman answers a second time, "Yea, Lord; thou knowest that I love thee" (see John 21:16).

The Savior again gives a brief response, but with relentless scrutiny He asks for the third time, "Peter, do you love me?" By now surely Peter is feeling truly uncomfortable. Perhaps there is in his heart the memory of only a few days earlier when he had been asked another question three times and he had answered equally emphatically—but in the negative. Or perhaps he began to wonder if he misunderstood the Master Teacher's question? Or perhaps he was searching his heart, seeking honest confirmation of the answer he had given so readily, almost automatically? Whatever his feelings, Peter said for the third time, "Lord, . . . thou knowest that I love thee" (John 21:17).

To which Jesus responded (and here again I acknowledge my non-scriptural elaboration) perhaps saying something like, "Then, Peter, why are you here? Why are we back on this same shore, by these same nets, having this same conversation? Wasn't it obvious then and isn't it obvious now that if I want fish I can get fish? What I need are disciples—and I need them forever. I need someone to feed my sheep and save my lambs. I need someone to preach my gospel and defend my faith. I need someone who loves me, truly loves me, and loves what our Father in Heaven has commissioned me to do. Ours is not a feeble message nor a fleeting task. It is not hapless nor hopeless nor is it to be consigned to the ash heap of history. It is the work of the Almighty and it is to change the world. So, for the second and presumably the last time, Peter, I am asking you to leave all this and to go teach and testify, labor and serve loyally, until the day in which they will do to you exactly what they did to me."

Then turning to all the Apostles, He might well have said, "Were you as foolhardy as the scribes and Pharisees were? As Herod and Pilate were? Did you, like they, think that this work could be killed simply by killing me? Did you, like they, think the cross and the nails and the tomb were the end of it all and each could blissfully go back to being whatever you were before? Children, did my life and my love not touch your hearts more deeply than that?"

Brothers and sisters, some of us endlessly ask God, "Do you love me?" That is manifestly the wrong question; that question He has endlessly answered—in scripture, in life, in the gift of His Only Begotten Son, and in ways, like His worlds, that are literally "without number." Surely the only *real* question is, "Do *we* love *Him*?"

NEITHER IS THERE SALVATION IN ANY OTHER:

FOR THERE IS NONE OTHER NAME

UNDER HEAVEN GIVEN AMONG MEN,

WHEREBY WE MUST BE SAVED.

—ACTS 4:12

———✦———

# ACTS

### ACTS 1

The book of Acts, which introduces the post-Resurrection portion of the New Testament, is technically called "The Acts of the Apostles." That is an important ecclesiastical declaration in the book, namely that the Apostles were ordained representatives of the Lord Jesus Christ and were thus authorized to lead the Church.

But consider what they faced. Consider the plight, the fear, the absolute confusion, the devastation of the members of the new little Christian Church after Christ was crucified. They may have understood something of what was happening, but they couldn't have understood it all. The people must have been very fearful and very confused, and the Brethren had their hands full trying to provide leadership.

The only contemporary example I can think of—and please do not misunderstand the comparison—might be the confusion and fear that reigned in our day after the martyrdom of the Prophet Joseph Smith. No one had had to face such a thought before. No one had even considered The Church of Jesus Christ of Latter-day Saints without Joseph as its prophet. And now this. It was a moment of almost spiritual bedlam in Nauvoo.

But God did something that taught a great lesson to the people. To counter Sidney Rigdon and a few others vying for the prophetic office, the Lord made His will and power manifest in the matter as Brigham Young was transformed in visage and countenance before the people. You know the story very well. By momentarily giving Brigham Young Joseph's appearance and very manner of speech—quite literally his mantle—God said to the people, "The keys of the kingdom are with the Twelve. Brigham is Joseph's rightful successor in leading the Church."

That is the obvious and very important declaration about Church governance that the Lord was making. But an even more important declaration was the manifestation of heavenly power itself. God's might and direct involvement in this issue was the truly important thing that was conveyed here—not that Brigham Young was to be in charge or even that Joseph Smith had been in charge. The message was: God is in charge.

Now that is exactly the point being made in the book of Acts. It is called "The Acts of the Apostles," and understandably so. It leads us to great respect for Peter, Paul, John, and the others. But not surprisingly, from the outset, from the first verse, the declaration is that The Church of Jesus Christ of Latter-day Saints will continue to be divinely led, not mortally led. And that was important for them to hear in that hour of terrible confusion and fear. Indeed, a more complete title for the book of Acts could appropriately be something like "The Acts of the Resurrected Christ Working through the Holy Spirit in the Lives and Ministries of His Ordained Apostles." Now, having said that, you can see why someone voted for the shorter title—but my suggested title is more accurate! Listen to Luke's opening lines. That is exactly what he said. These are lines you all know:

"The former treatise have I made, O Theophilus, of all that Jesus began both to do and teach,

"Until the day in which he was taken up, after that he through the Holy Ghost had given commandments unto the apostles whom he had chosen" (Acts 1:1–2).

The direction of The Church of Jesus Christ of Latter-day Saints is the same. The location of the Savior has been altered, but the direction and leadership of the Church is exactly the same. Then, having made that point, as if to prove in this most remarkable string of spiritual experiences all the way through the book, we get manifestations of the Lord's power through the Holy Ghost at every turn. It is, so to speak, the transformation of Brigham Young again and again, so to speak. The first teaching in the book of Acts from the resurrected Christ to the Twelve is that they "shall be baptized with the Holy Ghost not many days hence," and that "ye shall receive power, after that the Holy Ghost is come upon you" (Acts 1:5, 8).

After Jesus ascends to heaven before their very eyes, Peter gets the Church together—all one hundred and twenty of them. Can you see what an impact the troubles and the Crucifixion and the opposition had had on them? One hundred and twenty people gather, and Peter says, "This scripture must needs have been fulfilled, which the Holy Ghost by the mouth of David spake before concerning Judas" (Acts 1:16). In filling Judas's vacancy in the Twelve, they prayed exactly the way the Quorum of the Twelve and First Presidency pray today: "Thou, Lord, which knowest the hearts of all men, shew whether of these . . . thou hast chosen" (Acts 1:24). "Shew whether of these . . . *thou* hast chosen." And Matthias was called.

Luke is the author of the Gospel of Luke, obviously. But also remember that he is the author of the book of Acts and that those two books go together as two halves of a whole. Luke's is the most comprehensive of the four Gospels, constituting something that might be called "the acts of the Savior," followed by "the acts of the Apostles."

The book of Acts begins "The former treatise"—my book, my Gospel—"The former treatise have I made . . . of all that Jesus began both to do and teach, until the day in which he was taken up, after that he through the Holy Ghost had given commandments unto the apostles whom he had chosen: to whom also he shewed himself alive after his passion" (Acts 1:1–3).

"Alive after his passion," He showed himself with "many infallible proofs" (Acts 1:3). As a rule, we are not supposed to need proof in matters of faith. Proof is not going to be as essential as testimony, but it is interesting how much proof God has given us and will continue to give us regarding gospel issues. We are to have faith, and we do, but that faith is reinforced every single day of our lives with proof and evidence, documentation, miracles, and manifestation.

We start with the faith of a child, those little ones that He brought forward to sit on His knee. But eventually we are going to develop into gods and goddesses, kings and queens, priests and priestesses. That brings with it evidence and proof—infallible proof, if you want to use Luke's language.

In one of the earliest such manifestations after His Resurrection, Jesus came to the eleven, inviting them to touch His hands and feet as He sat to eat meat and honeycomb (see Luke 24:42). To those who doubted, Mark says He "upbraided them [for] their unbelief and hardness of heart" (Mark 16:14). The message is that if members of the Godhead go to the trouble of providing "many infallible proofs" (Acts 1:3) of truth, then surely we are honor bound to believe that truth as presented and may be upbraided if we do not. My testimony to you is that the gospel is infallibly true and that a variety of infallible proofs supporting that assertion will continue to come until Jesus descends as the ultimate infallible truth of all. Our testimonies are not dependent on evidence—we still need that spiritual confirmation in the heart of which we have spoken—but not to seek for and not to acknowledge intellectual, documentable support for our belief when it is available is to needlessly limit an otherwise incomparably strong theological position and deny us a unique, persuasive vocabulary in the latter-day arena of religious investigation and sectarian debate. Thus, armed with so much evidence, we ought to be more assertive than we sometimes are in defending our testimony of truth.

## ACTS 3

Picture a scene in Jerusalem not long after Jesus's ascension into heaven. Peter and John were about to enter the temple to worship and seek strength for the tasks that lay before them. A forty-year-old man, "lame from his mother's womb," asked alms of them as they passed.

There was nothing unique about his plea; the man had been begging every day for years in this same place. But Peter did not brush by. What would his petition mean, offered up in this holy house at the hour of prayer, if he suffered this man to offer up a similar petition in vain?

He turned to the invalid, "fastening his eyes on him" with a gaze that probed the deepest recesses of his soul. Finding faith there, Peter said deliberately and clearly: "Silver and gold have I none; but such as I have give I thee: In the name of Jesus Christ of Nazareth rise up and walk" (Acts 3:1–6). Peter had no money but he had riches: "such as he had" included every key to the kingdom of God on earth, priesthood power to raise the dead, faith to strengthen bones and sinews, a strong right hand of Christian fellowship. He could not give silver or gold but he could give that which is always purchased "without money and without price" (Isaiah 55:1)—and he gave it.

"And [Peter] took him by the right hand, and lifted him up: and immediately his feet and ankle bones received strength. And he"—the man, the limited man—"he leaping up stood, and walked, and entered into the temple, walking, and leaping, and praising God. And all the people saw him walking and praising God" (Acts 3:7–9).

There are a lot of verbs and verbals in those last two verses. Once I counted them and found at least eight. That is a lot—probably a little overdone. But this man has not had a verb in his life for forty years. He has scarcely even known a verb. And so Luke is going to put into his story all that he can. So the invalid is lifted, and his ankle bones are strengthened, and he stands, and he walks, and he leaps, and he enters, and he walks, and he leaps, and he praises God.

A great crowd gathers. Everyone knows this man. He has the prime spot in all of Jerusalem for begging: the steps of the temple. Only the best people go by—the best people on their way to do the best thing in the best place. If any passersby will be generous, surely it will be those on the way to the temple. When he saw Peter and John approaching, he thought perhaps he would get a little dinar, a little temple coin about the size of your little fingernail. But he ended up getting a lot more than that.

Suddenly (after 40 years!) he is now standing and leaping. The people say, "Isn't that old Simeon?" or whatever his name was. "Can this possibly be?" And they rush to get a closer view of this miracle. Luke records: "They knew that it was he which sat for alms at the Beautiful gate of the temple: and they were filled with wonder and amazement at that which had happened unto him. And as the lame man which was healed held Peter and John, all the people ran together" (Acts 3:10–11). He is the talk of the town.

But Peter wheels on the people as they gather. This great chief Apostle certainly was not a graduate of the Carnegie School of Public Relations. Ask the priest who found himself missing an ear for a moment.

Peter turns on these people and says, in essence, "How dare you? How dare you come running as if this were some strange, new phenomenon, something you have never seen before? In fact, you have seen it for the past three years. You have seen it at the hand of the living Son of the living God, and yet you crucified Him. Now you come acting as if this is something unique and wonderful? Where were you last week? Where were you last month? Where were you six months ago? And where will you be six months from now?" He is very exercised over their superficial wonder.

Bearing witness of the Savior, Peter says, "faith in his name hath made this man strong" (Acts 3:16). Praising Jesus's name and priesthood, Peter is modestly and appropriately brushing aside the role he himself played in the miracle that this Galilean fisherman had performed, a fisherman who speaks with an accent and is considered among the lowest in Israelite culture and society. He says instead: "I did not do this of my own strength, nor did I do it last week, nor will my brethren and I be doing it next week in and of ourselves. No, it will always be the same name, of the same Son of God, with the same priesthood power who will perform these miracles. It will be He whom you rejected and crucified, Jesus of Nazareth, Savior and King."

## ACTS 4

After Peter healed the lame man at the temple, the leaders of the Jews met and acknowledged they had a problem. The Pharisees and the Sadducees, who were the utmost of enemies, set aside their differences in a new common cause. Jesus had been a problem and they had dealt with Him.

But now Jesus's *followers* were a problem, something they hadn't counted on. Whoever this Peter was, and John, and a handful of others—were they now going to be a second generation of "problems"? "Now when they saw the boldness of Peter and John, and perceived that they were unlearned and ignorant men, they marveled; and they took knowledge of them, that they had been with Jesus" (Acts 4:13).

And then this point: "Beholding the man which was healed standing with them, they could say nothing against it" (Acts 4:14). They are irritated. They are more than irritated—they are angry. They are more than angry—they are harboring malice. They had dealt with that other one, called Jesus, and thought that messy business was over. But obviously it was not. Now they had a new set of problems to deal with in the form of His Apostles. But they can say nothing against this miraculous incident performed by one of those Apostles, evoking the cry, saying, "What shall we do to these men? for that indeed a notable miracle hath been done by them is manifest to all them that dwell in Jerusalem; and we cannot deny it" (Acts 4:16). Big problem.

They could say it did not happen. They could say it should not have happened. They could demand that everyone remain with the beliefs that had served them for three or four thousand years. In short, there were all kinds of things they could have said—except for one problem: this man who had been healed. Whoever he is, he is the problem because he just keeps jumping up and down. No one can get him to sit down. And who would deny him that right to jump anyway? He is in the middle of a large group and suddenly his head rises above the rest. He is testing those ankles. After forty years, it is fun for him to jump a little. He never knew life could be so fun. Yes, he is the problem these priests and scribes face now. No, I rephrase that—he is the *evidence* of the problem they face.

While he had the crowd's attention, Peter prophesied of the return of Christ, "whom the heaven must receive until the times of restitution of all things, which God hath spoken by the mouth of all his holy prophets since the world began" (Acts 3:21).

Peter used this great opportunity in the very moment to bear his testimony. That was very successful, inasmuch as they had three thousand baptisms the day before, and they were going to have five thousand as a result of this incident. That is not a bad weekend for the zone leaders to call in to their mission president: "We had a tough time of it here, President. We only got eight thousand this week!"

This is indicative of the power with which Peter and John were assuming their new leadership roles, inadequate as they were, in an effort to build up the faith of the people and build on the miracles they were able to perform in the Savior's name.

Of the several lessons that one might glean from this account, the first and foremost might be that you can't argue with the evidence. You can't tell this heretofore invalid man that the miracle of his ankle bones strengthening did not happen. Opponents might ask him not to act as if it happened, not to jump up and down as if it happened, not to tell other people that it happened—but there is a problem with such an approach. The ankle bones are strong. The evidence speaks for itself. The man *is* healed. He *is* leaping and jumping and following Peter and John into the temple. His head keeps popping up above the crowd. He is a happy man. Neither friend nor foe can argue with any of this.

I have cause to leap and shout with spiritually straight ankle bones, just like this man in ancient Jerusalem. Day after day and week after week I see the power of the gospel of Jesus Christ, its perfection, divinity, and healing influence upon mortal people like me and my family.

With joy, then, we ought to follow the Presiding Brethren into the temple, leaping and rejoicing that we have been made spiritually whole; mindful of the evidence of God's hand in our lives and of the divinity of The Church of Jesus Christ of Latter-day Saints. That serves as the vehicle for providing such priesthood power.

A second lesson that might come of that story is that in the gospel of Jesus Christ, you get a lot more than you counted on. This man, carried to the steps of the temple for 40 years, hoped for a coin, however limited in size or value it might be. On a good day, perhaps he would get two. But that is the level of his expectation.

Peter, taking the man by the hand, said, however, "I don't have money, but what I have, you can have." Then in the name of Jesus Christ and by the power of the holy priesthood, he changed that man's life—and his expectations—in an instant. I am confident that when he was carried to the temple that morning, just as he had been for 40 years, that fellow did not think that this day, instead of money he would be given freedom. How could he know that this day he was going to be made whole, that that evening he would walk home under his own strength and do so joyously for the rest of his life?

Whatever this good man expected that day, I do not think he expected such a gift. But that is true of all of us when we find the gospel. We get a lot more than we anticipated—and we get it forever.

⚜

Christ is the source of our strength—and inclination—to repent. Alma the Younger had been touched by all the teachings of his father, but it is particularly important that the prophecy he remembered at his lowest point was one regarding "the coming of one Jesus Christ, a Son of God, to atone for the sins of the world" (Alma 36:17). That is the name and that is the message that every person will hear if repentance is to be genuine and permanent.

When Alma remembered this, he cried out from the anguish of a hell that kept burning and a conscience that would not heal, "O Jesus, thou Son of God, have mercy on me" (Alma 36:18).

Perhaps such a prayer, though brief, is the most significant one that can be uttered in a fallen world. Whatever other prayers we offer, whatever other needs we have, all come back to that plea: "O Jesus, thou Son of God, have mercy on me."

The greatest of reassurances is that Jesus is prepared to provide that mercy. He paid for it with His very life in order to give it to us. The least we can do is ask for it and be worthy of it, to love it and appreciate the magnitude of the gift. "There is none other name under heaven given among men, whereby we must be saved" (Acts 4:12).

## ACTS 5

The tidal wave of conversion that swept Jerusalem under Peter's direction aroused the anger and fear of both Sadducee and Pharisee. But Peter's compelling declarations could not be silenced. In prison he overwhelmed his accusers with a piercing testimony of Jesus and found himself set free by angels as well as by mortal men. Such powers stunned Jewish lawyers, who marveled at these "unlearned and ignorant men" (Acts 4:13). They did not understand that in the gospel of Jesus Christ those have never been synonymous terms. The Spirit of the Lord attended the Twelve wherever they met, shaking both body and building with its power. Multitudes were brought to them and they were healed "every one" (Acts 5:16). Faith in Peter's faith brought the sick into the streets on their beds of affliction "that at least the shadow of Peter passing by might overshadow some of them" (Acts 5:15). One wonders if there is a single written line in any other record that stands as a greater monument to the faith and power of one mortal man bearing the holy priesthood of God.

With his own sense of urgency, Peter aggressively defied the injunction not to teach in the name of Christ, and he returned again and again to the temple, where his safety was never secure. There he testified plainly, "We ought to obey God rather than men. . . . We are his witnesses of these things" (Acts 5:29, 32). Imprisoned and beaten, forbidden to speak, Peter was as irrepressible as Abinadi of old. He and his brethren rejoiced that they were "counted worthy to suffer shame for his name. And daily in the temple and in every house, they ceased not to teach and preach Jesus Christ" (Acts 5:41–42).

## ACTS 9

On the doctrinal matter of priesthood keys and ordination to do this work: even the magnificence of the First Vision did not authorize Joseph Smith to teach the gospel or organize a Church or claim a following. It is as Paul experienced. Notwithstanding the marvel of the revelation on the road to Damascus in which the Lord Jesus Christ appeared to him, Paul was not authorized to preach or organize or recruit or otherwise put himself forward until he went—at the Lord's own direction—to Ananias and the other "disciples which were at Damascus" (Acts 9:19) who, as authorized priesthood officers, could receive him into Christ's Church. Upon his return to Jerusalem, Barnabas took him to the Twelve Apostles and, with their authorization, he began his missionary labors to the world—and not until (see Acts 9:3–19).

Until someone can speak not of unverifiable visions but rather of priesthood keys and the fruits of divinity that it has taken two hundred years for The Church of Jesus Christ of Latter-day Saints to produce, be leery and be warned of those who cry "Lo, here" and "Lo, there." Look for Apostles (at least twelve of them) and look for prophets who are ordained by one who had authority to do so. Look for the rest of the officers and procedures of the Church that Jesus Christ established in the meridian of time. It is not only your salvation at stake but that of your family, your children, and your children's children who are yet unborn.

WHO SHALL SEPARATE US FROM THE
LOVE OF CHRIST? SHALL TRIBULATION, OR
DISTRESS, OR PERSECUTION, OR FAMINE, OR
NAKEDNESS, OR PERIL, OR SWORD? . . . NAY, IN
ALL THESE THINGS WE ARE MORE THAN
CONQUERORS THROUGH HIM THAT LOVED US.

—ROMANS 8:35, 37

# ROMANS

## ROMANS 3

What conceivable historical, doctrinal, or procedural issue that may arise could ever overshadow or negate one's consuming spiritual conviction regarding the Father's merciful plan of salvation; His Only Begotten Son's birth, mission, Atonement, and Resurrection; the reality of the First Vision; the restoration of the priesthood; the receipt of divine revelation both personally and institutionally; the soul-shaping spirit and moving power of the Book of Mormon; the awe and majesty of the temple endowment; one's own personal experience with true miracles; and on and on and on? It is a mystery to me how those majestic, eternal, first-level truths so central to the grandeur of the *whole* gospel message can be set aside or completely dismissed by some in favor of obsessing over second- or third- or fourth-level *pieces* of that whole.

I readily acknowledge the very legitimate inquiries of many who are perfectly honest in heart. I also readily acknowledge that *everyone* has some gospel question or other yet to be answered. Nevertheless, we would hope for skeptic, believer, and everyone in between, that humility, faith, and the influence of the Holy Spirit would always be elements of every quest for truth, that foundational truths would *always* be the reference points in that quest, and that all other issues that may yet need resolving are pursued "by study and also by faith" (D&C 88:118). At the end of the day, all of us must make distinctions between the greater and the lesser elements of our testimony. For me the greater pillars include those majestic truths mentioned earlier, their irreplaceable centrality in my life, and the realization that I simply could not live, could not go on without them, or without the blessings I have known, or without the promises we have all been given in The Church of Jesus Christ of Latter-day Saints.

So, as we speak of questions, write this one from the Apostle Paul across the chalkboard of your mind: "For what if some [do] not believe? shall their unbelief make the faith of God without effect?" (Romans 3:3). The answer to that question is "No!" Not in my life! Not for me and my house! *No one's* unbelief has or can or will—ever—make my faith in God, my love of Christ, my devotion to The Church of Jesus Christ of Latter-day Saints "without effect." The truthfulness of this latter-day work is "in effect" and it will stay "in effect" as long as the sun shines and rivers run to the sea—and forever after that. Don't miss those blessings!

Don't feel abandoned or forsaken or forever damaged if you have made a mistake, even a serious mistake. Everyone has, with some mistakes of course being more serious than others. But as the Apostle Paul knew personally, "*All* have sinned, and come short of the glory of God" (Romans 3:23; emphasis added).

As much as our Father in Heaven warned against sin and continually pleads against committing it, He nevertheless knew—clear back in the premortal councils of heaven—that we would not do everything right. So He planned for and promised a way out of our problems, described in the scriptures as "*the* way." That way out of our problems—"the way, the truth, and the life" (John 14:6)—is the Atonement of His perfect, totally obedient Son, the only one in the entire family who would not transgress when He came to earth. Only that Son was worthy enough—and therefore capable of—lifting our sins from our shoulders and putting them on His.

We shouted for joy at that offer of help, and from that moment on we loved Christ (or certainly should have) because He first loved us. But to take full advantage of the Atonement of Jesus Christ and obtain forgiveness of those sins, we do have to do some very basic things. We *do* owe something for this gift. We must have faith in Christ and believe in His redeeming power. We must be honest about our mistakes—confront them, confess them, truly regret them, and forsake them. Then we must vow honestly to live as much like Christ as we possibly can, including following Him in the saving ordinances of the gospel.

## ROMANS 5

A vicarious blessing is one in which the faith, obedience, and righteous acts of one person bring blessings to another person. Christ's Atonement is that kind of vicarious act—because of *His* righteousness, blessings come to *us*. The Prophet Isaiah taught this principle of vicarious blessing when he said of the Messiah that it would be "with *his* stripes [that] *we* are healed" (Isaiah 53:5; emphasis added). Lehi taught that same lesson to his son Jacob when he said, "I know that thou art redeemed, *because of the righteousness of thy Redeemer*" (2 Nephi 2:3; emphasis added). Notice that he does not say it is because of *Jacob's* righteousness that he will be redeemed (though Jacob was righteous and so should all of the rest of us try to be), but rather Jacob is redeemed "because of the righteousness of [his] Redeemer." The Apostle Paul taught such a principle in one sentence: "By the righteousness of one [man] the free gift came upon all men" (Romans 5:18).

It ought not to be surprising that such a sacred, miraculous principle is at the heart of temple work. Our ancestors who lived before us and passed away without ever hearing the gospel nevertheless need the blessings of The Church of Jesus Christ of Latter-day Saints and its ordinances for their salvation as much as we do—but they are not in a position to obtain those ordinances now that they are deceased. So *they are totally dependent upon someone still living here on earth to obtain them in their behalf.* You are aware that when we go to the temple the first time, it is for our own blessings—our own ordinances.

But once we have had that initial experience in the temple, forever after our temple attendance is on behalf of someone else. We find their names, we bring that information to the temple, and we perform the ordinances in their behalf vicariously. That is why those who do their family history and then perform ordinances for those persons in the temple are often called "saviours . . . on mount Zion" (Obadiah 1:21), because, in a way directly comparable to the Savior's Atonement, our actions bring blessings to another person. Thus, in temple work we can in a small way do and be for our kindred dead what Jesus did and was for all mankind.

## ROMANS 8

"There is sunshine in my soul today," Eliza Hewitt wrote, "More glorious and bright/ Than glows in any earthly sky,/ For Jesus is my light" ("There Is Sunshine in My Soul Today," *Hymns* [1985], no. 227).

With radiance in every note, that marvelous old Christian hymn is virtually impossible to sing without smiling. But I wish to lift out of context just one line from it that may help on days when we find it hard to sing *or* smile and "peaceful happy moments" do *not* seem to "roll." If for a time you are unable to echo the joyous melodies you hear coming from others, I ask you to hold tenaciously to the line in this hymn that reassures "Jesus listening can hear/ The songs [you] cannot sing."

Among the realities we face as children of God living in a fallen world is that some days are difficult, days when our faith and our fortitude are tested. These challenges may come from a lack in us, a lack in others, or just a lack in life, but whatever the reasons, we find they can rob us of songs we so much want to sing, and darken the promise of "springtime in [the] soul" that Eliza Hewitt celebrates in one of her verses.

So, what do we do in such times? For one thing, we embrace the Apostle Paul's counsel and "hope for that [which] we see not, . . . [and] with patience wait for it" (Romans 8:25). In those moments when the

melody of joy falters below our power of expression, we may have to stand silent for a time and simply listen to others, drawing strength from the splendor of the music around us. Many of us who are "musically challenged" have had our confidence bolstered and our singing markedly improved by positioning ourselves next to someone with a stronger, more certain voice. Surely it follows that in singing the anthems of eternity, we should stand as close as humanly possible to the Savior and Redeemer of the world—who has absolutely perfect pitch. We then take courage from His ability to hear our silence and take hope from His melodious Messianic intercession in our behalf.

If we give our heart to God, if we love the Lord Jesus Christ, if we do the best we can to live the gospel, then tomorrow—and every other day—is ultimately going to be magnificent, even if we don't always recognize it as such. Why? Because our Heavenly Father wants it to be! He wants to bless us. A rewarding, abundant, and eternal life is the very object of His merciful plan for His children! It is a plan predicated on the truth "that all things work together for good to them that love God" (Romans 8:28). So keep loving. Keep trying. Keep trusting. Keep believing. Keep growing. Heaven is cheering you on today, tomorrow, and forever.

There is in the modern world so much sin and moral decay affecting everyone, especially the young, and it seems to be getting worse by the day. You and I share so many concerns about the spread of pornography and poverty, abuse and abortion, illicit sexual transgression (both heterosexual and homosexual), violence, crudity, cruelty, and temptation, all glaring as close as your daughter's cell phone or your son's iPad. Surely there is a way for people of good will who love God and have taken upon themselves the name of Christ to "stand together" for the cause of Christ and against the forces of sin. In this we have every right to be bold and believing, for "if God be for us, who can be against us?" You serve and preach, teach and labor in that confidence, and so do I. And in doing so I believe we can trust in that next verse from Romans as well: "He that spared not his own Son, but delivered him up for us all, how shall he not with him also freely give us all things?" I truly believe that if across the world we can all try harder not to separate *each other* "from the love of Christ," we will be "more than conquerors through him that loved us" (Romans 8:31, 32, 35, 37).

## ROMANS 10

The eternal challenge is real growth, real improvement, real change. That is what we are supposed to be seeking, person by person, member by member, throughout The Church of Jesus Christ of Latter-day Saints.

But what tools do we have to bring about this change? Not salaries or threats or coercion or lawsuits like most of the rest of the world uses. No, the stake or ward leader, the missionary, the teacher, the parent, the everyday member basically has one tool—we have words. Words directed by the Holy Ghost and infused with priesthood power, but words nonetheless.

A long time ago the Apostle Paul wrote to the Romans:

"For with the heart man believeth unto righteousness; and *with the mouth confession is made unto salvation*. . . .

"For whosoever shall call upon the name of the Lord shall be saved.

"How then shall they call on him in whom they have not believed? and how shall they believe in him of whom they have not heard? and how shall they hear without a preacher? . . .

*"Faith cometh by hearing, and hearing by the word of God"* (Romans 10:10, 13–14, 17; emphasis added).

Teachers and preachers. Listeners and learners. The power of the word, especially when it is the word of God. The Book of Mormon says that Alma, trying to do the very things we are trying to do in the modern Church—convert people, activate people, strengthen people, protect young people, fortify the Church and kingdom of God—learned that "the preaching of the word" had a greater tendency to touch the people and lead them to righteousness than did "the sword, or anything else, which had happened unto them—therefore Alma thought it was expedient that they should try the virtue of the word of God" (Alma 31:5).

The Prophet Joseph Smith and his brethren taught the same thing in the *Lectures on Faith*: "It is by words . . . [that] every being works when he works by faith. God said, 'Let there be light: and there was light.' Joshua spake, and the great lights which God had created stood still. Elijah commanded . . . and for the space of three years and six months . . . it did not rain; he again commanded and the heavens gave forth rain. . . . Faith, then, works by words; and with [words] its mightiest works have been, and will be, performed" (*Lectures on Faith* [1985], 72–73).

So, this is at least part of the reason we have conferences and meetings and classes of every kind—because we want settings in which we can use words in a hundred different ways to inspire, to motivate, to lead people upward.

Sometimes this actually works. You have had moments in your life when you were changed forever by something someone said—a sermon, a lesson, a testimony—that the Spirit of the Lord carried down into your heart and a miracle happened. Some kind of change resulted and you became better in some aspect of your life.

The classic scriptural example is the impact King Benjamin's masterful sermon in the Book of Mormon had on those who heard him. At the close of that great discourse, Mormon records this about the impact:

"And they all cried . . . saying: . . .We believe all the words which thou hast spoken . . . and . . . we know of their surety and truth. . . . The Spirit of the Lord Omnipotent . . . has wrought a mighty change in . . . our hearts. . . . We have no more disposition to do evil, but to do good continually. . . .

"And we are willing to enter into a covenant with our God to do his will, and to be obedient to his commandments in all things that he shall command us, all the remainder of our days" (Mosiah 5:2–5).

What a terrific response to a sermon! It is what every speaker or teacher or leader dreams of! That kind of response is what every stake president dreams might happen after a stake conference. That is what a bishop hopes for following sacrament meeting. That is what youth leaders want after a youth conference or an Aaronic Priesthood quorum meeting or a Young Women class. This is what missionaries hope will happen to their investigators.

Assuming the listener as well as the speaker has some responsibility in this, I encourage you to ponder this question: What can we do to make our Church experiences and the scriptural messages we hear mean something more like this in our lives? What can we do to encourage that "mighty change" spoken of in this experience? What can we do to make any change at all as a result of the many conferences and meetings, teachings and messages that faithful members of The Church of Jesus Christ of Latter-day Saints spend so much time sharing with each other?

YE ARE BOUGHT WITH A PRICE:

THEREFORE GLORIFY GOD IN YOUR BODY,

AND IN YOUR SPIRIT, WHICH ARE GOD'S.

—1 CORINTHIANS 6:20

# 1 CORINTHIANS

## 1 CORINTHIANS 1

What does it mean to belong, to be a member of Christ's true Church and be "called unto the fellowship of . . . Jesus Christ our Lord" (1 Corinthians 1:9)? Obviously, much of the joy and most of the meaning is yet to be fully realized. Surely it will be after death and beyond the veil that Latter-day Saints will see the eternal, saving implications of their earthly covenants. But what of our experience here and now while we face our daily challenges? What does membership mean to those who have joined, or are contemplating joining, Christ's true Church here on earth?

Let me share a personal response to those questions with two caveats. First, no single statement can do justice to what any of us feel about our membership in The Church of Jesus Christ of Latter-day Saints; a whole barrel of books could not do it, so certainly the little cup I am offering here will not be sufficient. Second, the most personal of responses—and consequently the most persuasive ones—often cannot be shared. Some are too sacred and others simply ineffable. In either case, all that can be put in print is, as a Book of Mormon prophet, Ammon, said, "the smallest part" of what we feel (Alma 26:16).

It *is* a soul-stirring reassurance to belong, to be part of the most cohesive, extended family association in all eternity. We speak of sealing ourselves to one another, and well we should. The Prophet Joseph Smith said we might more plainly refer to it as *welding* (see D&C 128:18). The bonding is eternal, and it finds its highest expression in the temples of the Lord—built, dedicated, and sanctified to the sealing of families to each other for this life and the next, where all that we have enjoyed in our mortal association is continued forever and ever with the people we love most of all—our own families.

We begin to build that shared strength by such habits as faithful, personal prayer, family prayer, daily scripture study, weekly family home evening, and acts of Christian love. These and so much more strengthen us individually and collectively, making it easier to avoid the unwholesome and unclean, making it easier to seek all that is "virtuous, lovely, . . . of good report or praiseworthy" (Articles of Faith 1:13). When public problems or private heartaches come—as surely they do come—our family will be most fortunate if in that hour we find ourselves in the company of Latter-day Saints.

What emerges from that special association—from feelings of safety and peace, of belonging and happiness and heavenly help—is an inexorable sense of purpose and direction. Some have felt the fears and frustrations of life more than others, but all of us feel them a little, and in such times we need the gospel compass to remind us who we are and where we must go.

Our basic message is that with a complete offering of His body, His blood, and the anguish of His spirit, Christ atoned for the initial transgression of Adam and Eve in the Garden of Eden, and also for the personal sins of everyone else who would ever live in this world from Adam to the end of time. Some of those blessings are unconditional, such as the gift of the Resurrection. Others of the blessings, at least the full realization of them, are very conditional, requiring the keeping of commandments, the performance of ordinances, and living the life of a disciple of Christ. Either way, the essential message of the gospel, the starting point for all other truths, is this from the Master's own lips: "I am the way, the truth, and the life: no man cometh unto the Father, but by me" (John 14:6). Thus, the Atonement of Christ, which makes that return to the Father possible, is rightfully seen as the central fact, the crucial foundation, the chief doctrine of the great and eternal plan of salvation.

Little wonder, then, that the greatest missionary the world has ever known wrote: "The preaching of the cross is to them that perish foolishness; but unto us which are saved it is the power of God. . . . For the Jews require a sign, and the Greeks seek after wisdom: but we preach Christ crucified" (1 Corinthians 1:18, 22–23).

Inherent in all of this is a rather simple definition of the gospel, at least when considered in its essence. The word *gospel* as we use it in English comes down to us through early scriptural language: language that meant literally "good news" or sometimes "glad tidings." The "good news" was that death and hell could be escaped, that mistakes and sins could be overcome, that there was hope, that there was help, that the insoluble was solved, that the enemy had been conquered. The good news, which culminated in the Atonement and the Resurrection of Jesus Christ, was that everyone's tomb could one day be empty, that everyone's soul could be pure again, that every child of God could again return to the Father who gave them life.

## 1 CORINTHIANS 6

There are things on which we have to take a firm stand. We know that some people are addicted to gambling, for instance, and we have to help, we have to say, basically, that this is a destructive behavior, and if you go down that road very far, there is often tragedy and dismay and disarray and divorce and all kinds of problems at the end. And we have to help with that. We are against domestic abuse. I am not making, necessarily, analogies here. I am just saying there are a lot of things we have to say the gospel is here to remedy, the gospel is here to bless and help. And if someone is suffering with this, we want to work with them, we want to help.

But we can't say, "Oh, it is okay. We will just have to let it go." Because some things you can't let go, (1) because they are commandments and (2) because the commandments are designed to lead to happiness. You may confront difficult issues, but stay close to your leaders. Keep your faith. I can promise you that happiness is in The Church of Jesus Christ of Latter-day Saints, not out of it. However hard it may seem to be in The Church of Jesus Christ of Latter-day Saints, it is a lot harder to be out of it, in terms of any chance for happiness. By hard, I mean something you may have a struggle with. Whatever the challenge, it is going to be better if we can stay in and talk and work.

This is not our Church. I love what Paul said to the Corinthians: "Ye are bought with a price" (1 Corinthians 6:20). We are indentured servants, if you will. We owe everything to the Savior who bought our salvation. And so it is not as if we can be whimsical and flit about and do exactly what we want. I don't know of anyone who can do that. We have been purchased. Death and hell and the adversary and dark eternity was one option, and that got paid for. We are indebted to the great living Son of God who paid that price, and we owe Him our allegiance.

## 1 CORINTHIANS 10

A loving Father in Heaven does not maliciously "lead us . . . into temptation" (Matthew 6:13) nor have any wish to ensnare us in evil. He has, however, allowed us to come to this mortal world in which we must face temptations of every kind, temptations from "men" and from "devils" (see D&C 46:7). The Lord's Prayer is a prayer for strength, for the ability to endure such difficult times. It is a special plea for protection from excessive or unremitting enticement that would threaten our ability to withstand. It is an expression of our desire to remain clean.

We do, of course, take comfort in knowing that the Lord will not allow us to be tempted beyond our capability to resist. Furthermore, for every temptation that an enemy places before us, the Lord has made an "escape, that [we] may be able to bear it" (1 Corinthians 10:13). If we then yield to temptation, it may well be that we did not recognize (or did not want) the opportunity to escape it. Nevertheless, if we do falter, the privilege of repenting is simply further confirmation that our Father in Heaven does not wish us to be entangled in sin. Through the gift of His Son, He has provided the means for us to be free from evil, even after the fact, if we are willing to pay the price.

Our own best efforts and good judgment coupled with honest prayer to our Heavenly Father will enable us to walk better the narrow path that is free from the heartache, sorrow, and despair that transgression inevitably brings. That is the personal ability and divine assistance for which Jesus prayed.

## 1 CORINTHIANS 11

The Apostle Paul taught the inspired concept that "Neither is the man without the woman, neither the woman without the man, in the Lord" (1 Corinthians 11:11). I know the truth of that in my own life. No prophet, no Apostle, no President of the Church, no mission president, no bishop, no deacons quorum advisor, no Scoutmaster, no seminary teacher, no one in all this world has taught me what Sister Holland has taught me.

She has been the light of my life for more than half a century, in a category of her own beyond any of those great fine teachers that I have had. I like to tell young adult men, you make sure you marry the right woman. You make sure you understand that this world and your world is not complete until you are equally yoked with a woman of faith. I don't care about how she looks. I don't care about her education. I don't care about her social status. I don't care about her income or what her parents were or were not. But I want her to have faith in the Lord Jesus Christ and a love of God Almighty, our Father. With her conviction of the Restoration, and her love for you, you will change the world. And you will start by changing your own.

## 1 CORINTHIANS 12

Obviously, part of the meaning of being a member of the Lord's Church is in that choice of language itself, coined originally by the

Apostle Paul, who knew so much about coming to Christ and making the covenants we all make at baptism.

"For as the body is one, and hath many members . . . so also is Christ. . . .

"For the body is not one member but many. . . .

"And the eye cannot say unto the hand, I have no need of thee: nor again the head to the feet, I have no need of you. . . .

"Now ye are the body of Christ, and members in particular" (1 Corinthians 12:12, 14, 21, 27).

It is an immensely satisfying thing to be needed in the body of Christ—and *everyone* is needed. Whether we function as an eye or arm is irrelevant; the fact is we are needed in this most majestic structure, and the body is imperfect without us. In The Church of Jesus Christ of Latter-day Saints—the restored ecclesiastical body of Christ—people need people, and everyone is welcomed. This includes (in Paul's assertion) not only the attractive, talented, "comely" members, but those of us who seem to have fewer gifts and face greater challenges, those who receive less honor and attention. *Every* member matters, and all are invited to serve, even as they are served by others. We speak often of "the *work* of the Lord" and "a *labor* of love." There is much to be done in The Church of Jesus Christ of Latter-day Saints to secure our happiness, guarantee our spiritual safety, and eventually usher in the millennial day. Everyone is needed and all can contribute in wonderful ways.

Latter-day Saints love and welcome and reach out to young and old in a way that Christians are commanded to do. Indeed, there are "no more strangers and foreigners" in the household of God (Ephesians 2:19). For we have been commanded to "meet together oft, to fast and to pray, and to speak one with another concerning the welfare of [our] souls" (Moroni 6:5). This is something more than boys' clubs or civic associations or political affiliations offer, worthy as those may be. It is more than house parties and welcome wagons provide, as kind as such expressions are. This fellowship is ultimately of the Spirit and comes because Christ is our eternal head.

Contrast the psychic turbulence experienced by so many in a wicked world with the serenity my wife and I saw while standing with our childhood playmates as they laid their firstborn child in the grave. This beautiful little thirteen-year-old girl, born just ninety days after our own first child, had fallen victim to Cockayne's syndrome a half dozen years earlier. There is no way to adequately describe the deterioration of that little body. Nor is there any way to tell the patience and pain of those parents as they carried legs that could not walk and finally fed with an eye-dropper a mouth that could not swallow.

But there was no existential anguish rending the air. Standing quietly—no, peacefully—at the casket with this little family now temporarily lessened by Patti's leaving were her Young Women class, her Sunday School teacher, and a favorite teenage home teacher. There also were the two with whom her father had served in the bishopric. Her mother's Relief Society associates dried their tears and slipped away to prepare a family luncheon. Fellow members in the body of Christ remembering, "And whether one member suffer, all the members suffer with it" (1 Corinthians 12:26).

That hopeful, trusting facing of the future is part of what it means to be a Latter-day Saint. It is part of knowing by divine revelation the answers (even in our childhood) to life's greatest questions.

## 1 CORINTHIANS 13

The first element of divine love—pure love—taught by Paul (and later Mormon) is its kindness, its selfless quality, its lack of ego and vanity and consuming self-centeredness. "Charity suffereth long, and is kind; charity envieth not, . . . is not puffed up, . . . seeketh not her own" (1 Corinthians 13:4–5). I have heard prophets and other leaders teach publicly and privately that most problems in love and marriage ultimately start with selfishness. In outlining ideal love in which Christ, the most unselfish man who ever lived, is the great example, it is not surprising that this scriptural commentary starts here.

There are many qualities you will want to look for in a friend or a close associate—to say nothing of a spouse and eternal companion—but surely among the very first and most basic of those qualities will be those of care and sensitivity toward others, a minimum of self-centeredness that allows compassion and courtesy to be evident. There are lots of limitations in all of us that we hope our sweethearts will overlook. I suppose no one is as handsome or as beautiful as he or she wishes, or as brilliant in school or as witty in speech or as wealthy as we would like, but in a world of varied talents and fortunes that we can't always command, I think that makes even more attractive the qualities we *can* command—such qualities as thoughtfulness, patience, a kind word, and true delight in the accomplishment of another. These cost us *nothing,* and they can mean *everything* to the one who receives them.

I like Mormon and Paul's language that says one who truly loves is not "puffed up." Puffed up! Isn't that a great image? Haven't you ever been with someone who was so conceited, so full of themselves that they made the Pillsbury Doughboy seem thin? Fred Allen said once that he saw such a fellow walking down Lovers' Lane holding his own hand. True love blooms when we care more about another person than we care about ourselves. That is Christ's great atoning example for us, and it ought to be more evident in the kindness we show, the respect we give, and the selflessness and courtesy we employ in our personal relationships.

Love is a fragile thing, and some elements in life can try to break it. Much damage can be done if we are not in tender hands, caring hands. To give ourselves totally to another person, as we do in marriage, is the most trusting step we take in any human relationship. It is a real act of faith—faith all of us must be willing to exercise. If we do it right, we end up sharing everything—all our hopes, all our fears, all our dreams, all our weaknesses, and all our joys—with another person.

In all that Christ was, He was not *ever* envious or inflated, never consumed with His own needs. He did not once, *not ever,* seek His own advantage at the expense of someone else. He delighted in the happiness of others, the happiness He could bring them. He was forever kind.

The second segment of this scriptural sermon on love says that true charity—real love—"is not easily provoked, thinketh no evil; rejoiceth not in iniquity" (1 Corinthians 13:5–6). Think of how many arguments could be avoided, how many hurt feelings could be spared, how many cold shoulders and silent treatments could be ended, and, in a worst-case scenario, how many breakups and divorces could be avoided if we were not so easily provoked, if we thought no evil of one another, and if we not only did not rejoice in iniquity but didn't rejoice even in little mistakes.

Temper tantrums are not cute even in children; they are despicable in adults, especially adults who are supposed to love each other. We are too easily provoked; we are too inclined to think that our partner meant to hurt us—meant to do us evil, so to speak; and in defensive or jealous response we too often rejoice when we see *them* make a mistake and find *them* in a fault. Let's show some discipline on this one. Act a little more maturely. Bite your tongue if you have to. "He that is slow to anger is better than the mighty; and he that ruleth his spirit than he that taketh a city" (Proverbs 16:32). At least one difference between a tolerable marriage and a great one may be that willingness in the latter to allow some things to pass without comment, without response.

Thirdly and lastly, the prophets tell us that true love "beareth all things, believeth all things, hopeth all things, endureth all things" (1 Corinthians 13:7). Once again that is ultimately a description of Christ's love—He is the great example of one who bore and believed and hoped and endured. We are invited to do the same to the best of our ability. Bear up and be strong. Be hopeful and believing. Some things in life we have little or no control over. These have to be endured. Some disappointments have to be lived with. These are not things anyone wants in life, but sometimes they come. And when they come, we have to bear them; we have to believe; we have to hope for an end to such sorrows and difficulty; we have to endure until things come right in the end.

One of the great purposes of true love is to help each other in these times. No one ought to have to face such trials alone. We can endure almost anything if we have someone at our side who truly loves us, who is easing the burden and lightening the load. In this regard, a friend from our BYU faculty, Professor Brent Barlow, told me some years ago about Plimsoll marks.

As a youth in England, Samuel Plimsoll was fascinated with watching ships load and unload their cargoes. He soon observed that, regardless of the cargo space available, each ship had its maximum capacity. If a ship exceeded its limit, it would likely sink at sea. In 1868, Plimsoll entered Parliament and passed a merchant shipping act that, among other things, called for making calculations of how much a ship could carry. As a result, lines were drawn on the hull of each ship in England. As the cargo was loaded, the freighter would sink lower and lower into the water. When the water level on the side of the ship reached the Plimsoll mark, the ship was considered loaded to capacity, regardless of how much space remained. As a result, British deaths at sea were greatly reduced.

Like ships, people have differing capacities at different times and even different days in their lives. In our relationships we need to establish our own Plimsoll marks and help identify them in the lives of those we love. Together we need to monitor the load levels and be helpful in shedding or at least readjusting some cargo if we see our sweetheart or friend is sinking. Then, when the ship of love is stabilized, we can evaluate long-term what has to continue, what can be put off until another time, and what can be put off permanently. Friends, sweethearts, and spouses need to be able to monitor each other's stress and recognize the different tides and seasons of life. We owe it to each other to declare some limits and then help jettison some things if emotional health and the strength of loving relationships are at risk.

Remember, pure love "beareth all things, believeth all things, hopeth all things, endureth all things," and helps loved ones do the same.

In Mormon's and Paul's final witnesses, they declare that "charity [pure love] never faileth" (Moroni 7:46; 1 Corinthians 13:8). It is there through thick and thin. It endures through sunshine and shadow, through darkest sorrow and on into the light. It *never* fails. So Christ loved us, and that is how He hoped we would love each other.

## 1 CORINTHIANS 14

"For if the trumpet give an uncertain sound, who shall prepare himself to the battle? . . . Seek that ye may excel to the edifying of the church" (1 Corinthians 14:8, 12).

Obviously, with such incredible forces at work in our time, it is going to require gospel instruction so powerful that absolutely nothing could shake the faith or divert the path of our young people when they walk out of a gospel class and reenter the world. That kind of teaching is easier said than done, but every one of us can be better, more powerful teachers than we are. In approaching such a daunting task, please remember this one thing: a student is not a container to be filled; a student is a fire to be ignited. As teachers of the gospel, we are to be spiritual arsonists. Our lessons are to be incendiary devices.

I have always been impressed that in almost every significant teaching situation in the Book of Mormon, the phrase used to describe that moment is that the individual was taught with "power and authority" (Helaman 5:18). That is my greatest desire in my own teaching, and I hope it is in yours.

Please don't misunderstand. I am not talking about raising the decibels of your voice, being theatrical in your presentation, or forcing false emotion. I am talking about something that is essentially a matter of spirit, a spirit that will be manifest in different ways by different teachers. You have to be yourselves. Learn all you can from great teachers, but of course, in the end, you have to teach naturally, teach your way. However, whatever approach that turns out to be, the result should be powerful, authoritative teaching.

## 1 CORINTHIANS 15

In our increasingly secular society it is as uncommon as it is unfashionable to speak of Adam and Eve or the Garden of Eden or of a "fortunate fall" into mortality. Nevertheless, the simple truth is that we *cannot* fully comprehend the Atonement and Resurrection of Christ and we *will not* adequately appreciate the unique purpose of His birth or His death without understanding that there were an actual Adam and Eve who fell from an actual Eden with all the consequences that Fall carried with it. I do not know the details of what happened on this planet before that, but I do know these two were created under the divine hand of God, that for a time they lived alone in a paradisiacal setting where there was neither human death nor future family, and that through a sequence of choices they transgressed a commandment of God which required that they leave their garden setting but which allowed them to have children before facing physical death (see 2 Nephi 2:19–29; Moses 5:10–11). To add further sorrow and complexity to their circumstance, their transgression had spiritual consequences as well, cutting them off from the presence of God forever. Because we were then born into that fallen world and because we too would transgress the laws of God, we also were sentenced to the same penalties that Adam and Eve faced.

What a plight! The entire human race in free fall—every man, woman, and child in it physically tumbling toward permanent death, spiritually plunging toward eternal anguish. Is that what life was meant to be? Is this the grand finale of the human experience? Are we all just hanging in a cold canyon somewhere in an indifferent universe, each of us searching for a toehold, each of us seeking for something to grip—with nothing but the feeling of sand sliding under our fingers, nothing to save us, nothing to hold on to much less anything to hold on to us. Is our only purpose in life an empty existential exercise—simply to leap as high as we can, hang on for our prescribed three score years and ten, then fail, then fall, and keep falling forever?

The answer to those questions is an unequivocal and eternal "No!" With prophets ancient and modern I testify that "all things have been done in the wisdom of him who knoweth all things" (2 Nephi 2:24). Thus, from the moment those first parents stepped out of the Garden of Eden, the God and Father of us all, anticipating Adam and Eve's decision, dispatched the very angels of heaven to declare to them—and down through time to us—that the entire sequence was designed for our eternal happiness. It was part of His divine plan, which provided for a Savior, the very Son of God Himself—another "Adam," the Apostle Paul would call Him (1 Corinthians 15:45)—who would come in the meridian of time to atone for the first Adam's transgression. That Atonement of Jesus Christ would achieve complete victory over physical death, unconditionally granting resurrection to every person who has been born or ever will be born into this world. Mercifully it would also provide forgiveness for the personal sins of all, from Adam to the end of the world, conditioned upon repentance and obedience to divine commandments.

As one of His ordained witnesses I declare that Jesus of Nazareth was and is that Savior of the world, the "last Adam" (1 Corinthians 15:45), the Author and Finisher of our faith, the Alpha and Omega of eternal life. "For as in Adam all die, even so in Christ shall all be made alive," Paul declared (1 Corinthians 15:22).

I testify of the Holy Resurrection, that unspeakable cornerstone gift in the Atonement of the Lord Jesus Christ! With the Apostle Paul, I testify that that which was sown in corruption will one day be raised in incorruption and that which was sown in weakness will ultimately be raised in power (see 1 Corinthians 15:42–43). I bear witness of that day when loved ones whom we knew to have disabilities in mortality will stand before us glorified and grand, breathtakingly perfect in body and mind. What a thrilling moment that will be! I do not know whether we will be happier for ourselves that we have witnessed such a miracle or happier for them that they are fully perfect. Until that hour when Christ's consummate gift is evident to us all, may we live by faith, hold fast to hope, and show "compassion one of another" (1 Peter 3:8).

BLESSED BE GOD, EVEN THE FATHER OF OUR

LORD JESUS CHRIST, THE FATHER OF MERCIES,

AND THE GOD OF ALL COMFORT;

WHO COMFORTETH US IN ALL OUR TRIBULATION,

THAT WE MAY BE ABLE TO COMFORT

THEM WHICH ARE IN ANY TROUBLE.

—2 CORINTHIANS 1:3–4

# 2 CORINTHIANS

## 2 CORINTHIANS 1

Our reliance upon the forgiving, long-suffering, merciful nature of God was taught from before the very foundation of the world. It was always to give us hope and help, a reason to progress and improve, an incentive to lay down our burdens and take up our salvation. May I be bold enough to suggest that it is impossible for anyone who really knows God to doubt His willingness to receive us with open arms in a divine embrace if we will but come unto Him. There certainly can and will be plenty of external difficulties in life. Nevertheless, the soul that comes unto Christ dwells within a personal fortress, a veritable palace of perfect peace. "Whoso hearkeneth unto me," Jehovah says, "shall dwell safely, and shall be quiet from fear of evil" (Proverbs 1:33).

That is exactly what Paul said to the Corinthians. Trying to help them keep their chin up—and the Corinthians had a lot to be grim about—he wrote:

"Blessed be God, even the Father of our Lord Jesus Christ, the Father of mercies, and the God of all comfort;

"Who comforteth us in all our tribulation, that we may be able to comfort them which are in any trouble, by the comfort wherewith we ourselves are comforted of God" (2 Corinthians 1:3–4).

## 2 CORINTHIANS 11

Virtually any religious faith of which I know, Christian, Muslim, Jew, non-monotheistic Eastern, or otherwise, has *some* tenet central to its belief that calls for kindness, compassion, patience, long-suffering, forgiveness, and, above all, love. Surely those would be virtues underlying *any* belief in *any* God that might be worshipped—at least we would hope so.

In The Church of Jesus Christ of Latter-day Saints, our position was conveyed very early by the Prophet Joseph Smith. He said: "I am bold to declare before heaven that I am just as ready to die in defending the rights of a Presbyterian, a Baptist, or a good man of any other denomination; for the same principle which would trample upon the rights of the Latter day Saints would trample upon the rights of . . . any other denomination. . . .

"Friendship is one of the grand fundamental principles of Mormonism to revolutionize . . . the world, and cause wars and contentions to cease, and men to become friends and brothers" (*The Joseph Smith Papers: History, 1838–1856,* volume E-1 [1 July 1843–30 April 1844], 1666, 1680).

Of course, nothing in that implies any lack of conviction or compromise in doctrine. In our Christian tradition no one could accuse the Apostle Paul of lacking conviction or being shy about doctrine. He was not anything if not bold, and as a result he had his share of opponents. Yet he who five times received thirty-nine-stroke lashings, who three times was beaten with rods, who was bruised with stones and repeatedly beaten by former friends and new enemies alike (see 2 Corinthians 11:24–27), and who ultimately died a martyr's death— yes, he who had so much conviction that troubles seemed nearly endless, nevertheless wrote this:

"Are they Hebrews? so am I. Are they Israelites? so am I. Are they the seed of Abraham? so am I. Are they ministers of Christ? . . . I am more" (2 Corinthians 11:22–23).

"[So] let [our] love be without dissimulation. . . . Be kindly affectioned one to another. . . . Bless them which persecute you: bless, and curse not. . . . Recompense to no man evil for evil. . . . If thine enemy hunger, feed him; if he thirst, give him drink: . . . Be not overcome of evil, but overcome evil with good" (Romans 12:9–10, 14, 17, 20–21).

*"If it be possible, as much as lieth in you, live peaceably with all men"* (Romans 12:18; emphasis added).

BEAR YE ONE ANOTHER'S BURDENS,

AND SO FULFIL THE LAW OF CHRIST.

—GALATIANS 6:2

# GALATIANS

## GALATIANS 6

What you ultimately believe about the Atonement of Jesus Christ is not going to be said in a classroom. It will come in your human relationships with people whose problems are, if not sinful, at least unfortunate. We all make mistakes. There is a burden there, in serious cases the burden of sin. The cry of Paul to the Galatians is, "Bear ye one another's burdens, and so fulfil the law of Christ" (Galatians 6:2).

If I have offended you, I am your burden. If I have done something wrong to you, if I have spoken despitefully to you, if I have hated you, or cursed you, I am your burden. You are mine. I am your burden, because I have hurt you. You are not as happy or as spiritual as you were. You think about me and you get mad. You burn the beans and kick the pots and pans. You are less than you were, because I did something to you.

You are part of my burden as I stand before the throne of judgment and I hear the Lord ask me, "Is every conflict in your life resolved? If you had problems in the past, did you take care of them? Is the slate clean?"

Before I can answer, might you cry out from somewhere back in the shadows of the hall, "I have a couple of things to say before Brother Holland gives his reply"?

At that point, if I haven't fully repented, you can keep me from the kingdom. I know I was wrong. I know I should not have in some way or another cursed you or hated you or despitefully used you. If I am your husband or wife, daughter or son, my transgression against you is even more serious.

But the point here is that my eternal salvation is at stake, and you hold the key to unlocking my prison door. As I understand it, unless we get that grievance worked out, both you and I are in trouble. If you don't forgive me, my progress could be blocked for a while. But at the same time, *your* progress is also stymied. So, we are both in trouble, unless we indeed understand the message of the baptismal covenant in this kingdom, and bear one another's burdens.

The way you can bear mine is to forgive the sin with which I hurt you. You shoulder the fact that I somehow used you and yet you forgave me of that.

At first blush, we say, "What sense does that make? You have committed some sin against me, but you want me to take that off your shoulder and, at least temporarily, place it on me? You want *me* to bear *your* burdens!" The Lord says, "Yes, in some strange way, that is what I want you to do, because that is what I do. So, forgive his offense. Take from him the things under your control that would keep him from the kingdom, and I will work out with him the rest of it which is under his control and mine."

This is the one way that we consciously, conspicuously, present ourselves as members of the body of Christ, one way that we actively participate in the Atonement of Jesus Christ on behalf of another. That is the sacrifice for sin we can make, the bearing of the burden of someone else's sorrow. In a small way, it is exactly what the Savior does in a universal way.

He says to us, "I am going to give you a chance to join me in the work of redemption. It may be very difficult to do. What you will have to do is forgive your son for coming home at 10:30 instead of 10:00. Even if he was in the wrong and should have obeyed your counsel. Nevertheless, you can help him work out the mistake by lifting it from his shoulders and giving him a chance to try again and do better the next time. If you can do this, you will know something about who I am and what price I paid for *your* mistakes.

After an experience visiting with men in a state prison, I thought of the divine law of justice and was more sobered than ever by the question of an ancient prophet, "What, do you suppose that mercy can rob justice? I say unto you, Nay; not one whit. If so, God would cease to be God" (Alma 42:25). Paul had warned the Galatians, "Be not deceived; God is not mocked: for whatsoever a man soweth that shall he also reap" (Galatians 6:7).

Paul meant that we reap in kind. That is, we do not plant thistles and expect to reap alfalfa. We do not sow discord and expect to reap harmony.

So we reap in kind, but we also almost always reap in greater quantity. That is, we sow a little thistle seed and get lots of thistles—great, big thistles, bushes and branches of them, for years and years to come, unless we root it out. Sowing a little discord reaps discord—big, painful, malicious, warring discord. And so on. Alma said God is just. Paul said we reap in kind exactly as we have sown. Hosea said we reap in quantity exceeding what we have sown. Of those men in prison, and ultimately of all of us, he said, "They have sown the wind, and they shall reap the whirlwind" (Hosea 8:7).

But this idea gives me great courage: as frightening as the thought of a just God might be, that is much less frightening than the thought of an unjust God. For all we have in Western Civilization that we owe to the Greeks, I for one am most grateful that I do not believe in the gods of Tantalus and Sisyphus and Prometheus. The frequent caprice and cruelty that marked their style indicated gods made in the image and likeness of men rather than vice versa. Without believing in God's eternal commitment to justice, we would have no assurance that our efforts to live honestly and righteously would count for anything.

UNTO EVERY ONE OF US IS GIVEN

GRACE ACCORDING TO THE MEASURE

OF THE GIFT OF CHRIST.

—EPHESIANS 4:7

# EPHESIANS

## EPHESIANS 2

Before the general use of concrete, the foundation walls of a temple were built upon a bed of rocks with particularly strong, substantial stones placed at the four corners of the structure. The final stone of the four was sometimes spoken of as the chief cornerstone, and its placement was a cause for celebration because the temple could now rise in glory. The Apostle Paul spoke of foundations and cornerstones in a verse of scripture often used by our missionaries. To new members he said:

"Now therefore ye are no more strangers and foreigners, but fellow-citizens with the saints, and of the household of God;

"And are built upon the foundation of the apostles and prophets, Jesus Christ himself being the chief corner stone;

"In whom all the building fitly framed together groweth unto an holy temple in the Lord" (Ephesians 2:19–21).

Notice if you will that the end purpose of membership in the Church of Christ is to "[grow] unto an holy temple in the Lord." Thus the temple, the earthly symbol of God's dwelling place, becomes the desired destination for all who want to be "of the household of God." It is a divinely designated home, the place of eternal families, and our Father in Heaven wants all His children to gather there as often as circumstances allow. Like our homes are supposed to be, the temple is a place of peace and spirituality, a place of revelation and purity and love. In the temple everything is "fitly framed together"—especially families but also the miter joints and carpet seams—and we are "no more strangers and foreigners" to His eternal purposes. What a majestic structure a temple is in the gospel of Jesus Christ.

In His plan for our salvation and the erecting of a temple-worthy life, our Heavenly Father gave us the greatest gift possible on which to build, not only a cornerstone but the chief cornerstone—the life, mission, atoning sacrifice, and Resurrection of His Only Begotten Son, the Lord Jesus Christ. He is the chief cornerstone of the Church that bears His name, and there is no other name given among men whereby we can be saved (see Acts 4:12). He is the author of our salvation and the finisher of our faith. He is the beginning and the end, the first and the last, the alpha and omega of our quest for eternal life.

## EPHESIANS 4

In New Testament times there was a true Church, of which Jesus Christ was the chief cornerstone and the personification of divinity, with mortal men called as prophets and apostles to form a foundational structure around Him. These Apostles, with other teachers and priests, pastors and members, constituted a figurative building—a church, if you will—fitly framed together, which Paul described as "for the perfecting of the saints, for the work of the ministry, for the edifying of the body of Christ" (Ephesians 4:12).

A fundamental truth is that the New Testament Church was expected to exist, or at least it is assumed it was expected to continue to exist, until that glorious final appearance of which these angels spoke of in the book of Acts. There were Jesus's teachings to be taught, His saving ordinances and sacraments to be embraced, and a community of believers to be established that would serve and strengthen individuals, families, neighborhoods, and nations by putting on what Paul called "the whole armour of God" (Ephesians 6:11).

Sadly, however, the Church did not withstand what Paul went on to call "the wiles of the devil" and "the rulers of the darkness of this world" (Ephesians 6:11–12). After Christ's ascension and the gradual, inexorable death of the early Apostles, the divinity of the Church and its orderly succession of ordained, authorized priesthood administers were gradually lost, removed from the human family. Without apostolic keys and authorized priestly oversight, over time the doctrine either eroded or in some cases was corrupted, and unauthorized changes to the saving ordinances were introduced. What then ensued was more than a millennium of institutional darkness, leading to the divisions and divergence and religious disarray of many kinds and dashing Paul's hopes that there would be a "unity of the faith" and a "knowledge of the Son of God" (Ephesians 4:13). It belabors the obvious to note that in the Christian world we do not enjoy anything remotely approximating a unity of faith today, nor a common church fitly framed together. Indeed, those in the contemporary religious culture—if we can call it that—particularly the young, seem well and truly "tossed to and fro, and carried about with every wind of doctrine" (Ephesians 4:14). But Paul still gives voice to all who would yearn for that "one Lord, one faith, one baptism" (Ephesians 4:5) of the original New Testament Church.

## EPHESIANS 6

Ever since my youth I have been impressed with Paul's call to all of us to be clothed with the "armour of God." He said:

"Finally, my brethren, be strong in the Lord, and in the power of his might.

"Put on the whole armour of God, that ye may be able to stand against the wiles of the devil.

"For we wrestle not against flesh and blood, but against principalities, against powers, against the rulers of the darkness of this world, against spiritual wickedness in high places.

"Wherefore take unto you the whole armour of God, that ye may be able to withstand in the evil day, and having done all, to stand.

"Stand therefore, having your loins girt about with truth, and having on the breastplate of righteousness;

"And your feet shod with the preparation of the gospel of peace;

"Above all, taking the shield of faith, wherewith ye shall be able to quench all the fiery darts of the wicked.

"And take the helmet of salvation, and the sword of the Spirit, which is the word of God" (Ephesians 6:10–17).

My point in noting this familiar call to arms is that it does not say very much about, well, arms. It says a lot about armor—about breastplates and helmets and shields of protection—but not much by way of weapons. In fact, if I read it correctly, there is only one element of offense mentioned in a metaphor otherwise devoted entirely to defense. The one actual weapon we are given is "the sword of the Spirit, which is the word of God" (Ephesians 6:17). Indeed, Paul goes on to plead that "utterance may be given unto me, that I may open my mouth boldly, to make known the mystery of the gospel, for which I am an ambassador in bonds: that therein I may speak boldly, as I ought to speak" (Ephesians 6:19–20).

In this war in which we are engaged, this fight over good and evil that began in heaven and continues on earth, we do not have a lot of weapons, certainly not the weapons traditionally granted to armies or navies or corporations or governments. To accomplish our purposes we don't, at least in the ecclesiastical realm, hire people or fire people. We don't yell at them or harangue them (at least we are not supposed to), and we don't force them to do anything. In a purely gospel sense, we not only can't force anyone to do anything, we shouldn't. Irony of ironies, that is part of what the great premortal war was over. So how does one motivate, inspire, stimulate, and move others? We are left with one principal asset—words. Energized by the Spirit and expressed with love, words are the only real sword we have in this divine battle.

Coupled with prayer and the power of the priesthood that ought to be in all of our lives, the greatest source of spirituality available to us is the word of God—the scriptures, the revelations. Martin Luther and the Reformers were closer to the truth than they knew when they taught that the scriptures are a means of grace. They did not have it entirely right, but they knew they were on to something—that the scriptures had a great central role in the Church of God, that hearing the word of God, and later when they could, reading the word of God, was a privilege every lay member of the Church was to enjoy. Every man or woman was to have a direct relationship with Deity through the study of the scriptures. That is a principle within the Reformation that set the stage for the Restoration.

WHEREFORE GOD ALSO HATH

HIGHLY EXALTED HIM, AND GIVEN HIM A NAME

WHICH IS ABOVE EVERY NAME:

THAT AT THE NAME OF JESUS

EVERY KNEE SHOULD BOW,

OF THINGS IN HEAVEN, AND THINGS IN

EARTH, AND THINGS UNDER THE EARTH.

−PHILIPPIANS 2:9-10

# PHILIPPIANS

Our first and foremost article of faith in The Church of Jesus Christ of Latter-day Saints is "We believe in God, the Eternal Father, and in His Son, Jesus Christ, and in the Holy Ghost" (Articles of Faith 1:1). We believe these three divine persons constituting a single Godhead are united in purpose, in manner, in testimony, in mission. We believe Them to be filled with the same godly sense of mercy and love, justice and grace, patience, forgiveness, and redemption. I think it is accurate to say we believe They are one in every significant and eternal aspect imaginable *except* believing Them to be three persons combined in one substance, a Trinitarian notion never set forth in the scriptures because it is not true.

So, any criticism that The Church of Jesus Christ of Latter-day Saints does not hold the contemporary Christian view of God, Jesus, and the Holy Ghost is *not* a comment about our commitment to Christ but rather a recognition (accurate, I might add) that our view of the Godhead breaks with post–New Testament Christian history and returns to the doctrine taught by Jesus Himself. Now, a word about that post–New Testament history might be helpful.

In the year AD 325, the Roman emperor Constantine convened the Council of Nicaea to address—among other things—the growing issue of God's alleged "trinity in unity." What emerged from the heated contentions of churchmen, philosophers, and ecclesiastical dignitaries came to be known (after another 125 years and three more major councils) as the Nicene Creed, with later reformulations such as the

Athanasian Creed. These various evolutions and iterations of creeds—and others to come over the centuries—declared the Father, Son, and Holy Ghost to be abstract, absolute, transcendent, immanent, consubstantial, coeternal, and unknowable, without body, parts, or passions and dwelling outside space and time. In such creeds all three members are separate persons, but they are a single being, the oft-noted "mystery of the trinity." They are three distinct persons, yet not three Gods but one. All three persons are incomprehensible, yet it is one God who is incomprehensible.

We agree with our critics on at least that point—that such a formulation for divinity is truly incomprehensible. How are we to trust, love, worship, to say nothing of striving to be like, One who is incomprehensible and unknowable? What of Jesus's prayer to His Father in Heaven that "this is life eternal, that they might *know* thee the only true God, and Jesus Christ, whom *thou* hast sent" (John 17:3; emphasis added)?

It is not our purpose to demean any person's belief nor the doctrine of any religion. We extend to all the same respect for their doctrine that we are asking for ours. (That, too, is an article of our faith.) But if one says we are not Christians because we do not hold a fourth- or fifth-century view of the Godhead, then what of those first Christian Saints, many of whom were eyewitnesses of the living Christ, who did not hold such a view either?

To acknowledge the scriptural evidence that otherwise perfectly united members of the Godhead are nevertheless separate and distinct beings is not to be guilty of polytheism; it is, rather, part of the great revelation Jesus came to deliver concerning the nature of divine beings. Perhaps the Apostle Paul said it best: "Christ Jesus . . . being in the form of God, thought it not robbery to be equal with God" (Philippians 2:5–6).

GIVING THANKS UNTO THE FATHER,

WHICH . . . HATH TRANSLATED US INTO THE

KINGDOM OF HIS DEAR SON: IN WHOM WE

HAVE REDEMPTION THROUGH HIS BLOOD.

—COLOSSIANS 1:12–14

# COLOSSIANS

## COLOSSIANS 1

Nothing is so pervasive in our lives, nothing so encompassing and enfolding and upholding, as the Savior of this world and the Redeemer of all humankind. One of His names is Alpha, the first letter of the Greek alphabet, which suggests commencement and inception. "I was in the beginning with the Father," He reveals (D&C 93:21), and, as the Firstborn, He stood at the right hand of the Father in the councils of heaven and in the work of creation. It was by our unity with Him (as He was one with the Father) that we survived a great conflict between good and evil before this world was created. By the "blood of the Lamb, and by the word of [our] testimony," we overcame the opposition of Satan, "that old serpent, called the Devil" (see Revelation 12:711), and we saw him cast out into the earth ahead of us.

Reaching back in time to scenes untouched by memory but still resonant in our souls, we realize that even then we recognized the role of One who, as both friend and brother, would pave for us the narrow path of perfection. However little we know of our premortal state, we know that this beloved Son of God strengthened our convictions and created this world to which we would come. He was "the firstborn of every creature" (Colossians 1:15).

## COLOSSIANS 3

Sin is the great cleaver. It is sin in your life or mine that will keep us from the unity God means us to have. It is the sin in your life or mine that will make it harder to administer justice, or charity, or long-suffering, or kindness, or patience. Surely if everyone were as Christ was, if we could all live as the Prince of Peace, then it would be a marvelously easy thing to be patient and kind, because we would have great cause to be so.

As Paul earnestly admonished the Colossians:

"Put on therefore, as the elect of God, holy and beloved, bowels of mercies, kindness, humbleness of mind, meekness, longsuffering;

"Forbearing one another, and forgiving one another, if any man have a quarrel against any; even as Christ forgave you, so also do ye.

"And above all these things put on charity, which is the bond of perfectness" (Colossians 3:12–14).

The task is to be like He was in a world that is not like He was. It is to be kind when people are unkind. It is to be patient when people are impatient with you. It is to bless those that curse you, and to pray for those that despitefully use you (see Matthew 5:44). Unity, Christ urgently sought.

FOR IF WE BELIEVE THAT JESUS DIED

AND ROSE AGAIN, EVEN SO THEM ALSO WHICH

SLEEP IN JESUS WILL GOD BRING WITH HIM.

—1 THESSALONIANS 4:14

# 1 THESSALONIANS

## 1 THESSALONIANS 4

Some gifts coming from the Atonement of Jesus Christ are universal, infinite, and unconditional. These include His ransom for Adam's original transgression so that no member of the human family is held responsible for that sin. Another universal gift is the resurrection from the dead of every man, woman, and child who lives, has ever lived, or ever will live on earth.

As the Apostle Paul assured the Thessalonians: "I would not have you to be ignorant, brethren, concerning them which are asleep, that ye sorrow not, even as others which have no hope. For if we believe that Jesus died and rose again, even so them also which sleep in Jesus will God bring with him" (1 Thessalonians 4:13–14).

Although the resurrection of the body is a free and universal gift from Christ, a result of His victory over death, the nature of the resurrected body (or "degree of glory" given it), as well as the time of one's resurrection, is affected directly by one's faithfulness in this life. The Apostle Paul made clear, for example, that those fully committed to Christ will "rise first" in the Resurrection (1 Thessalonians 4:16). Modern revelation clarifies the different orders of resurrected bodies, promising the highest degree of glory only to those who adhere to the principles and ordinances of the gospel of Jesus Christ.

GOD HATH FROM THE BEGINNING CHOSEN YOU

TO SALVATION THROUGH SANCTIFICATION

OF THE SPIRIT AND BELIEF OF THE TRUTH:

WHEREUNTO HE CALLED YOU BY OUR

GOSPEL, TO THE OBTAINING OF THE

GLORY OF OUR LORD JESUS CHRIST.

—2 THESSALONIANS 2:13-14

# 2 THESSALONIANS

## 2 THESSALONIANS 2

Every dispensation except the present one has ended in apostasy or in some kind of comparable disarray—Old Testament periods, the Book of Mormon era, even the meridian Church in Christ's time. We have long periods and short periods of truth, with major prophets and minor prophets to teach it, but such periods never last. They never succeed. Until now. Only this dispensation is going to succeed, ultimately. That is one of the reasons it is not only the last but the greatest dispensation. All those blessings from the past will be brought together in our time. Your time. This era.

People like Peter and James and John, and people like Isaiah and Ezekiel and Jeremiah, and people like Alma and Amulek and Nephi and Moroni have all waited for you. Because they did not succeed—and, to some degree, even though they knew they were not going to succeed—they knew theirs was not going to be a permanent dispensation. They knew the Church in those moments was not going to last.

In the New Testament, we have Peter and Paul, to say nothing of the Savior Himself, testifying in their own lifetime that apostasy would creep into the household of faith. Paul warned the Thessalonians not to be "shaken in mind, or be troubled, neither by spirit, nor by word, nor by letter as from us, as that the day of Christ is at hand. Let no man deceive you by any means, for that day shall not come, *except there come a falling away first*" (2 Thessalonians 2:2–3; emphasis added). And there *was* a falling away, an apostasy in Paul's time, just as there was in every other dispensation. But perhaps there was one thing more than any other that kept those prophets going, kept them from being overly discouraged.

I think those Saints of earlier dispensations were committed, and stayed faithful, not because *they* would succeed, but because *you* in our day would. That knowledge was one great motivation that kept them going.

When we serve in the kingdom of God in our modern day, we are representing not simply the President of The Church of Jesus Christ of Latter-day Saints, our leaders, and other contemporary members; we are representing all those ancient prophets as well. We are saying, in effect, "Peter, we are going to finish the work because you were not able to do so, even though you gave your life for it." Tradition has it that Peter was crucified upside down after being imprisoned in Rome.

In the same vein we could say, "Paul, we are going to finish the work because you did not get that opportunity, even though you gave your life for it." The tradition is that Paul was beheaded, drawn (eviscerated), and quartered (cut in four parts). Then the four parts of his body were taken to the four corners of Rome, with his head being placed on a stake in the middle of the city just to remind people what it meant to be a bold Christian in those days.

When my time comes, I want to stand worthily not only before the Father and the Son, which is our ultimate accounting, but I also want to stand worthily before the prophets, pioneers, and early missionaries who paid this kind of price for their faith. I can envision them saying to me, "Jeff, you were born in the greatest of all dispensations and your call to serve came in the greatest of all times. Did you take advantage of it? Did you pursue the cause as faithfully as we did? Did you represent the Lord—and us—with devotion and commitment and loyalty?"

I probably won't be asked to die the way some of them did. I am not likely to be crucified upside down or beheaded. But I will stand before these men and women—a whole series of people who went before us—who did face those fates. I truly believe I will be called upon to answer not only for the significance of the work in our day, but also for the significance it had for theirs.

Brethren and sisters, in a very real sense, we are carrying the weight of *every* dispensation on our shoulders because this is the last and the greatest of them all, into which all earlier truths will be gathered into one. It is in our day that the most comprehensive, global missionary work for the living, and all of the vicarious temple work for the dead, will be done. That is the moment into which you have been born.

FOR THERE IS ONE GOD,

AND ONE MEDIATOR BETWEEN GOD AND MEN,

THE MAN CHRIST JESUS;

WHO GAVE HIMSELF A RANSOM FOR ALL,

TO BE TESTIFIED IN DUE TIME.

1 TIMOTHY 2:5–6

# 1 TIMOTHY

## 1 TIMOTHY 5

With current statistics telling us that "worldwide there are 40 million abortions per year" and that "41 percent of all births in the United States [are] to women who [are] not married" (Joyce A. Martin and others, "Births: Final Data for 2013," *National Vital Statistics Reports,* vol. 64, no. 1 [Jan. 2015]), we should be declaring boldly that inherent in the very act of creation is, for both parents, a lifelong commitment to and responsibility for the child they created. No one can with impunity terminate that life, neglect that care, or shirk that responsibility. Paul wrote to Timothy, "But if any provide not for his own, and specially for those of his own house, he hath denied the faith, and is worse than an infidel" (1 Timothy 5:8). If Paul could see our day, surely he would repeat that counsel and would mean more than providing physical nourishment, essential as that is. If we want democracy to work and society to be stable, parents must nourish a child's mind and heart and spirit as well. Generally speaking, no community of whatever size or definition has enough resources in time, money, or will to make up for what does not happen at home.

JESUS CHRIST . . . HATH ABOLISHED DEATH,

AND HATH BROUGHT LIFE AND IMMORTALITY

TO LIGHT THROUGH THE GOSPEL.

—2 TIMOTHY 1:10

# 2 TIMOTHY

## 2 TIMOTHY 1

Many at home and abroad have been alarmed by international events and the almost wholesale use of the word *terror*. Not many years ago that word was reserved almost entirely for B-grade movie advertisements and Stephen King novels. Now, sadly, it is daily fare in our newspapers and so common in conversation that even young children are conscious that the world in which we live can be brutally, criminally affected by people called "terrorists." And there are other disasters of other kinds, natural and otherwise, that remind us that life can be fragile, that life can present fateful turns of events.

Against that backdrop, I know that many of you have wondered in your hearts what all of this means regarding the end of the world and your life in it. In recent times, I have heard very fearful and even dismal opinions coming from young people especially, wondering whether there is any purpose in going on a mission or getting an education or planning for a career if the world we live in is going to be so uncertain. I have even heard sweethearts say, "We don't know whether we should get married in such uncertain times."

Worst of all, I have heard reports of some newlyweds questioning whether they should bring children into a terror-filled world on the brink of latter-day cataclysms. May I tell you that, in a way, those kinds of attitudes worry me more than global pandemics and international terrorists worry me.

We must *never*, in *any* age or circumstance, let fear and the father of fear (Satan himself) divert us from our faith and faithful living. As

Paul told Timothy, "God hath not given us the spirit of fear; but of power, and of love, and of a sound mind" (2 Timothy 1:7).

There have *always* been questions about the future. Every young person or every young couple in every era has had to walk by faith into what has *always* been some uncertainty—starting with Adam and Eve in those first tremulous steps out of the Garden of Eden. But that is all right. This is the plan. It will be okay. Just be faithful. God is in charge. He knows your name and He knows your need.

*Faith* in the Lord Jesus Christ—that is the first principle of the gospel. We must go forward, as it says in K. Newell Dayley's hymn commemorating our pioneers of the past, with "faith in every foot-step." But like those pioneers, we do have to keep taking them—one step and then another and then the next. That is how tasks are accomplished, that is how goals are achieved, and that is how frontiers are conquered. In more divine language, that is how worlds are created and it is how *your* world will be created.

God expects us to have enough faith and determination and enough trust in Him to keep moving, keep living, keep rejoicing. In fact, He expects us not simply to *face* the future (that sounds pretty grim and stoic); He expects us to embrace and *shape* the future with power and love and a sound mind—to love it and rejoice in it and delight in your opportunities.

God is anxiously waiting for the chance to answer our prayers and fulfill our dreams, just as He always has. But He can't if we don't pray, and He can't if we don't dream. In short, He can't if we don't believe.

## 2 TIMOTHY 3

How can we receive inspiration and guidance from heaven? One quick rule of thumb is don't go where the Spirit can't go; don't say what the Spirit can't say; don't be what the Spirit would never be. And the reverse side of that formula is, of course, to be where the Spirit can be and go where the Spirit can go. Cultivate the habits that you know will bring the Spirit into your life. Some of those habits are basic for everyone. Obviously, prayer is one of those. But although prayer is of utmost, eternal importance, sometimes we are in a setting where we cannot pray publicly. We can pray privately. We can pray in our heart. But we often find ourselves in meetings or other places where it is impossible to drop to one's knees and offer a prayer.

However, in those situations where public prayer is impossible but in which we still need instant inspiration, one can almost always find such in the scriptures. We can all rely on the promise of the Lord, "*All scripture* is given by inspiration of God, and is profitable for doctrine, for reproof, for correction, for instruction in righteousness" (2 Timothy 3:16; emphasis added). Any one of us can open to any page of the scriptures (or any section of the application on our hand-held devices) and there will be something on that page that will bless us.

We should partake of the sacrament every Sabbath day. After these, we can add any number of other habits. We should be kind and loving toward all people. We should serve others and especially care for the poor. We should do family history and go to the temple as faithfully as we can. We should not use language that is alienating to the Spirit. We should avoid anything pornographic like the plague that it is. There are many, many more virtues that could be used. If we can do these, we are in a position to receive spiritual help from heaven. We can at least say, "Lord, I have done what I can do. I have done everything I know to do. Can you now help me where I am still lacking?"

We won't be perfect, no one is. But we can repent and forgive, and we can keep trying. This places us in a position to receive the Spirit of the Lord.

In my long-ago, now nearly forgotten youth, I loved sports of any and all kinds. I was always involved in sports—football or basketball or baseball or tennis—it was always some kind of sport. One thing the coaches always said to us was: "Put yourself in a position to win. You might not always be ahead in every game or match you play. You might be a little behind from time to time. But stay in the hunt. Stay in the pursuit. Work hard and keep yourself close. Put yourself in a position that you can still win at the end."

That is a poor analogy, especially when we are speaking of spiritual matters, but it comes to mind from my youth. Put yourself in a position to win. Stay close. Don't let the opposition get so far ahead that you cannot catch up. Don't you get irreversibly far behind. Keep working. Keep trying. Fight to stay close. In the end, often the way will open for you to be victorious.

NOT BY WORKS OF RIGHTEOUSNESS WHICH

WE HAVE DONE, BUT ACCORDING TO HIS

MERCY HE SAVED US, BY THE WASHING OF

REGENERATION, AND RENEWING OF THE HOLY

GHOST; WHICH HE SHED ON US ABUNDANTLY

THROUGH JESUS CHRIST OUR SAVIOUR.

—TITUS 3:5–6

# TITUS

## TITUS 1

In explicit contradiction to the Lord's instructions, Saul, king of Israel, brought back from the Amalekites "the best of the sheep and of the oxen: to sacrifice unto the Lord [his] God." Samuel, in utter anguish cries:

"Hath the Lord as great delight in burnt offerings and sacrifice, as in obeying the voice of the Lord? Behold, to obey is better than sacrifice, and to hearken than the fat of rams.

"For rebellion is the sin of witchcraft, and stubbornness is as iniquity and idolatry. Because thou hast rejected the word of the Lord, he hath also rejected thee from being king" (1 Samuel 15:15, 22–23).

Why is rebellion (or stubbornness or disobedience in our ordinances) like witchcraft? Because it makes a statement about our loyalty and our understanding of what God is really like and what He really wants. Saul who understands the method but not the meaning of his sacrifice, and the Latter-day Saint who faithfully goes to sacrament meeting but is no more merciful or patient or forgiving as a result, are precisely the same as the witch and the idolater. "They profess that they know God; but in works they deny him, being abominable, and disobedient, and unto every good work reprobate" (Titus 1:16). They go through the motions of the ordinances without loyalty to or understanding of the reasons for which these ordinances were established—obedience, gentleness, loving kindness in the search for forgiveness of our sins. If Cain or Saul (or the rest of us) can't remember that, then surely it would be better to offer no sacrifice at all. Ordinances pursued in error and altered in meaning mark an apostate priesthood and an idolatrous nation.

THAT THE COMMUNICATION OF THY

FAITH MAY BECOME EFFECTUAL BY THE

ACKNOWLEDGING OF EVERY GOOD THING

WHICH IS IN YOU IN CHRIST JESUS.

—PHILEMON 1:6

# PHILEMON

## PHILEMON 1

Anyone could be pleasant, patient, and forgiving on a good day. A Christian has to be pleasant, patient, and forgiving on all days. Christ's forgiveness of His tormentors was perhaps the quintessential moment of His ministry. Pre-figuring the eternal forgiveness He would offer all of us, this specific act on the cross was as perfect in its example as it was difficult to endure.

Is there someone who needs forgiveness from you in a more personal way? Is there someone in your home, someone in your family, someone in your neighborhood who has done an unjust or an unkind or an un-Christian thing? Is it possible that even this very moment, in the rush to get to work or to some meeting, some unkind word was spoken and the vault of human pain increased yet again? All of us are guilty of such transgressions, so there surely must be someone who yet needs your forgiveness. And please don't ask if that is fair—if the injured should have to bear the burden of forgiveness for the offender.

Don't ask if "justice" doesn't demand that it be the other way around. No, whatever you do, don't ask for justice. You and I know that what we plead for is mercy, and that is what we must be willing to give.

This was exactly what the Apostle Paul asked of one of his converts, Philemon. When justice would have demanded punishment for Onesimus, a runaway slave, Paul sent him back to his owner with the plea to treat him "not now as a servant, but above a servant, a brother beloved" (Philemon 1:16). Mercy was what Paul said, "for love's sake I rather beseech thee" (Philemon 1:9).

My beloved brothers and sisters, I testify that forgiving and forsaking offenses, old or new, is central to the grandeur of the Atonement of Jesus Christ. I testify that ultimately such spiritual repair can come only from our divine Redeemer, He who rushes to our aid "with healing in his wings" (Malachi 4:2). We thank Him, and our Heavenly Father who sent Him, that renewal and rebirth, a future free from old sorrows and past mistakes, are not only possible, but they have already been purchased, paid for, at an excruciating cost symbolized by the blood of the Lamb who shed it.

We can almost hear the Savior say, as did the Apostle Paul, "If he hath wronged thee, or oweth thee ought, put that on mine account. I . . . have written it with mine own hand, I will repay it: albeit I do not say to thee how thou owest unto me even thine own self besides" (Philemon 1:18–19).

With the apostolic authority granted me by the Savior of the world, I testify of the tranquility to the soul that reconciliation with God and each other will bring if we are meek and courageous enough to pursue it. "Cease to contend one with another," the Savior pled (D&C 136:23). If you know of an old injury, repair it. Care for one another in love.

CHRIST BEING COME AN HIGH PRIEST

OF GOOD THINGS TO COME,

BY A GREATER AND MORE PERFECT

TABERNACLE, NOT MADE WITH HANDS.

—HEBREWS 9:11

# HEBREWS

If you will understand the price that was paid for your salvation voluntarily against injustice, against unfairness, paid by the only Man in the world who did not have a sin in the world to repent of and could have gotten off scot-free—when you think of the Father and the Son arranging a plan just for you, that will be the beginning of your understanding about your self-worth.

And that is why one of the greatest warnings in the scripture is, do not "crucify . . . the Son of God afresh" (Hebrews 6:6). If we truly understood the Atonement of Jesus Christ, we would never ever dare say anything about our lack of worth, any lack in how God sees us. Only our adversary, Lucifer, would try to plant the seeds of doubt and darkness about our self-worth. There is certainly nothing in the gospel, nothing in the plan of salvation from beginning to end, that says anything other than that we are children of God and matter to Him more than anything in the world: more than all the flowers in the spring, more than the sun that comes up every morning, more than all the planets in their orbit. Those are almost incidental to the real meaning of life which is our worth and meaning to our Father in Heaven. The adversary would try to convince us otherwise. Resist his lies. Don't crucify Christ afresh. Love yourself in the eternal way He loves you.

## HEBREWS 9

On those days when we have special need of heaven's help, we would do well to remember one of the titles given to the Savior in the epistle to the Hebrews. Speaking of Jesus's "more excellent ministry" and why He is "the mediator of a better covenant" filled with "better promises" (Hebrews 8:6), this author—presumably the Apostle Paul—tells us that through His mediation and Atonement, Christ became "an high priest of good things to come" (Hebrews 9:11).

Every one of us has times when we need to know things will get better. Moroni spoke of it in the Book of Mormon as "hope for a better world" (Ether 12:4). For emotional health and spiritual stamina, everyone needs to be able to look forward to some respite, to something pleasant and renewing and hopeful, whether that blessing be near at hand or still some distance ahead. It is enough just to know we can get there, that however measured or far away, there is the promise of "good things to come."

My declaration is that this is precisely what the gospel of Jesus Christ offers us, especially in times of need. There *is* help. There *is* happiness. There really *is* light at the end of the tunnel. It is the Light of the World, the Bright and Morning Star, the "light that is endless, that can never be darkened" (Mosiah 16:9). It is the very Son of God Himself. To any who may be struggling to see that light and find that hope, I say: Hold on. Keep trying. God loves you. Things will improve. Christ comes to you in His "more excellent ministry" with a future of "better promises." He is your "high priest of good things to come."

## HEBREWS 10

We want to hold fast to the spiritual impressions we have had and the inspired teachings we have heard. But it is inevitable that after heavenly moments in our lives, we, of necessity, return to earth, so to speak, where sometimes less-than-ideal circumstances again face us. The author of Hebrews warned us of this when he wrote, "Call to remembrance the former days, in which, after ye were illuminated, ye endured a great fight of afflictions" (Hebrews 10:32). That post-illumination affliction can come in many ways and it can come to all of us. Surely every missionary who has ever served soon realized that life in the field was not going to be quite like the rarified atmosphere of the Missionary Training Center. So, too, for all of us upon leaving a sweet session in the temple or concluding a particularly spiritual sacrament meeting. Remember that when Moses came down from his singular experience on Mount Sinai he found his people had "corrupted themselves" and had "turned aside quickly" (Exodus 32:7–8). There they were at the foot of the mountain, busily fashioning a golden calf to worship, in the very hour that Jehovah, at the summit of the mountain, had been telling Moses, "Thou shalt have no other gods before me," and "Thou shalt not make unto thee any graven image" (Exodus 20:3–4). Moses was *not* happy with his flock of wandering Israelites that day!

If in the days ahead you not only see limitations in those around you but also find elements in your own life that don't yet measure up to the messages you might hear on a general conference weekend, please don't be cast down in spirit and don't give up. The gospel, the Church itself, these wonderful semiannual gatherings are intended to give hope and inspiration. They are not intended to discourage you. Only the adversary, the enemy of us all, would try to convince us that the ideals outlined in general conference are depressing and unrealistic, that people don't really improve, that no one really progresses. And why does Lucifer give that speech? Because he knows *he* can't improve, *he* can't progress, that worlds without end *he* will never have a bright tomorrow. He is a miserable man bound by eternal limitations and he wants you to be miserable too. Well, don't fall for that. With the gift of the Atonement of Jesus Christ and the strength of heaven to help us, we *can* improve, and the great thing about the gospel is we get credit for *trying*, even if we don't always succeed.

We cannot sign on for a battle of such eternal significance and everlasting consequence without knowing it will be a fight—a fight we win but a fight nevertheless that will have more than one round to the contest before it is over. The Apostle Paul says to those who thought a new testimony and baptism into the Church would put them beyond trouble, "Call to remembrance the former days, in which, *after ye were illuminated,* ye endured a great fight of afflictions" (Hebrews 10:32; emphasis added).

I love that counsel! Paul is saying what the Lord said, "Don't let your guard down." To these new converts, or new missionaries, or newly wedded couples, he pleads: "For ye have need of patience, that, after ye have done the will of God, ye might receive the promise. . . . If any man draw back, my soul shall have no pleasure in him. . . . *We are not of them who draw back unto perdition*" (Hebrews 10:35–36, 38–39; emphasis added).

There is the ultimate call to hang in there, to hang on, to keep believing. He is saying: "Sure it can be tough—before you join The Church of Jesus Christ of Latter-day Saints, while you are trying to join, and after you have joined. Before you go on a mission, while you are on your mission, after you get home from it. Before you marry, while you are dating, and after you are married." But when it is challenging, Paul says: "Don't 'draw back,' don't panic, don't retreat. Don't forget the answers you have had and the miracles you have seen. Don't distrust the spiritual experience you have already had, even as you wait for another." That tenacity is what saved Moses when the adversary confronted him. That is what saved Joseph Smith, and it is what will save you.

## HEBREWS 11

I hear frequently from people, especially young people, who wonder about their faith and how to improve it. Sometimes they speak of a crisis of faith, but often enough it is just plain old faith they want to enhance, with or without the crisis part.

First of all, may I thank everyone, young or old, new convert or longtime member, who cares enough to inquire and has an honest desire to grow. If it takes a "crisis" to prompt that, so be it, because "without faith it is impossible to please [God]" (Hebrews 11:6). But frankly I feel obliged to say that if by *crisis* you mean the trial of your faith then welcome to life, to the journey that sometimes takes you through a lone and dreary waste, a wilderness. If faith is going to be faith, it has to be tested, and it has to be tried. It has to enter the crucible of refinement or else you have a pretty cheap, even shoddy version of faith. So let's stop talking about a crisis of faith and just talk about plain old faith in the open marketplace of religious ideas, because for me comfortable faith or convenient faith or untested faith or untried faith is no faith at all—at least it is hard to know whether it is really faith or not. Maybe it is, but how would you know if it weren't challenged?

The cold-blooded first issue of faith is do you *want* to believe? Paul said that "faith is the substance of things *hoped* for, the evidence of things not seen" (Hebrews 11:1; emphasis added). Alma said, "if ye have faith ye hope for things which are not seen, which are true" (Alma 32:21). Moroni said he would show the world that "faith is things which are hoped for and not seen" (Ether 12:6).

What is the operative word in those passages? *Hope!* If you hope the gospel is true, then there is a delightful journey to begin, but if you hope it is not true, then there is a very different kind of conversation to have.

In keeping with the Savior's own experience, there has been a long history of rejection and a painfully high price paid by prophets and apostles, missionaries and members in every generation—all those who have tried to honor God's call to lift the human family to "a more excellent way" (1 Corinthians 12:31).

"And what shall I more say . . . of [them]?" the writer of the Book of Hebrews asks.

"[They] who . . . stopped the mouths of lions,

"Quenched the violence of fire, escaped the edge of the sword, . . . waxed valiant in fight, turned to flight . . . armies . . . ,

"[Saw] their dead raised to life: . . . [while] others were tortured . . .

"And . . . had trial of cruel mockings and scourgings, . . . of bonds and imprisonment:

"They were stoned, . . . were sawn asunder, were tempted, were slain with the sword: . . . wandered about in sheepskins and goatskins; being destitute, afflicted, [and] tormented;

"([They] of whom the world was not worthy:) . . . wandered in deserts, and in mountains, and in dens and caves of the earth" (Hebrews 11:32–38).

Surely the angels of heaven wept as they recorded this cost of discipleship in a world that is often hostile to the commandments of God. The Savior Himself shed His own tears over those who for hundreds of years had been rejected and slain in His service.

DRAW NIGH TO GOD,

AND HE WILL DRAW NIGH TO YOU. . . .

HUMBLE YOURSELVES IN THE SIGHT OF

THE LORD, AND HE SHALL LIFT YOU UP.

—JAMES 4:8, 10

# JAMES

## JAMES 1

I hope you read regularly—I invite you to read regularly—the account of the First Vision to Joseph Smith as recorded in the Pearl of Great Price. It is purely and simply one of the most moving pieces of scripture in all of the standard works. I know of few accounts in all of human history that are as inspiring. There is so much we could say about it, but let me focus on the opposition that this lad faced almost literally from the moment he turned to the first chapter of James, fifth verse, and read there could well be considered the most important scriptural verse in human history.

"If any of you lack wisdom, let him ask of God, that giveth to all men liberally, and upbraideth not; and it shall be given him" (James 1:5).

There it is—twenty-six words, four short, tidy clauses with only three nouns, four pronouns, and five verbs. It is simple enough for a child to understand and yet it changed the world, or, more correctly, it is in the process of changing the world. My hope is that it is in the process of changing you. It is on the strength of that little verse that the Restoration of the gospel would begin to roll forth to fill the earth. But we know from Joseph's experience that such rolling forth would be opposed every step of the way. We know that from what happened when Joseph tried to put this verse of scripture into practice.

In his own description of the experience, Joseph said he had gone into the woods near his home to do as the book of James had invited him to do—to seek his Father in Heaven in the first vocal prayer he had ever uttered. Making certain he was alone, he had scarcely begun his prayer when he felt a power of astonishing influence come over him. He found himself unable to speak, with "thick darkness," as he described it, gathering around him. This influence was so strong and so terrifying that Joseph was absolutely certain he was going to be destroyed. But he *exerted all his power* to call upon God to deliver him from this opposition, and as he did so a pillar of light brighter than the noonday sun descended gradually until it rested upon him. At the very moment of the light's appearance, he found himself delivered from the destructive power that had held him bound. What then followed is the greatest epiphany that has ever occurred since the events that surround the Crucifixion, Resurrection, and Ascension of Jesus Christ in the meridian of time. The Father and the Son appeared to Joseph Smith, and the dispensation of the fulness of times had begun (see Joseph Smith—History 1:15–17).

It is loyalty—loyalty to true principles and true people and honorable institutions and worthy ideals—that unifies our purpose in life and defines our morality. Where we have no such loyalties or convictions, no standards against which to measure our acts and their consequences, we are unanchored and adrift, "driven with the wind and tossed," says the scripture (James 1:6), until some other storm or problem or appetite takes us another direction for an equally short and unstable period of time.

How much pressure is too much pressure to remain true? How much disappointment is too much disappointment to stand firm? How far is too far to walk with a discouraged friend, or a struggling spouse, or a troubled child? When the opposition heats up, and the going gets tough, how much of what we thought was important to us will we defend and how much, in that inevitable tug and pull of life, will we find it convenient to give away?

## JAMES 2

As a rule, Latter-day Saints are known as an industrious people, a works-conscious people. For us, the works of righteousness, what we might call "dedicated discipleship," are an unerring measure of the reality of our faith; we believe with James, the brother of Jesus, that true faith always manifests itself in faithfulness (see James 2, especially verses 14, 17–18, 20–26). We teach that those Puritans were closer to the truth than they realized when they expected a "godly walk" from those under covenant (D&C 20:69).

Salvation and eternal life are free; indeed, they are the greatest of all the gifts of God (see 2 Nephi 2:4; D&C 6:13; 14:7). Nevertheless, we teach that one must prepare to receive those gifts by declaring and demonstrating faith in the Lord Jesus Christ—by trusting in and relying upon "the merits, and mercy, and grace of the Holy Messiah" (2 Nephi 2:8). For us, the fruits of that faith include repentance, the receipt of gospel covenants and ordinances (including baptism), and a heart of gratitude that motivates us to deny ourselves of all ungodliness, to take up our cross daily (see Luke 9:23), and to keep His commandments—*all* of His commandments.

## JAMES 3

It is with a deep realization of the power and sanctity of words that I wish to caution us, if caution is needed, regarding how we speak to each other and how we speak of ourselves.

There is a line from the Apocrypha which puts the seriousness of this issue better than I can. It reads, "The stroke of the whip maketh marks in the flesh: but the stroke of the tongue breaketh the bones" (Sirach 28:17). With that stinging image in mind, I was particularly impressed to read in the book of James that there was a way I could be "a perfect man."

Said James: "For in many things we offend all. *[But] if any man offend not in word, the same is a perfect man,* and able also to bridle the whole body."

Continuing the imagery of the bridle, he writes: "Behold, we put bits in the horses' mouths, that they may obey us; and we turn about their whole body.

"Behold also the ships, which though they be so great, and are driven of fierce winds, yet are they turned about with a very small helm. . . ."

Then James makes his point: "The tongue is [also] a little member. . . . [But] behold, how great a [forest] a little fire [can burn].

"And the tongue is a fire . . . among our members, . . . it defileth the whole body, . . . it is set on fire of hell.

"For every kind of beasts, and of birds, and of serpents, and of things in the sea, . . . hath been tamed of mankind:

"But the tongue can no man tame; it is an unruly evil, full of deadly poison.

"Therewith bless we God, even the Father; and therewith curse we men, which are made after the similitude of God.

"*Out of the same mouth proceedeth blessing and cursing.* My brethren, these things ought not so to be" (James 3:2–10; emphasis added).

Well, *that* is straightforward! Obviously, James does not mean our tongues are *always* iniquitous, nor that *everything* we say is "full of deadly poison." But he clearly means that at least some things we say can be destructive, even venomous—and that is a chilling indictment for a Latter-day Saint! The voice that bears profound testimony, utters fervent prayer, and sings the hymns of Zion *can be* the same voice that berates and criticizes, embarrasses and demeans, inflicts pain and destroys the spirit of oneself and of others in the process. "Out of the same mouth proceedeth blessing and cursing," James grieves. "My brethren [and sisters], these things ought not so to be."

Is this something we could all work on just a little? Is this an area in which we could each try to be a little more like a "perfect" man or woman?

Husbands, you have been entrusted with the most sacred gift God can give you—a wife, a daughter of God, the mother of your children who has voluntarily given herself to you for love and joyful companionship. Think of the kind things you said when you were courting, think of the blessings you have given with hands placed lovingly upon her head, think of yourself and of her as the god and goddess you both inherently are, and then reflect on other moments characterized by cold, caustic, unbridled words. Given the damage that can be done with our tongues, little wonder the Savior said, "Not that which goeth into the mouth defileth a man; but that which cometh out of the mouth, this defileth a man" (Matthew 15:11). A husband who would never dream of striking his wife physically can break, if not her bones, then certainly her heart by the brutality of thoughtless or unkind speech. Physical abuse is uniformly and unequivocally condemned in The Church of Jesus Christ of Latter-day Saints. If it is possible to be more condemning than that, we speak even more vigorously against all forms of sexual abuse. Today, I speak against verbal and emotional abuse of anyone against anyone, but especially of husbands against wives. Brethren, these things ought not to be.

In that same spirit we speak to the sisters as well, for the sin of verbal abuse knows no gender. Wives, what of the unbridled tongue in *your* mouth, of the power for good or ill in *your* words? How is it that such a lovely voice, which by divine nature is so angelic, so close to the veil, so instinctively gentle and inherently kind, could ever in a turn be so shrill, so biting, so acrid and untamed? A woman's words can be more piercing than any dagger ever forged, and they can drive the people they love to retreat beyond a barrier more distant than anyone in the beginning of that exchange could ever have imagined. Sisters, there is no place in that magnificent spirit of yours for acerbic or abrasive expression of any kind, including gossip or backbiting or catty remarks. Let it never be said of our home or our ward or our neighborhood that "the tongue is a fire, a world of iniquity . . . [burning] among our members" (James 3:6).

May I expand this counsel to make it a full family matter. We must be so careful in speaking to a child. What we say or don't say, how we say it and when is so very, very important in shaping a child's view of himself or herself. But it is even more important in shaping that child's faith in us and their faith in God. Be constructive in your comments to a child—always. Never tell them, even in whimsy, that they are fat or dumb or lazy or homely. You would never do that maliciously, but they remember and may struggle for years trying to forget—and to forgive. And try not to compare your children, even if you think you are skillful at it. You may say most positively that "Susan is pretty and Sandra is bright," but all Susan will remember is that she isn't bright and Sandra that she isn't pretty. Praise each child individually for what that child is and help him or her escape our culture's obsession with comparing, competing, and never feeling we are "enough."

In all of this, I suppose it goes without saying that negative speaking so often flows from negative thinking, including negative thinking about ourselves. We see our own faults, we speak—or at least think—critically of ourselves, and before long that is how we see everyone and everything. No sunshine, no roses, no promise of hope or happiness. Before long we and everyone around us are miserable. These things ought not to be.

## JAMES 4

Heaven only knows how much the world uses envy and pride and worldly glamour in our society. We have to walk away from these things, but this will not be easy to do. We will need the gifts of heaven, the power of God's grace and priesthood, and the atoning power of the Savior, which compensates where we try and try but seem to fall short.

James knew all this. He said: "The spirit that dwelleth in us lusteth to envy . . . but he giveth more grace. Wherefore he saith, *God resisteth the proud, but giveth grace unto the humble.* Submit yourselves therefore to God. . . . *Draw nigh to God, and he will draw nigh to you. . . .*

Humble yourselves in the sight of the Lord, and he shall lift you up" (James 4:5–8, 10; emphasis added).

Isn't that a tremendous thought? If we would not lift ourselves up with these cursed temptations of envy and pride, God would gladly step in and do the lifting for us! Only He can lift us up where He wants us and where we really want to be. We can't get there by clawing or clamor, by cattiness or cutting others down. We certainly can't get there by vaunting ourselves "up."

Furthermore, I believe with all my heart that this is a challenge we will face again and again. We should not be discouraged if the challenge returns tomorrow just when we thought we gave it such a good effort today. I say this out of the honesty—and experience—of my own heart. I struggle with these issues just as you do, and just as everyone does. So don't give up hope and don't think you are the only one who feels these things or struggles with these temptations. We all do, but every effort is a godly one, and every victory is counted for our good. And if we turn around to face the same challenge again tomorrow, so be it. We will work again, with all our heart, to strip away anything that keeps us from truly being meek and lowly—in all the right ways— before God. His grace *is* sufficient to help us succeed at that.

CHRIST ALSO SUFFERED FOR US,

LEAVING US AN EXAMPLE,

THAT YE SHOULD FOLLOW HIS STEPS.

—1 PETER 2:21

# 1 PETER

## 1 PETER 2

We have no personal obligations in life that transcend the covenants we have made to the Lord. And the covenants we have made are based on the two great commandments: to love God and to love each other. Such love includes being gentle, long-suffering, and forgiving.

We all say we will be long-suffering: "Sure, I will be long-suffering—until a trial of some kind comes along." Then we don't want to suffer, and we don't want it to last very long. We all pledge to have more patience. We pull out those wonderful descriptions of Joseph in Liberty Jail, or quote section four of the Doctrine and Covenants, with which we send the missionaries out into the field. That tried-and-true passage lists a whole host of virtues that we make covenants to acquire. There is nothing there about hostility. There is nothing there about divisiveness. There is nothing there about contention.

The very first thing that the Savior teaches when He comes to the Nephites is to say, "There will be no contention here." He has much to teach them. He will give the Sermon at the Temple—equivalent to the Sermon on the Mount. He will speak about the law of Moses and how it relates to the gospel. He will talk about the last days and the gathering of Israel. He will gather the children together and will conclude the day by implementing the sacrament among them, but He wasn't going to do anything—not *anything*—until all contention was eliminated from among them (see 3 Nephi 11:28–30).

In one of the finest things ever said about the Savior, Peter said in the short phrase that "when he was reviled, [he] reviled not again; when he suffered, he threatened not; but committed himself to him that judgeth righteously" (1 Peter 2:23).

Living the gospel is not limited to times when it is convenient, when it is comfortable, when the sea is calm and there is no wind blowing. Anyone can hold the tiller of their ship when there is no wind. Anyone can take the boat into the bay when there is not a wave or a ripple in sight. The Lord needs people who can handle their ship in a storm. He needs people who can be reliable in the hard times, in the challenging times. That is when we have to be at our best. "If, when ye do well and suffer for it, yet take it patiently, this is acceptable with God" (1 Peter 2:20).

We will never be the Church God intended us to be if the first little thing that comes along can disrupt us, can divide the quorum or upset the Relief Society or the ward or the stake. Satan must laugh at all the ways he and his minions can cause contention and get people to take their eye off of the covenants they have made and the love that was to accompany them.

Jesus Christ is the Shepherd of our souls (see 1 Peter 2:25). It is an unusual title. Think of the Good Shepherd. It is a variation on that. But I like the addition that He is also the bishop—as well as the Shepherd of our souls. It is a wonderful title because I have always loved bishops, and I love that eternal idea of a shepherd.

As for bishops, they are probably the most overworked people in The Church of Jesus Christ of Latter-day Saints. A bishop is the point of contact between formal Church life and a member's day-to-day struggles. I have been a bishop, and I know how that responsibility feels. I can understand this Bishop and Shepherd of our souls who won't go to bed at night until He has all the sheep back in the fold, who is restless and anxious, looking in dark places and distant locations until He finds every single one of His sheep. We may voluntarily run, we may willfully hide, or we might innocently just be lost, but somehow forever and forever that Bishop is looking for us. I know, whatever situation I am in, that Bishop is going to find me. The Shepherd of my soul will bring me home.

FOR HE RECEIVED FROM GOD

THE FATHER HONOUR AND GLORY,

WHEN THERE CAME SUCH A VOICE

TO HIM FROM THE EXCELLENT GLORY,

THIS IS MY BELOVED SON,

IN WHOM I AM WELL PLEASED.

—2 PETER 1:17

# 2 PETER

I want you to know that I have not given my life to a fairy tale. This work is not a joke we are trying to play on someone. As the Apostle Peter said, "For we have not followed cunningly devised fables, when we made known unto you the power and coming of our Lord Jesus Christ, but were eyewitnesses of his majesty" (2 Peter 1:16). This gospel is not a "cunningly devised fable," as some accuse it of being. That idea offends me; it is an insult to me. I was not born yesterday. During the course of my life, I have read several books; I have been to two or three good schools; I even had the privilege of presiding over a good school. Along the way, I have met kings and queens, princes, and prime ministers.

So, this is not my first rodeo, as they say; I am not foolish enough to go off on some wild-goose chase. Rather than racing around the world at my age, I could be home, doing whatever it is that people do when they are octogenarians. So why am I *not* home? It is because this is the very Church and kingdom of God on earth. I will say that until I have no breath left in my lungs or words upon my lips to say it. This is not "a cunningly devised fable." It is God's very truth!

I am not deluded, and neither are you. Now, you may not be as strong in the faith as you need to be, but you can become stronger. The truth has a way to make you strong, and this is God's truth.

There are multitudes of men and women—in and out of The Church of Jesus Christ of Latter-day Saints—who are struggling vainly against obstacles in their path. Many are fighting the battle of life—and losing. Indeed, there are those among us who consider themselves the vilest of sinners.

We have all known such people. We have all spoken with those who do not think they have been forgiven—or worse, who do not think they can be forgiven.

How many broken hearts remain broken because those people feel they are beyond the pale of God's restorative power? How many bruised and battered spirits are certain that they have sunk to a depth at which the light of redeeming hope and grace will never again shine?

The "good news" of the gospel is that there is a way back, that there is repentance and safety and peace because of Christ's gift to us. The good news is that the nightmares—large ones, little ones, every fear and concern—can end, and a safe loving light can shine in that "dark place, until the day dawn[s]," clean and clear and gloriously bright, and "the day star arise[s] in your hearts" (2 Peter 1:19).

That is the message all the world must hear.

IF ANY MAN SIN, WE HAVE AN ADVOCATE WITH

THE FATHER, JESUS CHRIST THE RIGHTEOUS:

AND HE IS THE PROPITIATION FOR OUR

SINS: AND NOT FOR OURS ONLY, BUT ALSO

FOR THE SINS OF THE WHOLE WORLD.

—1 JOHN 2:1-2

———— ✳ ————

# 1 JOHN

## 1 JOHN 1

By taking the sacrament each week, we focus our attention on the Savior's atoning sacrifice, acknowledging our dependence on His mercy and forgiveness. That is directly related to our Christian observance of Sunday as the day of the Resurrection. The sacrament is a weekly reminder that directs our thoughts to the Savior—toward our one great source of salvation, and our need to repent so that we might qualify for the full blessings of His Atonement and Resurrection.

Although we should be repenting all the time, the Sabbath and the sacrament give us the opportunity to really set aside worldly cares and concentrate on our spiritual improvement. Hence the Lord's statement to confess our sins before the Lord: "If we confess our sins, he is faithful and just to forgive us our sins, and to cleanse us from all unrighteousness" (1 John 1:9). Think for a moment how different our lives could be if through repentance we were made clean each and every Sabbath, and could start each week absolutely pure, renewed, and refreshed and totally confident of our standing before God. That sounds wonderful to me. It *is* wonderful. Thank heaven for Sundays and the sacrament.

## 1 JOHN 3

As Omega, a name taken from the last letter of the Greek alphabet, Christ is the terminus, the end cause as well as the end result of mortal experience. At His coming we will know what we might have become. John wrote, "Now are we the sons of God, and it doth not yet appear what we shall be: but we know that, when he shall appear, we shall be like him; for we shall see him as he is" (1 John 3:2).

When that day comes, we hope we will be very much like Him—not in sovereignty or station or degree of sacrifice, but perhaps in some portion of virtue and love and obedience. He will come to reign as the Messiah, Lord of lords and King of kings, and we will call him Master. In this finality, which is for the redeemed a beginning, the Lord of this earth will come.

GRACE BE WITH YOU, MERCY, AND PEACE,

FROM GOD THE FATHER, AND FROM

THE LORD JESUS CHRIST, THE SON OF

THE FATHER, IN TRUTH AND LOVE.

—2 JOHN 1:3

# 2 JOHN

## 2 JOHN 1

I am not certain just what our experience will be on Judgment Day, but I will be very surprised if at some point in that conversation, God does not ask us exactly what Christ asked Peter: "Did you love me?" I think He will want to know if in our very mortal, very inadequate, and sometimes childish grasp of things, did we at least understand *one* commandment, the first and greatest commandment of them all—"Thou shalt love the Lord thy God with all thy heart, and with all thy soul, and with all thy strength, and with all thy mind" (Luke 10:27)? And if at such a moment we can stammer out, "Yea, Lord, thou knowest that I love thee," then He may remind us that the crowning characteristic of love is always loyalty.

"And this is love," wrote the Apostle John, "that we walk after his commandments. This is the commandment, That, as ye have heard from the beginning, ye should walk in it" (2 John 1:6). So we have neighbors to bless, children to protect, the poor to lift up, and the truth to defend. We have wrongs to make right, truths to share, and good to do. In short, we have a life of devoted discipleship to give in demonstrating our love of the Lord. We can't quit and we can't go back. After an encounter with the living Son of the living God, nothing is ever again to be as it was before. The Crucifixion, Atonement, and Resurrection of Jesus Christ mark the beginning of a Christian life, not the end of it. It was this truth, this reality, that allowed a handful of Galilean fishermen-turned-again-Apostles to leave those nets a second time and go on to shape the history of the world in which we now live.

The voice of Christ comes ringing down through the halls of time, asking each one of us while there is time, "Do you love me?" And for every one of us, I answer with my honor and my soul, "Yea, Lord, we do love thee." And having set our "hand to the plough" (Luke 9:62), we will never look back until this work is finished and love of God and neighbor rules the world.

FOLLOW NOT THAT WHICH IS EVIL,

BUT THAT WHICH IS GOOD.

HE THAT DOETH GOOD IS OF GOD:

BUT HE THAT DOETH EVIL HATH NOT SEEN GOD.

—3 JOHN 1:11

— ✴ —

# 3 JOHN

## 3 JOHN 1

I ask us to consider the obligation we have to help our children know the truths of the gospel by declaring them and handing them down "from generation to generation as long as the earth shall stand" (see 2 Nephi 25:21–23). The Apostle John expressed it well when he wrote, "I have no greater joy than to hear that my children walk in truth" (3 John 1:4).

I offer a simple reminder that The Church of Jesus Christ of Latter-day Saints is always only one generation away from extinction. That does not change, however many decades we have seen since that first grand vision opened up to young Joseph Smith. The Church was true in 1830, it was true in 1840, it was true in 1900, and it is true today. But we are always just one generation away from extinction. To destroy this work, all we would have to do, I assume, is stop teaching our children for one generation. Let everything stop, close the books, seal up your heart, keep your mouth shut. In one generation it would then be 1820 all over again. We could search the scriptures, read of prayer, and go into a grove of trees to pray. With the blessings of the Lord, we could then find six people who would—when baptized— organize a church and take the gospel to all. Of course, it won't hap- pen, but it could happen if we ceased to accept the obligation upon us to teach the gospel, especially to our children.

We don't need to spell out what a break in that generational testi- mony can mean. Suffice it to say, it means apostasy. It can be personal apostasy, it can be familial apostasy, it can be dispensational apostasy, but it is apostasy, a break in the tie from generational to generation.

The bond protecting against such a break is, of course, very important in our theology. Joseph Smith said that we might well have rendered this bond as *welding,* and maybe that is a more graphic image than *sealing. Sealing* has several applications, not the least of which is the royal seal by the king—in this case the King of kings and Lord of lords. There is also the image of being sealed together, locked, linked, bound, tied, in a way that does not let evil in, that does not allow for personal or familial or dispensational apostasy, and that keeps those generations linked for time and all eternity.

May I read from the Prophet Joseph what our responsibility is to the living as well as to the dead. We all know the language pertaining to salvation for the dead. We all understand our obligation to seal our deceased families back through every generation. What I am not sure we have understood—in those revelations regarding baptism for the dead, and all the other saving ordinances, including endowments and sealings in the temple—is the language from the lips of the Prophet Joseph Smith himself about what our obligation is to the living—indeed, the living in our own households; indeed, the children at our knee who eat at our table and pray at our bedside. Let me give you that language from Doctrine and Covenants 128:17. Quoting Malachi, the Prophet Joseph Smith said: "Behold I will send you Elijah the prophet before the coming of the great and dreadful day of the Lord: And he shall turn the heart of the fathers to the children, and the heart of the children to their fathers, lest I come and smite the earth with a curse."

Now, I think everyone understands that scripture, especially as it pertains to work for the dead. But what is the meaning for your family in the world of the living? The Prophet Joseph goes on to say:

"I might have rendered a plainer translation to this, but it is sufficiently plain to suit my purpose as it stands. It is sufficient to know, in this case, that the earth will be smitten with a curse unless there is a welding link of some kind. . . . It is necessary in the ushering in of the dispensation of the fulness of times, which dispensation is now beginning to usher in, that a whole and complete and perfect union, and welding together of dispensations, and keys, and powers, and glories should take place, and be revealed from the days of Adam even to the present time. And not only this, but those things which never have been revealed from the foundation of the world, but have been kept hid from the wise and prudent, shall be revealed unto babes and sucklings in this, the dispensation of the fulness of times" (D&C 127:18).

As I understand it, the latter portion of that scripture has nothing to do with work for the dead or sealing back through generations to Adam. No, it has to do with things that have been hidden from the wise and prudent and that are to be "revealed unto babes and sucklings in this, the dispensation of the fulness of times," in your home and mine, today.

This can help us understand why The Church of Jesus Christ of Latter-day Saints leaders talk so much about family. Why does this Church take the stand it takes on things that relate to family—like abortion and premarital chastity? Is it really just a modern phenomenon to offset movies and magazines and trouble in the schools, difficulty in the streets, problems in the community? No, this theological emphasis is as old as the family of man.

I would suggest that Adam and Eve left the garden primarily for two reasons, and, as I read it, they had a lot of other reasons to stay. They could swim in the lagoon every morning and pluck wild berries for lunch, avoiding all the problems of growing old with all the difficulties you and I know about.

But in pursuit of eternal progress, they chose to leave for two reasons: to have a family and to gain eternal knowledge. If they had stayed in the garden, scripture tells us they would not have had children and they could not have become like the gods, never knowing good from evil. And against all of those other very attractive and very accommodating and very pleasant reasons to stay in the garden, they willingly left paradise in order to work out their salvation.

Is it just coincidence that the great biblical and scriptural stories are family stories? Was it happenstance that Satan began immediately to try to rend the family, to break the generational link, immediately turning Cain against Abel? Why did Abraham's own father try to take his life? Was it because Satan knew what Abraham was going to be and how the entire population would be blessed by Abraham's seed (Jesus)? We see David's tragedy and then see it compounded in his son, Absalom. This was followed by difficult family experiences Solomon had that finally led to the rending of the kingdom. These are all part of a generational pattern. The Book of Mormon is from beginning to end a profound statement about essentially one family (with the Jaredites thrown in for good behavior) that was involved in a warring experience pitting good against evil in an attempt to keep their generational experience intact. At book's end it is the loneliest of scenes, that of a father and son corresponding, until the father is gone, and later so the son is, too.

We need to do better than this in our day. May we all experience that great joy of knowing that our children "walk in truth" (3 John 1:4) because we have done our best to teach it to them.

NOW UNTO HIM THAT IS ABLE TO KEEP

YOU FROM FALLING, AND TO PRESENT YOU

FAULTLESS BEFORE THE PRESENCE OF HIS

GLORY WITH EXCEEDING JOY, TO THE ONLY WISE

GOD OUR SAVIOUR, BE GLORY AND MAJESTY,

DOMINION AND POWER, BOTH NOW AND EVER.

—JUDE 1:24–25

# JUDE

## JUDE 1

Without safety ropes, harnesses, or climbing gear of any kind, two brothers—Jimmy, age fourteen, and John, age nineteen (though those are not their real names)—attempted to scale a sheer canyon wall in Snow Canyon State Park in my native southern Utah. Near the top of their laborious climb, they discovered that a protruding ledge denied them their final few feet of ascent. They could not get over it, but neither could they now retreat from it. They were stranded. After careful maneuvering, John found enough footing to boost his younger brother to safety on top of the ledge. But there was no way to lift himself. The more he strained to find finger or foot leverage, the more his muscles began to cramp. Panic started to sweep over him, and he began to fear for his life.

Unable to hold on much longer, John decided his only option was to try to jump vertically in an effort to grab the top of the overhanging ledge. If successful, he might, by his considerable arm strength, pull himself to safety.

In his own words, he said:

"Prior to my jump I told Jimmy to go search for a tree branch strong enough to extend down to me, although I knew there was nothing of the kind on this rocky summit. It was only a desperate ruse. If my jump failed, the least I could do was make certain my little brother did not see me falling to my death.

"Giving him enough time to be out of sight, I said my last prayer—that I wanted my family to know I loved them and that Jimmy could make it home safely on his own—then I leapt. There was enough adrenaline in my spring that the jump extended my arms above the ledge almost to my elbows. But as I slapped my hands down on the surface, I felt nothing but loose sand on flat stone. I can still remember the gritty sensation of hanging there with nothing to hold on to—no lip, no ridge, nothing to grab or grasp. I felt my fingers begin to recede slowly over the sandy surface. I knew my life was over.

"But then suddenly, like a lightning strike in a summer storm, two hands shot out from somewhere above the edge of the cliff, grabbing my wrists with a strength and determination that belied their size. My faithful little brother had not gone looking for any fictitious tree branch. Guessing exactly what I was planning to do, he had never moved an inch. He had simply waited—silently, almost breathlessly—knowing full well I would be foolish enough to try to make that jump. When I did, he grabbed me, held me, and refused to let me fall. Those strong brotherly arms saved my life that day as I dangled helplessly above what would surely have been certain death" (from correspondence in the possession of Jeffrey R. Holland).

My beloved brothers and sisters, we have promised to *always* remember the brotherly hands and determined arms that reached into the abyss of death to save us from our fallings and our failings, from our sorrows and our sins. "Now unto him that is able to keep you from falling, and to present you faultless before the presence of his glory with exceeding joy, to the only wise God our Saviour, be glory and majesty, dominion and power, both now and ever" (Jude 1:24–25).

Jesus still stands triumphant over death, although He stands on wounded feet. I thank Him and the Father, who gave Him to us, that He still extends unending grace, although He extends it with pierced palms and scarred wrists. I thank Him and the Father, who gave Him to us, that we can sing before a sweat-stained garden, a nail-driven cross, and a gloriously empty tomb:

*How great, how glorious, how complete*
*Redemption's grand design,*
*Where justice, love, and mercy meet*
*In harmony divine!*

("How Great the Wisdom and the Love,"
   *Hymns* [1985], no. 195)

I AM ALPHA AND OMEGA,

THE BEGINNING AND THE ENDING,

SAITH THE LORD, WHICH IS, AND WHICH WAS,

AND WHICH IS TO COME, THE ALMIGHTY.

—REVELATION 1:8

# REVELATION

## REVELATION 1

I testify of Christ as "Alpha and Omega, the beginning and the ending" (Revelation 1:8) of everything that matters to me. He is literally the beginning and literally the end. He was there in the beginning, He is there through the mortal journey, right up to these latter days, and He will be there triumphant in the end to rule as Lord of lords and King of kings.

He is the start and the finish of everything that matters. He is the beginning and the end. He is Alpha and Omega—Christ and His gospel, His Atonement and His teachings, what He represents of the Father and what He gives to us as His brothers and sisters. He and His gift and His gospel are everything of significance to me. He is the set of brackets, the bookends, if you will, of everything that I hold dear, from anything I know about what happened before and everything I hope that will yet happen in my life in time and eternity. It is all focused on Him, the beginning and the end of everything.

## REVELATION 12

An idea I have spent a lot of time thinking about is introduced in the book of Revelation with these very familiar lines:

"And there was war in heaven: Michael and his angels fought against the dragon; and the dragon fought and his angels,

"And prevailed not; neither was their place found any more in heaven.

"And the great dragon was cast out, that old serpent, called the Devil, and Satan, which deceiveth the whole world: he was cast out into the earth, and his angels were cast out with him" (Revelation 12:7–9).

One does not have to be a trained theologian to understand where that battle took place. The confrontation in which the righteous fought against "that old serpent, called the Devil and Satan, which deceiveth the whole world," is rightfully referred to as the war in heaven. However, I confess that I am a little uncomfortable with that phrase, as if because it started in heaven it also ended there. This war has not concluded. Though I do not wish to introduce any new doctrine or be iconoclastic regarding Biblical imagery, it would seem that, technically speaking, it may be more appropriate to call this a battle because the war is still very much on.

At the end of that battle, and I choose to call it that, there was a great momentary, triumphant, exalting cry by the victors:

"Now is come salvation, and strength, and the kingdom of our God, and the power of His Christ;

"For the accuser of our brethren is cast down, which accused them before our God day and night.

"For they have overcome him by the blood of the Lamb, and by the word of their testimony; for they loved not their own lives, but kept the testimony even unto death" (JST, Revelation 12:9–11).

That is a statement about Christ before He ever came to earth, a statement about His blood before He ever had any, a statement about our testimony in Him before we ever knew fully what that would mean. It meant something there; but it would come to mean more here. His mission, our belief and faith in Him, His success and salvation and Atonement in this life would obviously take on much more with the passage of time.

There was a resplendent and resounding cry through the heavens at least for a time that Christ—and we—had won. Success in this conflict came through the strength and power of Christ and our loyalty to Him. In His gospel, we found something to love more than anything else, something we were willing to fight for even, as it were, to the death. Above all else we wanted to preserve, retain, and protect the things that we had been taught and the plan that had been presented by a loving Father, championed by a loving Son, opposed by a rebellious one.

The meaning of this chapter is made more clear by the verses that follow:

"For when the dragon saw that he was cast unto the earth, he persecuted the woman which brought forth the man child. . . .

"Therefore, the dragon was wroth with the woman, and went to make war with the remnant of her seed, which keep the commandments of God, and have the testimony of Jesus Christ" (Revelation 12:13, 17).

Who is it that the dragon wishes to fight in this world? Whom would he win; whom would he destroy? What battle would he hope to be victorious in? He fights against those who keep the commandments of God and have a testimony of Jesus. Who was it that he fought before? Those who keep the commandments of God and have a testimony of Jesus. Who is it that he fights now? Those who keep the commandments of God and have a testimony of Jesus.

The war has not ceased. The terrain and a few of the tactics have changed, but the war that started a long time ago is still on. In it you and I are marked men and women. I say that with the understanding that all of us who were entitled to come here and keep our second estate rejoiced in the knowledge that we were those who loved not our lives unto death but overcame there the accuser of our brethren, day and night, and we overcame him through the Lamb. Just as we were objects of his opposition and persecution and betrayal then, so we are objects of his persecution and terror and betrayal here.

This chapter in Revelation has become increasingly important to me as I ponder the nature of our work, what it is we are supposed to be doing, what I believe we face and how serious and dangerous it can be.

If we understood what we may have understood once before, we would be far more fearful, far more faithful, and surely far more fit for the battle than some of us now are.

If it is true that Satan wanted to destroy us once before and that he still wants to do so now, what does that tell us about him? It says something about his tenacity; it says something about his convictions; it says something about his unwillingness to yield or submit or give up until the very last triumphant moment when Christ comes and the devil is cast into outer darkness forever. But until that moment, he believes he is in this war, believes that he still has not only a fighting chance but an almost overwhelming opportunity for victory.

He understands that he has lost the Savior of this world and a number of righteous men and women from Adam and Eve down to the present. But he believes he has not lost you and me. He thinks that our own sons and daughters are perfectly fair game; and if there are those among us who keep the commandments of God and have a testimony of Jesus, he will simply roll out heavier artillery and go after them as well. Satan is proud and relentless. He believes he will yet win the major portion of the children of God. He took a third of them once before, and he thinks he can take a goodly number the second time around.

We understand that part of the nature of the battle in the premortal existence was the controversy over agency. We sometimes speak of agency as if it were an end in itself; but agency is not an end but a very significant and important and fundamental means to an end. The issue at that time had to do with choices, including the ability to carry out those choices, but behind that issue was the simple proposition that by choosing correctly and living with those choices faithfully, you and I can become like God.

Outside of this The Church of Jesus Christ of Latter-day Saints, that idea would be branded as heretical; it was, in fact, part of that for which Christ was put to death. The suggestion that we can acquire divine attributes, that we can grow and develop and progress, that we can move through whatever stages of existence there are until we become like God, is what the premortal conference, confusion, and ultimate battle were about. It is still what the battle is about here. Lucifer does not want you or me to become like God. He doesn't want anyone to be like God. He doesn't even want God to be like God. *He* wants to be God. He had the audacity to say, in effect, "I will do it. Send me; but I want the honor and the glory and the kingdom and the crown. In the meantime, you, Father, can step down."

We believe that with effort and grace, with knowledge and ordinances and obedience to the principles of the gospel of Jesus Christ, we can become like our Father in Heaven, but we do not want to take His place; we do not want to claim His honor or His glory, nor will we ever set Jesus aside—or Michael or Enoch or Adam or Abraham or Moses. No, we believe that all, each in his or her own place, can have the great promise of being a god or a goddess, a king or a queen, a priest or a priestess. And that is what Satan is opposing. He cannot live with the idea that anyone would have power or kingdoms or principalities but him. If he cannot have it all, he is determined not to give any inheritance to someone else.

May I encourage all of you to bear witness of the Savior of the world. There is a powerful spirit that comes in the very name of Jesus Christ. The spirit that attends that name will help you speak and will convey its own power whenever you bear your testimony of the Son of God, His mission, and His Church—The Church of Jesus Christ of Latter-day Saints. Even though the veil of forgetfulness is drawn over our minds and we do not remember our premortal existence, nevertheless every single human being on this planet sat with us in those premortal councils and heard the Father and the Son teach the plan of salvation. As we know from the book of Revelation, two-thirds of that spiritual family remained faithful and earned the right to come to the earth. Every mortal on this earth earned his or her right to be here because of their testimony of Jesus in that premortal world (see Revelation 12). So everyone you see on the streets and in shops coming and going in all directions once knew the name of Jesus Christ and bore testimony of His divinity. Therefore, if we can bear our testimony effectively and spiritually, many of them will recall those feelings. Some may even hear an echo of their own premortal experience when you bear witness in Christ's name.

## REVELATION 22

One of the arguments often used in any defense of a closed canon is the New Testament passage recorded in Revelation 22:18: "For I testify unto every man that heareth the words of . . . this book, If any man shall add unto these things, God shall add unto him the plagues that are written in this book." However, there is overwhelming consensus among virtually all biblical scholars that this verse applies only to the book of Revelation, *not* the whole Bible. Those scholars of our day acknowledge a number of New Testament "books" that were almost certainly written *after* John's revelation on the Isle of Patmos was received. Included in this category are at least the books of Jude, the three Epistles of John, and probably the entire Gospel of John itself. Perhaps there are even more than these.

But there is a simpler answer as to why that passage in the final book of the current New Testament cannot apply to the whole Bible. That is because the whole Bible as we know it—one collection of texts bound in a single volume—did not exist when that verse was written. For centuries after John produced his writing, the individual books of the New Testament were in circulation singly or perhaps in combinations with a few other texts but almost *never* as a complete collection. Of the entire corpus of 5,366 known Greek New Testament manuscripts, only 35 contain the whole New Testament as we now know it, and 34 of those were compiled after AD 1000 (see Bruce M. Metzger, *Manuscripts of the Greek Bible: An Introduction to Greek Paleography* [1981], 54–55).

The fact of the matter is that virtually every prophet of the Old *and* New Testament has added scripture to that received by his predecessors. If the Old Testament words of Moses were sufficient, as some could have mistakenly thought them to be (see Deuteronomy 4:2, for example), then why the subsequent prophecies of Isaiah or Jeremiah, who follow him? To say nothing of Ezekiel and Daniel, of Joel, Amos, and all the rest. If one revelation to one prophet in one moment of time is sufficient for *all* time, what justifies these many others? What justifies them was made clear by Jehovah Himself when He said to Moses, "My works are without end, and . . . my words . . . never cease" (Moses 1:4).

Continuing revelation does not demean or discredit existing revelation. The Old Testament does not lose its value in our eyes when we are introduced to the New Testament, and the New Testament is only enhanced when we read the Book of Mormon: Another Testament of Jesus Christ. In considering the additional scripture accepted by Latter-day Saints, we might ask: were those early Christians who for decades had access only to the primitive Gospel of Mark (generally considered the first of the New Testament Gospels to be written) offended to receive the more detailed accounts set forth later by Matthew and Luke, to say nothing of the unprecedented passages and revelatory emphasis offered later yet by John? Surely, they must have rejoiced that ever more convincing evidence of the divinity of Christ kept coming. And so do we rejoice—until "the day star arise in [our] hearts" (2 Peter 1:19).

# SCRIPTURE INDEX

# SUBJECT INDEX